BERNARD ASHMOLE
1894–1988

An Autobiography

Bernard Ashmole about 1960

BERNARD ASHMOLE
1894–1988

An Autobiography

Edited by Donna Kurtz

Oxbow Books 1994

Published and distributed by
Oxbow Books, Park End Place, Oxford
(Phone: 0865-241249: Fax: 0865-794449)

Distributed in the United States of America by
The David Brown Book Company, PO Box 5605, Bloomington, IN 47407
(Phone: 812-331-0266; Fax: 812-331-0277)

© Bernard Ashmole Estate and the individual authors 1994

ISBN 0 946897 68 9

Printed in Great Britain
at the Short Run Press

Contents

Preface	vii
Introduction	xv

PART I: ONE MAN IN HIS TIME. THE AUTOBIOGRAPHY OF BERNARD ASHMOLE

I.	Parentage and Childhood: School and Oxford	1
II.	The First War	10
III.	Oxford, Greece and Italy	18
IV.	The British School in Rome	36
V.	'High and Over', 1929 and the Thirties	51
VI.	University College; Interlude at Denham; the British Museum	62
VII.	The Second War	74
VIII.	The Air Defence of Great Britain	111
IX.	After the Second War	120
X.	The Department of Greek and Roman Antiquities, British Museum	129
XI.	Return to Oxford, Lincoln Professorship	135
XII.	Retirement from Oxford	144
XIII.	Paul Getty	155
XIV.	Retirement in Scotland	162
Appendix I: Adventures of Air-crews of 84 Squadron		166
Appendix II: The Log of the *Scorpion*		174

PART II

The Published Writings of Bernard Ashmole	191
"Aim and Method in the Study of Ancient Art, the Value of Casts" Excerpts from the unpublished Inaugural Lecture of Bernard Ashmole at University College, London 24 October 1929	195

PART III

An Appreciation *by Martin Robertson*	199
Bernard Ashmole and the British Museum *by Ian Jenkins*	203
The Ashmole Archive at King's College, London *by Geoffrey Waywell*	211

'High and Over', Amersham, Bucks., The Residence of Professor Bernard Ashmole', reprinted from *Country Life* 19 September 1931   217

PART IV

List of Illustrations   225
General Index   228
Geographical Index   234

Preface

ASHMOLE IS A GREAT NAME. Whether or not descent from an uncle of Elias Ashmole, who founded Oxford University's Ashmolean Museum in 1683, encouraged Bernard to study antiquities in the university, is not revealed in *One Man in his Time*. Nor is the great reputation which the twentieth-century Ashmole had achieved as early as the 1930s. During the following half century Ashmole's reputation as a world authority on ancient Greek sculpture grew and his advice was actively sought by young students, senior scholars and others who shared his interest in art, including J. Paul Getty.

Personal achievement is understated in the autobiography, particularly in scholarship, and this will puzzle readers who knew Ashmole as a scholar. Part of the explanation must lie in natural modesty, but part may also be attributable to Ashmole's professional association with Beazley who was nine years his senior and who became something of a legend in academic circles. In 1985 Ashmole told me that there were few people who were more closely associated with Beazley than the German scholar Ernst Pfuhl and himself. In the autobiography Ashmole, on stepping down from the professorship at Oxford, expresses satisfaction that his successor, Martin Robertson, and the new Reader, John Boardman, would 'carry on the Beazley tradition'. He never speaks of his own tradition, yet in England and America today great authorities on Greek sculpture and architectural sculpture were profoundly influenced by Ashmole. His influence on the continent almost certainly would have been greater if the years of his most active work had not been blighted by world wars.

Ashmole's name is often associated with Beazley's. The two men were the outstanding classical archaeologists in Britain during much of the twentieth century. They both enjoyed long lives during which they were both close friends and colleagues. Both were art historians rather than field archaeologists and both held the Lincoln Professorship of Classical Archaeology and Art at Oxford. It is natural for comparisons to be drawn. Beazley's dedication to scholarship is generally agreed to have been complete. His publications were phenomenally numerous and his manner by all accounts was that of an academic aesthete. In contrast, scholarship of classical antiquity was only one aspect of Ashmole's life and the number of his publications is smaller, but his impact on the teaching of classical archaeology in the University of Oxford was greater. On more than one occasion he said he thought it was a deplorable modern trend for scholars to be judged by bulk and speed of publication. His manner was relaxed, yet authoritative, and he was a brilliant lecturer who could communicate even the most esoteric aspects of Greek architectural techniques to the general public who were charmed by his unpretentious style. He often said he thought lecturers should try to entertain as well as to educate and proudly revealed that his own lecture style was strongly influenced by military service where he had learned to speak loudly and clearly and to repeat often.

Ashmole's first publication dates from 1921 when he was twenty-seven. What makes it remarkable is not so much the quality of scholarship, which is high, as the perseverance to produce it despite the profound disruption to his life and to his university career brought about by the outbreak of war. Less than a year after he came up to Oxford, in the autumn of 1913, war was declared. By the autumn of 1914 Ashmole had already volunteered for service in the Infantry. Seriously injured and much decorated for his valour, he was one of the few who survived the war to return to Oxford on demobilization in 1919.

In *Goodbye To All That* Robert Graves described Oxford immediately after the war. It is a personal account which historiographers of the university now see as the glamorous and romanticized vision of a poet. They detect among the new intake of students in 1919 a sombre sobriety, a sense of relief, of purpose and determination. Ashmole's own words – 'Oxford was a sad and empty place after the war' – seem to confirm their view and to heighten the contrast between the university of war veterans in 1919 and the university of the younger men and women who came up in 1922, much celebrated by Evelyn Waugh in *Brideshead Revisited*. Throughout his life Ashmole maintained close ties with his undergraduate college (Hertford) which remembered him as charming, diffident and one of its great supporters.

With the 'new' Oxford Ashmole seems to have had little connection even though he did return again, in 1922, after a two-year study tour on the continent, to read for a graduate degree in classical archaeology. Graduate studies were not prominent in the university until the 1960s, and Ashmole's decision to take a higher degree was probably stimulated by the war's unwelcome curtailment of his undergraduate career. When he took the degree in 1923 he was offered a post in the Coin Room of the university's Ashmolean Museum. Later he applied a knowledge of numismatics to the study of Greek sculpture in a 'multi-media' approach which would be considered very modern today.

Early years at Oxford, later a professorship in the university, residence there for fifteen years after retirement, and sustained interest in its work, even from the distance of Scotland, did not make Ashmole an 'Oxford man'. To many his character seemed better suited to a career in the diplomatic service than to one in an academic community; he was a practical man rather than an aesthete; and he spent as many years in London as he did in Oxford. There he held the two leading posts in classical archaeology, serving as Keeper of the Greek and Roman Department of the British Museum and as Yates Professor of Classical Archaeology at University College, and he was offered the directorship of the Warburg

Institute, which he declined. Fritz Saxl, the Warburg's first director, was a personal friend and Ashmole's work on Cyriac of Ancona had revealed his scholarship of the post-antique.

The most remarkable professional achievement of Ashmole's London years was the evacuation, protection and reinstallation of the Greek and Roman galleries of the British Museum during and immediately after the second World War. As Keeper he was responsible for thousands of objects, including the Elgin Marbles. In the autobiography he describes how the treasured sculpture from the Parthenon was lowered into the tunnels of the London underground and how, after the war, it was brought up again with the help of Ashmole's ingenious invention of a 'wooden horse'. He ends his extraordinary account with these words: "So even today it is useful to know something about the seige of Troy. Virgil tells us that the Trojans fitted wheels to the Wooden Horse for a similar reason".

Ashmole openly acknowledged his personal commitment to London in later years by giving much of his library to the Classics Department of University College and most of his photographic archive to King's College. He was an excellent photographer. Early interest and considerable expertise probably came from his father who was a director of the then embryonic photographic firm Ilford in north London. At the beginning of his professional career Ashmole had mastered the art of capturing the true quality of ancient marbles whose planes and textures are notoriously difficult to reproduce successfully. He greatly admired the photography of the American Alison Frantz and together they set out to produce, with Nicholas Yalouris what Ashmole called: "a simple, fully illustrated account in English of the sculptures of the temple of Zeus at Olympia, which would serve as an introduction for students and for the many others who are interested in them." *(Olympia, The Sculptures of the Temple of Zeus).*

In addition to using photographs in his own publications from as early as 1921, he made them available to other scholars. Like other art historians of his generation Ashmole created a large photographic archive, but his prints were his own work, not those of professional photographers purchased or given in exchange for information. Beazley's photographic archive in Oxford has a significant collection of Ashmole's prints of Greek and Roman sculpture. The two men had collaborated in publication from time to time. Their chapters in the *Cambridge Ancient History* (1932), which were published separately as *Greek Sculpture and Painting* in 1932 and reprinted in 1966, became a standard textbook which is still valued today. Ashmole also gave to the British Museum his negatives of the sculptures of the Mausoleum at Halikarnassos but the greatest part of his original collection is now in King's College, London, where it forms the nucleus of the Ashmole Archive (described by Geoffrey Waywell in pages 209–13).

Between Oxford of youth and London of early middle-age came a brief interlude of five years in Rome. At the age of thirty-one he had been elected Director of the British School which had been founded in 1889 to give British artists and architects opportunities to develop their styles while working in one of the world's oldest and most beautiful cities. Although archaeologists later came to play an important role in the school it was the artists and architects who gave it a more colourful image than the sister institution in Athens with which Ashmole was also closely involved over a longer period of time. He served on its Board of Trustees and Managing Committee for many years and in 1960, at the age of sixty-six, was its Visiting Professor. At that time he delighted and impressed the students by organizing and participating in expeditions which were often very physically demanding.

Ashmole's time in Rome was relatively short and his association with the school in later life was not as close because his academic interests became predominantly Greek. The period of his directorship in Rome did, however, have considerable influence because many future luminaries of the British art world were either students or visitors to the school. Barbara Hepworth and Rex Whistler were there. The sculptor John Skeaping made a fountain for the school, David Evans a portrait head of Bernard's wife Dorothy, which she disliked and Bernard helped her to bury in the school's garden, and Wilson Parker a portrait bust of Bernard which found somewhat greater favour.

Another student was the New Zealander Amyas Connell who later became one of the best known British architects of the International Style. Connell's enthusiasm for Le Courbusier's radical new designs in new materials complemented Ashmole's admiration for the clean geometrical forms of classical Greek buildings and his genuine interest in technological applications. Together they designed a residence for the Ashmole's, 'High and Over', which was begun in 1929 and completed in 1931. Modern architecture hardly existed in England before the 1930s. The house was revolutionary. To the account published in *Country Life* in 1931 (reproduced here on pages 217–222) can be added Nicholas Pevsner's words: "The bare concrete walls, the sharply cut-in horizontal windows, the meeting of unrelieved cubic shapes, the fully glazed staircase, all these are now familiar features – they were shockingly new in England then."

In the autobiography Ashmole tells us that Amyas Connell once said "I want anyone to be able to see that this is the Ashmoles' house." Today, softened by the matured gardens which Ashmole landscaped on a bare hillside with the same attention to form and function which he required of the house, the classic lines reveal clearly the spirit of the man who wrote *Architect and Sculptor in Classical Greece* and designed the Duveen Gallery in the British Museum for the post-war display of the Parthenon sculptures.

From the early years of his professional life Ashmole seems to have blended authority with personal warmth. It is characteristic of his effect on younger people that he inspired Connell to launch his career in England with such a bold private commission. Although already an expert on ancient art by the mid-twenties Ashmole had flourished in the *avant garde* atmosphere of the School at Rome because he welcomed new ideas and had an excellent sense of humour. Costumed as a court jester, or as the British Red Lion, he took great pleasure in the School's social as well as academic life. Some twenty years later Ashmole was perhaps able to relive this flamboyant period when he was invited to advise on the costumes and sets of Michael Korda's famous, but unfinished film 'I Claudius'. Even in advanced old age Ashmole was handsome, courteous and so lively that he continued to attract young and old, academics, artists, and those who shared his many and varied interests.

Throughout his professional life he had keen interest in architectural design and technique and was particularly pleased to be elected an Honorary Associate of the Royal Institute of British Architects in 1927. He wrote about some of the greatest buildings of classical antiquity – the temple of Zeus at Olympia, the Parthenon on the Acropolis of Athens and the Mausoleum at Halikarnassos, one of the Seven Wonders of the ancient world – and had particular interest in the practical problems of their construction. In London and Oxford he actively collaborated with architects to design galleries. Many of the features of these galleries can be found in 'High and Over'.

Complementing the interest in architecture was a sensitivity to nature which may have encouraged Ashmole's son Philip to become an ornithologist. To those who disliked the sharp lines of 'High and Over' Ashmole replied that the house would in time fit the landscape. Today it does. The once barren hill is heavily wooded, gardens embrace the house, and one's eyes are led from the large round pool below – now the dominant feature of the site – up the steps towards the great cypress trees in front of the house. Ashmole would be pleased; water was important to him. Wherever he lived he wanted fountains and pools and a view of a river or stream. On seaside holidays he amused himself and his children by diverting streams onto banks, and in a time of great crisis during World War II when he came upon a tributary of the River Tigris he tells us:

> ... I suddenly had a strange experience...; as a child I had a recurrent dream that I was walking with my father beside a river full of fish, and that I killed them by throwing stones. I may have had the dream two or three times, perhaps forty years before, and had never recalled it since; yet now it dawned on me that this was, with absolute certainty, the river of my dream. I naturally (and as it turned out wrongly) supposed that this might mark some great moment in my life, and was particularly careful to see that it was not my last.

In the British School at Rome Skeaping's fountain had been Ashmole's inspiration. In the early years of married life in Oxford Ashmole had wanted to live in a 12th-century inn (now the Trout Inn) at Godstow, on the banks of the River Thames. At 'High and Over', which looked out onto the valley of the River Misbourne, he designed a fountain inside the house and built several pools outside. Later, in Oxford, home was the Mill House overlooking Iffley Lock and the River Thames. There Ashmole made ingenious use of a natural spring in the cellar of the house by diverting the flow to the desired place in the garden and casting the basin of the fountain in concrete in an inverted umbrella frame. And in Scotland home was on the Green by the River Tweed. Christmas 1985 Ashmole gave me what he called 'a little dilapidated book which was a great comfort during the Second War'. The book was a special Forces' paperback edition of

Robert Gibbings's *Sweet Thames Run Softly* with engravings of river birds which he particularly recommended.

Retirement was long and productive. It began in Oxford in 1961, continued in Scotland, at Peebles from 1970, and did not end until about 1986. At the age of ninety he could be persuaded to consider writing a handbook on Greek sculpture for students but his modesty would not let him accept the offer of a *Festschrift* in his honour. Throughout these years Ashmole remained keenly interested in the potential offered by new technologies, whether they analysed the physical structure of ancient marbles, detected forgeries or computerized data on antiquities.

It is to the period of retirement that his association with J. Paul Getty belongs. Getty had a particular interest in Greek and Roman antiquities. They had met in 1952, when Ashmole was showing Getty the Parthenon sculptures in the British Museum. Getty is said to have asked how much it would cost to buy them, and Ashmole is said to have replied – even more than you, Mr Getty, can pay. Ashmole's period of advising Getty on antiquities dates from the 1970s when Getty was living in England, at Sutton Place and Ashmole was living in Scotland. Getty is said to have asked his chauffeur to offer an honorarium for the first consultation. Ashmole graciously declined, adding that a bottle of claret would be ample reward. Getty appreciated the gesture, sent the claret, and the two became friends. In acknowledgement of the part Ashmole had played in forming his collection of classical antiquities the first issues of *The J. Paul Getty Museum Journal* (1974) were dedicated to him. Neither Getty nor Ashmole saw the new museum housed in a reproduction of a Pompeian villa high over the Pacific coast at Malibu in California, but its architecture, landscaping and commitment to the education of the general public would surely have pleased both of them greatly.

Also to the period of retirement belong some of Ashmole's publications which are today considered to be the most important: *Cyriac of Ancona*, Italian Lecture, British Academy (1960), *The Classical Ideal in Greek Sculpture* (1964), and *Architect and Sculptor in Classical Greece* (1972)). During these decades he also undertook extensive lecture tours, served on the Managing Committee of the British School in Athens, edited the Oxford Monographs on Classical Archaeology and directed the early development of the Beazley Archive. Even from Scotland he gave advice by telephone and by letter in a distinctively elegant handwriting that never seemed to falter despite great age.

> Dorothy and I feel, as we grow very old, that one can only pray for an old age where one doesn't become entirely senile, doesn't suffer intense pain, and will die suddenly, preferably together. But who can hope for it?
>
> *Bernard, writing 9 November 1982*

> He died at 94 without long illness or pain with his children near him... All the letters received express love and admiration and in spite of two wars, I can say that he lived a lovely life.
>
> *Dorothy, writing 4 March 1988*

Bernard's wish was fulfilled. Dorothy died not long after and their ashes were interred at Iffley, in the landscaped grounds of the 12th-century church of St Mary which overlook the River Thames and adjoin the grounds of the Mill House where they had lived from 1956 to 1972.

Donna Kurtz
Oxford, Summer 1993

Introduction

> I have been asked by some of my grandchildren to write an account of my life; and I have done so because it has covered a period not only of unparalleled technical developments but also of catastrophic events in the world at large, some of the effects of both of which I have directly experienced.
>
> Because I aim to make the record as accurate as possible, I have set down any brief remark that could be remembered exactly, but otherwise have not attempted to recall, or to invent, any dialogue, although this might have made the narrative more vivid.
>
> *Bernard Ashmole, 1981*

Ashmole wrote the autobiography, *One Man in His Time*, between 1981 and 1984. It is printed here in full, including Appendices describing events in World War II, and forms Part I of this book. However, the title of the book as a whole has been altered to avoid confusion with other autobiographies. Part II includes a list of Ashmole's publications and an excerpt from a lecture delivered in 1929 on the importance of plaster casts for the study of ancient Greek and Roman sculpture. This is published here in recognition of a renewed interest in the art historical and educational value of casts which would have delighted him. Part III has appreciations of different aspects of Ashmole's academic work, one by a member of his own generation, Martin Robertson, and two by younger men with special interest in Greek sculpture, Geoffrey Waywell and Ian Jenkins. Part IV are indexes whose length and breadth testify to the varied experiences of *One Man in His Time*.

One Man in His Time may surprise those who knew Ashmole as one of the greatest authorities on ancient Greek sculpture. His original preface, which is quoted in full above, prepares the reader. His is not the story of a scholar aesthete, but of a man who lived through, and experienced first hand, exciting and often terrible times, some of them the most momentous of the twentieth century.

Born in 1894 Ashmole, like other young men of his generation, served in World War I. He was badly injured on the Somme and honoured for distinguished service.

> His Majesty the King has been graciously pleased to confer the Military Cross on the undermentioned Officers and Warrant Officers in recognition of their gallantry and devotion to duty in the field.

> Temp. Lt. Bernard Ashmole, R. Fus.
> For conspicuous gallantry and devotion to duty. He displayed great courage and skill in forming his company up for attack under heavy fire. Later, although wounded, he continued in command until he was wounded a second time and collapsed.
>
> *Supplement to the London Gazette, 17 April 1919*

Unlike so many of his contemporaries Ashmole was able to resume studies at university and soon to embark on a remarkable career. At the age of forty-six he would not have been expected to serve in World War II, but in 1940 Ashmole joined the RAF, despite the fears of his family. Quickly he rose from the rank of Flying Officer to Wing Commander. He was mentioned in Dispatches and awarded the Greek Distinguished Flying Cross by the King of the Hellenes for 'great valour and audacity during flights against the enemy'. Later, in 1957, he was appointed CBE for services to the British Museum during the war.

Nearly half of *One Man in His Time* is the story of service to his country on the field of battle, from the Somme to Sumatra. The Editor is particularly grateful to Robert J. O'Neill, Chichele Professor of the History of War in the University of Oxford, for reading Ashmole's accounts of the two world wars and confirming their unique importance.

Writing in his eighties and looking back over a long life of varied experiences, which he did not record in diaries, Ashmole could be expected to provide a personal and highly selective account. There are surely events which others will have remembered differently, but Ashmole's aim, as stated in his own preface, to be as accurate as possible, probably more than compensates. Furthermore, he had demonstrated throughout his professional life a commitment to a precise, clear, and elegant style, whether he was writing about the technology of the ancient Greeks who built the Parthenon or about the young New Zealander Amyas Connell boldly experimenting with designs in reinforced concrete.

Ashmole's aim to record accurately and his personal modesty can mislead the reader. His self-effacing manner was understood within his family, but in a publication such as this it could be seen as a weakness. For that reason the Ashmole family asked the Editor to introduce the autobiography with a discussion of the man and his achievements. Unlike Martin Robertson's appreciation, which can be found in Part III, the Editor's takes the perspective of a younger generation whose professional work, and personal life, were profoundly influenced by him.

One Man in His Time was not intended for publication. As Ashmole explained in his preface, some of his grandchildren asked him to write an account of his life; he agreed to do this because it covered the most eventful period of the twentieth century. I became aware of the autobiography only after the publication of Martin Robertson's obituary for Ashmole which was published in the *Proceedings of the British Academy* in 1989. Since both Bernard and Dorothy had not only encouraged me to come to Oxford as a young student, but had shown me great kindness and affection, I had a personal interest in making *One Man and His Time* more widely available. Throughout the preparation of this book I have had the full cooperation of the Ashmole family, particularly of Bernard's eldest daughter, Dr Stella Ring, and her son, James, who were able to make many trips to Oxford: James had in fact given extensive help to Bernard in the preparation of the manuscript, before it was distributed to members of the family; Philip Ashmole corrected the proofs and contributed to the Indexes. Most of the illustrations published here were provided by the Ashmoles.

David Brown, Director of Oxbow Books, has also taken a personal interest in the publication. He knew Ashmole when he was an Assistant Keeper in the Ashmolean Museum's Department of Antiquities. Martin Robertson and John Boardman have advised on many aspects of the production. Geoffrey Waywell and Ian Jenkins not only contributed to Part III, they also welcomed the Editor's suggestion of celebrating Ashmole's centenary with a symposium on Greek architectural sculpture in the British Museum.

Others, to whom the Editor owes thanks are: M. Cayhill, E. Clay, B. F. Cook, D. Conran, S. Dodgson, L. Friedman, C. Gooch, M. Graham, A. D. Harvey, S. and D. E. L Haynes, I. P. Hiley, P. Howard, J. Inskeep, A. W. Johnston, A. Mace, A. Matthews, M. Moloney, K. O'Brien, R. J. O'Neill, N. Pollard, V. Prentice, S. C. Raftree, A. Rooke-Matthewes, E. Southworth, G. Vaughan, G. Waddell, J. Walsh, H. Waterhouse, E. Waywell, L. Wiener, R. L. Wilkins, D. F. Williams, H. A. Williams, T. P. Wiseman. Organizations to which the Editor owes thanks are: Athenaeum, British Academy, *Country Life* Magazine, Hertford Society, Liddell Hart Centre for Military Archives, Ministry of Defence, Oxfordshire County Library, Public Record Office, Royal Institute of British Architects, the British Architectural Library, and *The Times* Newspapers.

The following publications have been consulted in preparation of the Introduction.

J. BOARDMAN, "Classical Archaeology in Oxford" in *Beazley and Oxford*, ed. D. C. Kurtz (Oxford, 1985) 43-55.
A. D. HARVEY, "Oxford Before Evelyn Waugh: the Undergraduate Intake of 1919", *Oxford Magazine* (Nought Week, Trinity Term, 1992) 3-4.
M. KORDA, *Charmed Lives* (London, 1980)
R. MILLER, *The House of Getty* (London, 1985)
H. C. O'NEILL, *The Royal Fusiliers in the Great War* (London, 1922)
R. F. OVENELL, *The Ashmolean Museum 1683-1894* (Oxford, 1986)
J. SKEAPING, *Drawn From Life: An Autobiography* (London, 1977)
H. WATERHOUSE, *The British School at Athens – The First Hundred Years* (London, 1986)
L. WHISTLER, *The Laughter and the Urn: The Life of Rex Whistler* (London, 1985)
T. P. WISEMAN, *A Short History of the British School at Rome* (London, 1990)

Part I

One Man in his Time
The Autobiography of Bernard Ashmole

Chapter I

Parentage and Childhood
School and Oxford

I was born on June 22nd, 1894, into a world where the motor car was barely invented, where there were no telephones, and domestic lighting was either by candles, paraffin lamps, or flat-flame gas-burners; heating was by open fires or closed stoves burning coal, coke or wood, and central heating was almost unknown, except in greenhouses. Gas street-lighting had just come in, and the lamplighter, who came round at dusk with a long pole, was a familiar sight. Another daily visitor was the milk cart, and one of my earliest memories is of lying awake before anyone else was astir, listening for its arrival. It was a two-wheeled float, low-slung and open at the back, with a large brass churn standing on it; from this the milkman dipped with a half-pint ladle and filled any receptacle – jug, mug or basin – that the householder produced. The modern bicycle was just being perfected, although the freewheel was not generally introduced until about 1900 and the three-speed gear later still. The first typewriter, a Remington, appeared in my father's office about 1902. I remember about 1904 the first public telephone and the first motor-bus, solid-tyred, and the top open to the weather, as they all were until the First War. Flying was still believed by many to be an impossibility; radio was in the distant future; television then, and for many years, a fanciful prophecy.

We lived in Ilford, at that time a small independent town, not part of London as it is today. I was the youngest of a family of five, my oldest sister being seventeen years older than I and my only brother six. My father, William Ashmole, was an auctioneer and estate agent. He was the son of another William Ashmole, a builder, and his wife Charlotte Hunsdon. William's father Samuel was host of the Angel Inn at Ilford. Samuel, the son of Thomas Ashmole and Elizabeth Erpe, had moved south about 1800 from Findern in Derbyshire, whither his forebears had moved from Lichfield in the early eighteenth century. His father Thomas and other relations are buried at Findern; they were descended from an uncle of Elias Ashmole, the founder of the Ashmolean Museum.

My father, quiet and modest, was a keen cricketer and swimmer; the year I was born he was awarded the Royal Humane Society's certificate for rescuing a would-be suicide from the deepest part of our little river Roding. He was Churchwarden and Lay-reader, Chairman for forty years of the local Gas Company, and a Director of the infant photographic company, Ilford Ltd., now

*The Ashmole family in 1896.
William and Caroline, father and mother, are seated left and right. Gordon sits beside his father, Muriel beside her mother, Constance stands behind, Gladys and Bernard are seated in front.*

grown gigantic. From the age of fifteen he wrote a perfect copperplate hand, and did exquisite illuminated lettering; he had strong literary and antiquarian interests, and taught us to appreciate both literature and architecture. I remember him taking me to see Dance's grim Newgate Prison (on the site of the present Old Bailey) just before it was demolished, and the Roman Catholic Cathedral at Westminster just after it was built. He also ran a little Literary Society to which the dozen members would read papers from time to time on literary and antiquarian subjects, and these I was allowed to attend.

My mother was Caroline Sarah Wharton Tiver, daughter of John James Tiver and Sarah Ann Shrubsole Wharton; she had a twin sister Sarah Caroline Wharton Tiver, through whom I had the supreme good fortune of meeting Dorothy. Aunt Sarah used to be a visitor at Dorothy's home, because the sisters were related to her grandmother; Dorothy and I are thus distantly related, being stepsecond cousins once removed. My mother had evidently been strictly brought up in a religious household which had endowed her with keen common sense and simple piety. Physically she was small but extremely active; she ate little, was extraordinarily alert, woke at six every morning, enjoyed excellent health, never had a tooth decayed or stopped, and retained her own teeth until her peaceful death at the age of eighty-eight. We had family prayers every morning before breakfast, and her clear and simple reading every day at that time of a passage from the Authorized Version of the Gospels, had a deep influence, I hope on my character and certainly on my writing of English.

On Sundays we were not allowed to read ordinary books or play ordinary games, and of course cards were taboo. Fortunately when I grew a few years older Dr Kitto's essays on the Old Testament passed muster. Dr Kitto had a delightful way, appealing to the logic in a child's mind, of rationalizing the miracles in the Old Testament; all the plagues of Egypt could be comfortably explained, and as for the Israelites' crossing of the Red Sea, that could be through the combination of a very low tide and a very strong east wind. I was also allowed a copy of Layard's *Nineveh* which described his excavations and certainly gave me a taste for archaeology; but no childish fantasy could have foreseen that one day I should be part of a garrison defending Nineveh itself.

When I was three or four we moved a mile further from London to Seven Kings, then little more than a hamlet but due to be developed by the extension of the Great Eastern Railway and the building of a new railway station in 1899. There we lived in a modest house, Thornfield, in Aldborough Road, but, in the custom of those days, had two servants (housemaid and cook), a children's nurse, and also a groom (appropriately named Gee) who looked after the small garden and a pony (for a "governess cart") which lived in a stable at the back of the garden; this opened onto a lane which served the stables of other houses in the road. Next door lived my Godfather, Mr Farey, a spice-merchant in the City, whom I remember chiefly as owning a greenhouse in which he grew tomatoes, then a novelty. Not far away was *The Cauliflower* public house, which figures in stories by W. W. Jacobs the humorous writer, a local resident, then well-known, now almost forgotten.

Our summer holiday was usually in the Isle of Wight, but one summer we

*William Ashmole (father),
about 1900.*

*Caroline Ashmole (mother),
about 1940.*

Gordon Ashmole (brother), about 1935.

went to Newquay in Cornwall. We stayed in lodgings and it was usual to take one's linen; our luggage, for a family of two parents, a nurse and five children, consisted of several large trunks and a Gladstone bag or two. We went by train to Liverpool Street and were met there by a Great Western Railway horse-bus painted, of course, in their cream-and-chocolate livery; the luggage was piled on the roof and we drove across London to Paddington. It was misery to a child, for the granite setts with which London was then paved, combined with the metal-tyred wheels to produce a motion distinctly nauseating; I was never sick, but felt like death. Since all the traffic was horse-drawn, the streets of London were plentifully strewn with horse manure, but street sweepers were steadily at work, and also crossing sweepers where pedestrians crossed, giving them a penny. Because of the paving and horses' hooves the streets were noisy, and well-to-do people would have a thick layer of peat or straw laid down in the road opposite their house when anyone was seriously ill.

The G.W.R. was then regarded as the queen of railways, and Brunel's hallmark was still clear upon it, especially in its fine stations and the general layout of the line. Morale was high; the splendid engines came in with their brass and copperwork highly polished, their paint glisteningly clean. The corridor train with flexible connections between coaches had not yet been invented, and therefore it had no heating nor restaurant car. In cold weather carriages on the long-distance trains were each provided with a large copper foot-warmer; luncheon, if notice was given before starting, was handed in when the train stopped at Swindon, in the form of a covered basket with standard chicken and ham, neatly laid out with crockery and cutlery, the basket being collected at the journey's end.

The Great Northern Railway, considered more austere, was esteemed for its efficiency and the power of its engines; it was said that if the Flying Scotsman ran more than five minutes late into Edinburgh there was a headline in the local paper.

There were other, inferior railways: our own line, the Great Eastern; the South Eastern and Chatham; or, lowest of all, the London, Chatham and Dover, so notorious for its poor time-keeping as to be the target of a music-hall song. It ran something like this:

I went down to Dover in record time
On the London and Chatham and
    South Eastern line,
It took me all night and the most of
    next day
Aytooral, Aytooral, Aytooral Aytay.

In 1903 we moved from Seven Kings to Wanstead, which was about three miles away and more rural, but was near enough for my father to walk to and from his office in Ilford, partly through the fine Wanstead Park, which had a lake and heronry and was on the site of the two hundred acre grounds of the famous Wanstead House. This, built in 1715, had been the seat of the Child family, who must have also been responsible for the perfect Georgian church, complete with high pulpit (somehow embodying a large gilded palm tree), box-pews, and a grandiose monument with a life-size statue in the chancel. In the churchyard was a stone structure like a huge sentry box, to be used as a shelter by those keeping watch against body-snatchers – the London hospitals were not far distant. Wanstead House had survived for little more than a century and was demolished in 1822 because of the reckless gambling of the last heir. All that remained was a circular lake once in front of the house, and a deep hollow, once its cellars but now one of the greens on the golf-course.

Constance Ashmole (sister), about 1917.

At Wanstead we rented Stone Hall, a splendid early eighteenth-century house, built of brick despite its name, with much panelling; the dining room had a massive moulded plaster ceiling embodying the initials C. R. (said to be for Charles Rayner, not Carolus Rex) and the billiard-room, above, a boldly carved overmantel with wooden figures of the Seasons. Stone Hall was part of a group of three or four eighteenth-century houses, including one, Sheridan House, which had belonged to the playwright. There was a fair-sized garden which could take a tennis-court, a kitchen-garden behind it, a stable block and a little coachman's cottage; altogether a wonderful playground. I think we no longer kept a horse, but a brick-built refuse-bin in the stable-yard was large enough to conceal a child, as I was glad to find when pursued by Runagles, the gardener, after I had shot him, when bending, with my new air-gun.

The move enabled me to go as a day-boy to Forest School, a minor Public School, so called because it was on the borders of Epping Forest. The Reverend R. C. Guy was the Headmaster and part-owner, one of a family of twenty-two which included some well-known athletes. The teaching here was uneven in quality, and some of the masters seemed to be young, able men in their first post; in fact several of them attained some distinction later. A. de V. Wade, for instance, became a distinguished Civil Servant in Africa, Edwin Glasgow the Administrative Director of the National Gallery. The elderly second master, C. A. Eves, gave me some special tuition in 1911, my last year at school, and by his clear mind and gentle exposition made me understand less dimly what was the purpose of mathematical studies.

At this time too I was introduced to Macaulay's Essays, and carried a copy about with me until I had read them all – some more than once. This enabled me to write an essay myself in a style much like Macaulay's and may well have given people the impression that I had a better brain than I really had; but it did give me a good idea how to handle material and set it out in a clear orderly way, and may well have had a permanent effect on my way of writing.

It was now thought that I showed enough promise to try for a scholarship at a university. In southern England at that time Oxford, Cambridge and London stood alone, and because of the family connection through Elias Ashmole, Oxford was chosen. It was evidently found that the teaching at Forest School was not of a high enough standard; my father got in touch with a private tutor, the Reverend F. P. Long, and it was agreed that I should go and live in his household in Oxford, where several other students were receiving tuition. Mr Long was a fine scholar and an interesting character. He was, among other things, the translator for the Oxford Press of Caesar's Gallic War into English, which accurately transforms what was for most schoolboys a boring text-book into an absorbing narrative in modern language. I owe a great debt to Mr Long for this example of imaginative scholarship, but above all for teaching me to translate the other way round, English into Latin, and its value as a mental exercise in analysing the exact meaning of a piece of English prose. At the end of 1912 I was offered a small Exhibition at Pembroke College which it was thought wise not to accept; but in March 1913 I was awarded the Essex Scholarship in Classics at Hertford College, and went up in October.

Oxford then was what would today be considered old-fashioned; the famous Dr Spooner was still Warden of New College, and the Principal of Hertford was the elderly Henry Boyd, benevolent and dignified, who always wore a top hat when out of doors, and being wealthy was alleged to be financ-

Gladys Ashmole (sister), about 1917.

ing the College, then a poor one, out of his own pocket. In some of the colleges there still resided a few of the old bachelor Fellows appointed before the ban against marriage was lifted; one such was Bidder of St John's, a passionate gardener who started the rock-garden there, now dedicated to him and still greatly admired. He was completely toothless; when a tooth showed signs of decay it was removed, since he held that a metal stopping would spoil his palate for port, but this did not prevent him enjoying a good meal with hardened gums.

At Hertford I made many new friends. At that time it was a small college and there was a pleasant custom that in their first year all Freshmen were invited to breakfast in twos and threes by second and third-year men. Among the Freshmen my chief friend was Percy Campbell, the Senior Scholar in mathematics, who had the most stimulating, acute and unconventional mind imaginable. We used to have little coffee parties in our rooms of an evening to discuss with three or four friends all manner of subjects; this was indeed one of the main educational advantages of Oxford. Percy was the son of J. E. Campbell, the mathematician, Fellow of the Royal Society, Fellow of the College since 1891, and among the first to live in Oxford as a married Fellow when this became permissible. Mr Campbell and his wife Sarah used to entertain undergraduates to tea on Sundays, and I, and eventually Dorothy, came to know them well. From this sprang a lasting friendship of our two families and our lives have been intertwined for many years. Percy was killed in October 1914, having been in the Special Reserve who, on the outbreak of war were immediately drafted into Regular units; his brother Pat trained and served with distinction as an officer in the Artillery, and has recently written two books on his experiences. When I joined the Air Force in 1940 and went abroad, Pat, who was Second Master of a school at Gerrards Cross, took our son Philip as a weekly boarder and brought him up with his own three sons for more than three years. He acted almost as a foster-father, and – I think Philip would agree – instilled in him intellectual and moral principles which have stood him in good stead ever since. Our debt to Pat and his wife Camilla is incalculable.

The other Fellows of Hertford were an interesting group. Norman Whatley, the Dean, was afterwards Headmaster of Clifton. The Chaplain, John McLeod Campbell, became a close friend, married us, and was godfather to our first daughter, Stella. He served with the 51st Highland Division at the Front and we occasionally met each other in France; he was afterwards head of Trinity College, Kandy, Ceylon, Chaplain

Bernard Ashmole, about 1938.

to the Speaker of the House of Commons, and then Master of the Charterhouse in London. Canon E. A. Burroughs, afterwards Bishop of Peterborough, went out of his way to encourage the young, and in addition to giving tuition, entertained them regularly, in succession, with cocoa-parties in the evening, thus letting them come to know one another and stimulating them to show their own characters. After the War he gave me, and inscribed, a fine India-paper copy of *An Englishman in Greece*, an anthology by Rennell Rodd, which was a constant companion to Dorothy and me on our travels there, and is still treasured.

Altogether Hertford was a most friendly place, the dons obviously doing their best to make Freshmen feel at home, whilst the weekly tutorial, when one read an essay or took a prose to one's tutor and discussed it with him, somehow enhanced the feeling of community as well as being one of the most effective ways yet discovered of imparting knowledge and raising standards of scholarship. My own tutor, J. D. Denniston, was a fine scholar of Greek and Roman literature and grammar; I fancy he soon realised that I was unlikely to do very well in Honour Mods, knew that I had a leaning towards antiquities, and after consulting Professor Percy Gardner, advised me to take Pass Mods in two terms, with the aim of leaving enough time after taking Greats to study for a Diploma in Classical Archaeology. Percy Gardner had been the prime mover in introducing Greek Art as a subject for examination in Oxford; he had been an Assistant Keeper in the Medal Room at the British Museum before becoming a Professor, and he now introduced me to the study of Greek coins, from which I have learned much, especially that every detail, however small, in any work of Greek art, may be important in interpreting it, and should never be ignored.

In the Christmas holidays of 1913 I had been staying with the de Peyers at Newent in Gloucestershire, and in the following summer invited them up for Eights Week. Everard de Peyer, my future father-in-law, was a Chartered Accountant, whose work was connected largely with breweries, and who spent most of his time travelling up and down the country by rail auditing their accounts. His father, Carl Ferdinand de Peyer, had been correspondent to a Swiss newspaper, had married an Englishwoman and settled in London; he belonged to a Swiss family which had been ennobled by one of its members, a doctor, having discovered the 'patches' named after him. The family still flourishes in Switzerland, the main branch being at Schaffhausen, where there is a family museum. Everard de Peyer's over-riding ambition was to establish a comparable branch of the family in England. He had remarkable business ability, had steadily built up a fortune, and it was not until he was over forty that he married Edith Mabel Starkey, twenty years his junior; she was the elder daughter of Thomas Starkey, head of what was then the main brewery in the West Country, Starkey, Knight and Ford. He had bought Newent Court as a country seat, and now had a thriving family of three daughters and three sons.

Eights Week started, and Mrs de Peyer, with her two elder daughters, Hilda and Dorothy, was driven up from Newent in their Napier car, known in the family as 'the hearse', which recalled, in its coachwork and capaciousness, the days of the horse-drawn carriage. We watched the races from the Hertford barge. This was the last full array on the Isis of the College barges with their elegant guests; and the last of the old Oxford. We dispersed for the Long Vacation little knowing – knowing not at all – that most of us would never see one another again, or that to those who survived, our care-free world would seem like the distant past. On August 4th war with Germany was declared.

Chapter II

The First War

SOON AFTER WAR WAS DECLARED, and after consulting the College, I went down to Colchester, where a battalion of Royal Fusiliers was forming, was interviewed by the Colonel, provisionally accepted, and early in October 1914 was commissioned in the Infantry. Our early training was in Colchester, but in the new year we moved to Codford in the valley of the river Wylie. The training was hard but well planned, and we finished with a final bout based on our depot at Colchester, about a week of marching – a very tough unit capable of averaging twenty miles a day with the full kit of eighty pounds. Morale was excellent.

In the summer of 1915 the Battalion crossed to France. We were part of the 53rd Brigade of the 18th Division, under General Leo Maxse, one of the most enterprising Generals on the Front, but, like all the Higher Command, whether on the British or the German side, frustrated by the stagnation of trench-warfare which no-one knew how to break.

We were posted to Fricourt, a few miles east of Albert, where we took over from the French; it was a curiously quiet part of the lines since both sides had realised the futility of firing off small-arms ammunition without any possibility of result. Ammunition for artillery hardly existed on the British side and it used to be a joke that our supporting batteries of eighteen-pounders were allotted a single shell a day. The Germans had field artillery and light howitzers, and apparently plenty of ammunition, but used it sparingly except for an evening or a morning "hate". The reason was perhaps partly the character of the line in this sector, for earlier in the war when the lines had, as it were, crystallized, there had been intense mining and counter-mining here, and the opposing trenches were now in effect on the opposite lips of a large mine-crater, at a guess about thirty yards across, anyhow too wide apart to throw a hand-grenade. Sixty years later, when our daughter Silvia was living in Augsburg, where her husband directed the Opera, I was introduced during an interval to a friendly German of about my own age who had recently retired from being Mayor of Augsburg, having been appointed by the Americans, as a known anti-Nazi, when they invaded Germany. After a minute or two we discovered that we had both actually been in this same sector at Fricourt in 1915, opposite each other on the lip of the crater.

When we took over Fricourt mining had not ceased entirely, but was confined to small explosions deep underground which caused us no alarm whatever, but which we imagined were a private war – it certainly seemed a separate one from ours – between the engineers on opposite sides trying to blow in the heads of each other's mine-shafts; whether they were successful or not and whether anyone was ever hurt we never knew. Sadly enough not everything was so innocuous. The first casualty in my platoon was a Corporal Tarry. In those early days, when things seemed so quiet, people became careless; front-line trenches were normally about six feet deep but had a firing-step towards the enemy from which one could look over no-man's-land, but thus exposing one's head. Tarry was doing just this when an enemy sniper spotted him; the bullet struck Tarry sideways in one temple, passed behind his eyes and emerged through the other temple, blinding him completely. Within a week he was, we were told, about again, but without sight.

Far the worst weapon that the Germans brought against us was the *Minenwerfer*, nicknamed "the Minnie". This was a canister of high explosive of enormous size – a mine in fact – which was flung a hundred yards or more from some great catapulting machine. It turned over and over in the air and, when it had fallen, detonated with such a violent explosion that the nerves of anyone within a fairly large radius were literally shattered; one could not imagine anything more demoralizing. They were sometimes nicknamed "oilcans", and were thought to have quite a thin casing, but after one such explosion I remember a piece of metal a foot long and weighing three or four pounds landing near: it was red-hot and a good half-inch thick. Howitzer shells were not particularly alarming unless they actually landed in the trench, since they buried themselves in the soil before exploding. The shell from a field-gun – the "whizz-bang" – had a vicious sound from its high velocity, but its velocity also gave it a flattish trajectory, so that it did not normally fall right into the trench; but shells from a trench-mortar were lobbed, and, if they fell near you, could kill or mutilate instantly. As an example of the coolest courage, and also of Cockney humour, it would be hard to surpass our Mess-Batman Frost. In the trenches one day he came out from a dug-out carrying a couple of mugs of tea on a board that did duty as a tray; the shell from a German trench-mortar fell right into the trench and right between Frost's feet. It was a dud. "Blimey," he said, "I very nearly dropped it!"

We were in and out of the trenches

Bernard in the uniform of the Eleventh Royal Fusiliers, 1914.

for several months. At one period a German regiment of fine marksmen, presumably recruited from hunting country, moved in, and it was perilous to put one's head above the parapet even for a second. About the same time our Company was issued with two rifles fitted with telescopic sights, and I was appointed sniping-officer, which could be worked in easily with the ordinary watch-keeping duties of constantly walking up and down one's own section of the trenches. I was given three or four of the best shots in the Company to train whilst we were out of trenches for the ordinary week's rest, and when we were back again in the front line we devoted ourselves to making "hides" – watching-posts from which we could study the German parapets with a telescope through the hours of daylight. Naturally most of the construction of these had to be done at night, and the purpose was not only to make them as inconspicuous as possible, but also to build dummy posts so as to divert attention from the real ones. We also decided that firing must never be done from the watching-posts but only from other separately made places for the rare shots when we thought we had identified enemy sniping-posts. By sheer good luck the intense German activity died down. Evidently it was because the German regiment opposite us had been relieved by another not so determined or skilful. The tragedy was to come; our finest shot, Corporal Matson, was killed instantly by a bullet through the head when watching from one of the hides.

The winter was grim, and the trenches, whatever one did, knee-deep in mud and constantly tending to collapse. Yet I never remember either then or in the following winter, which was more severe, feeling really cold. This was partly because we were so fit, partly because we had thigh-length waders and inside them long thick woollen stockings impregnated with whale-oil. Duty was usually two hours on and two hours off, and in the two hours off one crept into a dug-out and went to sleep immediately, yet had the feeling of enjoying every moment of it, taking it in solid chunks. An hour before sunset and an hour before dawn everyone stood-to, and at morning stand-to the ration of rum was served, or unsweetened lime-juice for those who did not take rum. Despite its magic I think everyone vowed that after the war they would never voluntarily see another dawn.

Bernard in the rifle-butts at Colchester, 1915.

We moved to another sector of the line not far away where the trenches were further apart, perhaps two or three hundred yards, and in the spring the battalion of the Northamptonshire Regiment which alternated with us in the trenches was doing its week of duty when it was raided by the Germans, using, for the first time it was said, tear-gas. Our gas-masks, which were thought to be proof against the deadly chlorine gas, were fairly primitive, being a large pad of flannel soaked in some chemical solution; but they were useless against the not deadly but completely disabling tear-gas. The German artillery fire was limited to a small sector of the Northants line, but when this had been thoroughly saturated the raiding party – no doubt with protective masks – arrived, took prisoner a number of the British blinded by the gas, and then retired. This was clearly designed to discover what units were manning that sector, and so inferring the presence of the larger units to which they belonged. When we took over the trenches again there was still a strong sweet odour of the tear-gas, but it no longer produced tears.

Soon after this there happened the worst personal experience that I had during the war. My very dear friend, Nelson Neate, who commanded a platoon in our D Company (I commanded one in C Company) decided to try out the new rifle-grenades with which we had just been issued. A rifle-grenade is usually an iron case, much like a corn-cob in shape, with a rod attached to its base; the rod is thrust into the barrel of a rifle which has been fixed at the appropriate angle and loaded with a blank cartridge. When the trigger is pressed the grenade itself with its rod should soar into the air and come down a couple of hundred yards away, exploding on impact. Nelson pressed the trigger, but the grenade exploded prematurely at the muzzle of the rifle, wounding him and fracturing his skull. I did what I could; a stretcher-bearer was soon on the spot, and Nelson was carried from the trenches and taken to the nearest hospital behind the lines. There I was able to go and visit him after we were relieved from our tour of duty. His mind wandered a little and we talked of the happy times we had had together whilst training in Essex and Wiltshire; after some weeks and a move to a hospital at the Base he partly recovered. Most people would have been content to be sent back to England, but he was the most courageous of people and determined to get back to the Front as soon as possible. This was not to be for some months, and when eventually he did rejoin the Battalion he took part in an attack in another sector of the Somme in May 1917 and was reported "missing"; his body was never found.

When the grenade exploded I was stooping down just below the blast of shrapnel, unhurt but badly shocked; I too was sent back to Base and did not rejoin the Battalion until the first offensive on the Somme was over, and I was then just in time to take part in the battle for Thiepval in September, which was only the second occasion on which the newly-invented tanks were used in battle. The name "Tank", now commonplace, was devised to conceal that anything unusual was afoot. I acted as liaison-officer between our own battalion and the Northants on our flank. This was necessary because in those days, before the invention of radio, communication was by land-line, and the light wires were the first things to be severed by shellfire, so that no-one knew what was happening except immediately around him. Incidentally, I doubt if anyone has ever adequately praised the signallers in the First War, who repaired their lines, usually at night, under always difficult and often most dangerous conditions.

I was able to report to the two commanding officers more or less what was going on, and I was able to see at first hand the difficulties the tanks were meeting; their engines were not powerful enough to haul them out of the collapsed trenches and great shell-holes in which they were bogged down, and they were naturally a prime target for enemy gunfire.

The front lines became static again, and faced each other immobile through the bitter winter of 1916–1917. It was extraordinary to see the duck-boards, essential in communication-trenches over the mud earlier on, now frozen solid and so slippery that it was almost impossible to walk on them. The duck-boards ran across open country as well as in the trenches, and one had to keep to them because the land around was almost everywhere deeply pitted with shell-holes and virtually impassable. It was thus not only dangerous but painful to relieve another unit in the trenches, or for that matter to be relieved by them.

The anger and exasperation at the frequent falls were naturally extreme, and the language fearful; yet strangely enough the incident I remember most vividly coming down from the front line one moonlit night was an infantryman, loaded as we all were with rifle, ammunition, and kit, slipping off the duck-boards and rolling into a shell-hole. It was as if he had exhausted all his expletives, and I heard him say, not very loudly but with the most intense depth of feeling "Oh God! I *am* hurting myself."

The misery of the trenches was not so much the discomfort, fear, even terror, though these were occasionally acute, but the knowledge of the continuing casualties, and of the certainty that sooner or later one's own turn would come; my own tour of nineteen months was unusually long. On the other side was the comradeship, the humour, and the constant spectacle of unspectacular courage and endurance; and there was also considerable comfort to be had, absurd though it may now seem, in the familiar sophism, said to have been invented by the French, and current in two or three slightly different versions:-

> When you are a soldier you are one of two things: you are either at the Front or behind the lines. If you are behind the lines you needn't worry. If you are at the Front you are one of two things: you are either in a danger zone or one that is not dangerous. If you are in a zone that is not dangerous you needn't worry. If you are in a danger zone you are one of two things: either you are wounded or you are not. If you are not wounded you needn't worry. If you are wounded you are one of two things: either seriously wounded or slightly wounded. If you are slightly wounded you needn't worry. If you are seriously wounded one of two things is certain: either you recover or you die. If you recover you needn't worry; if you die you can't worry. So there is no need to worry at all.

And then the rats. They swarmed everywhere and the stories and jokes about them were endless. "Look at the size of that rat, Bill! No, not *that* one, the one that's carrying your kit bag." I'm afraid it is only too clear what they mainly fed on: but they would eat anything – leather, clothes, candles (blowing out the flame, it was said, when necessary) and each other. I had had a wonderful gift by post, a wooden box containing a gross of bars of Bournville chocolate, a couple of bars for every man in my platoon. At night it lay on the shelf in my dug-out; in the morning the end of the box had gone, and with it more than a hundred bars of chocolate. Round Christmas time we held a famous strong-point just behind the lines, Mouquet Farm; it wasn't a building any longer, just the cellars with a great pile of rubble on top that made it seem safe and warm. We had a tinned Christmas pudding and a joint of meat; even rats couldn't open the tin, but the only way of saving the meat was to hang it by a long thin wire from the ceiling.

We sometimes tried to kill a few, going out at night with sticks and electric torches. One night we flung open the door of a barn, and when we looked in the whole floor – thirty feet long at a guess – was gently undulating; we could hardly believe our eyes. It was a complete carpet of rats, literally thousands of them.

Early in the New Year of 1917 my own Company Commander, Captain Hoare, was killed by a howitzer shell which fell near and buried him in the collapsed trench. He was a splendid soldier, not a Regular, never over-demonstrative, but always calm and practical. Our senior platoon commander, Geoffrey Cumberlege, had been made Battalion Adjutant; so I now commanded C Company.

Our Regular Officers were fine examples of the Regular Army: Colonel Carr, commanding, steady and kind; his second-in-command, Major Meyrick, equally efficient and with a dry but keen sense of humour; Minchin, our Quartermaster, as good a specimen as one could want of an officer who had worked his way up from the ranks; and Wilkin, our transport officer, a veteran from the Boer War. Transport was by horses or mules; motor-cars, even the famous Model T Ford (known to us as "the flying bedstead") being quite rare still. Periodically, when we were out of trenches, a new batch of horses would be sent up from the Base to replace those that had been killed, and company commanders would go down to have a look at them with the possibility that one of the new batch – nominally for pulling Service waggons – might be better as a charger than the one they had already; and this sometimes proved to be so, for they were naturally a pretty mixed lot. One indeed bolted with me in the Forest of Crecy, in a rainstorm; but since the Forest is planned on a grid system, with rides stretching for miles in a straight line, all I had to do was to stay on its back until the beast was exhausted.

The village to which we came for our rest periods out of trenches was Franvillers, where we had quarters for both men and officers. We were on excellent terms with the villagers – to whom we brought a touch of prosperity – and we even introduced a system of token paper-money for small change, which was redeemed by our Quartermaster. The officers of our Company had a modest house and spruced it up: we found a French wallpaper with a design of foliage not unlike a William Morris paper, and papered the little room used for a Mess. I was also able to buy a table for it from a little antique shop in the village. It was in Louis

XVI style, two or three inches at the lower end of its six legs had rotted away, and, as I discovered later, it had had five successive coats of paint of different colours, which argued a respectable age. It was of oak, circular, about five feet in diameter and hinged in the middle so as to fold up in a semi-circle, one of the most simple and pleasing designs possible. It was eventually sent back to England, and we have since used it with pleasure as a dining-table in Rome, Amersham, London and Oxford for more than fifty years, although its slender legs were all broken off in transit to Rome.

As spring drew nearer the lines of trenches became more flexible. There was a successful attack here and there which moved them forward – or backward – a few hundred yards; and there seemed to be prospects of a more general movement. An attack by our own Brigade was planned for February 17th. We were still not far from Albert, in the neighbourhood of Miraumont; our trenches ran along the edge of a ravine called Boom Ravine, with some dug-outs in the side of it. The attack was to be made in one long line, in which it was naturally important there should be no gaps. A sergeant and I were up in front of the trenches early in the night of the 16th, and had pegged out with tapes the line from which our men were to advance, the plan being that the bulk of the Company should rest well behind the front line during the night and move up in time to form for the attack. Things were made very difficult by the thaw which had now set in, and the ground was both muddy and sticky. Evidently the enemy either knew or suspected our plans, and about an hour before we were due to form put down a heavy barrage on and behind our front line. The result was that my Company could not get through, and the sergeant and I waited hopelessly for them to arrive.

Geoffrey Cumberlege came and I explained the situation to him; he was encouraging but of course could do nothing about it. Strangely enough at this point I felt no fear, only great anxiety that we should leave a gap in the line of attack. I don't understand the psychology, but I think it was partly this anxiety and partly the conviction that the shell fire was so heavy it was no good being frightened. I was wounded in the knee by a piece of shrapnel but not at all seriously, and when zero-hour came and only a few men had managed to get through, the handful of us went over the top together. I suppose we made twenty or thirty yards under machine-gun fire when I was hit by a bullet coming from somewhere on my left, which knocked me over; but I felt no pain, simply a heavy blow. It struck the inside of my right thigh and then went through my trouser pocket in which I was carrying a large magnetic compass and a handful of spare revolver cartridges; some of these must have exploded and blown a large flesh-wound just under my hip, filling it with metal fragments, but mercifully not damaging an artery or the hip itself. I rolled or was flung into a shell hole and this may have saved my life, since the area was still swept by machine-gun fire. Some time after, I have no idea how long, I was found by our Medical Officer Major J. C. Sale. It would be impossible to exaggerate his courage, efficiency and kindness, which was felt then and always throughout the Battalion; my only regret is that perhaps I did not express my gratitude warmly enough then, or later, for all that he had done. Stretcher-bearers took me to a Casualty Clearing Station, and there a doctor extracted some of the pieces with which my wound was filled. It was probably unwise to use a general anaesthetic since the aim was, naturally, to keep casualties moving back from the line as quickly as possible; and I remember telling him in a friendly way how much I disliked him for hurting me so much. But I don't suppose it was really any worse than an ordinary visit to a dentist, and to compensate for the pain there was the comforting thought that one was still alive.

We were taken back to Rouen, thence by hospital-ship to London and to a nursing home in Mandeville Place, off Wigmore Street. My wound being large and dirty went septic, and, penicillin not having been discovered, was treated for about a week effectively with a solution newly invented in Edinburgh University, and called therefore Eusol; during that time I lost exactly a stone in weight which I have never regained. When convalescent I had a series of small operations on my thigh to relieve pain caused by damage to nerves or to remove pieces of metal still embedded deeply, all of which emerged later on.

When I was fit again for home service I was posted to an A4 Battalion at Clipston in Northants. These were young men conscripted – conscription, at that grim stage in the war with the outcome still uncertain, had become essential – but excellent material for training, and I commanded what seemed under the circumstances a happy company, and extraordinarily smart; I have rarely seen better parade ground drill. It was a Rifle Regiment, the 52 Rifle Brigade, which has a slightly different small-arms drill, and marches at a quicker step than an ordinary infantry regiment; this, even when a little lame, it was not difficult to acquire. When they were trained, I took over a draft to France – a distressing job to anyone knowing what awaited them. I was later posted back to Regimental Headquarters in Colchester, and continued with a similar task of training recruits.

In the autumn of 1918 came the epidemic of "Asian" Influenza, which spread over the whole of Britain and infected many thousands; in some families two or three people died. Resistance lowered by years of strain and privation seems to have made people particularly vulnerable, but that is not the whole story, for, curiously, it often attacked and killed the young and vigorous. In our depot at Colchester was Joe Grimmett, with whom I had become particularly friendly. He was a perfect specimen of the gentle giant, and a most congenial companion with a fine dry sense of humour; a Canadian, who had been sparring-partner of Jack Dempsey, the boxing champion, thus in good health and training. He caught the infection and died within a week. People were naturally anxious, and when I had it too, Father came down to Colchester on October 31st to see me. Then on November 11th came the Armistice, and although there were scenes of wild rejoicing in London, most people's feelings were of deep relief and thankfulness not openly expressed.

When demobilization was ordered, students were given a high priority, and I was released in January 1919 to return to Oxford.

Chapter III

Oxford, Greece and Italy

OXFORD WAS A SAD and empty place after the war. Only a handful of its undergraduates had come back to the College and the University was slow in reviving. It was impossible to forget all those who had given their lives, or my own special friends, Nelson Neate and Percy Campbell. Irreparable is a feeble word for the losses that Britain suffered in talent and in the promise of future generations – and from which we still suffer seventy years later.

Many of the Dons had been in the Services, the younger mostly at the Front, and it is misleading to suggest, as does Vera Brittain's *Testament of Youth*, that the advent of a new wild batch of undergraduates from the Forces was anticipated with foreboding; or, in my experience, that the Freshmen were oblivious of what survivors had suffered and concerned only with their own prospects. Among new Hertford Freshmen was Neville Hadcock, with whom I became particularly friendly, and since he had a car we did some expeditions together, including one to stay with Dorothy's people at Newent. He was a Roman Catholic and a keen student of mediaeval architecture and monastic foundations, having already produced a detailed reconstruction of Hexham Priory which was not far from where

Oxford, High Street, 1920

Hertford College, Oxford. Senior and Junior commonrooms dining together, 1919. Front row from left: J.D. Denniston, Tutor in Classics; John McLeod Campbell (Chaplain of 51st Highland Division in World War I, later Principal of Trinity College, Kandy, Ceylon and Master of The Charter House, and Stella's god-father); L.H.D. Blacker, Senior Scholar; Cannon Burroughs, Classical Tutor, afterwards Bishop of Peterborough; R.T. Peel, Chairman of Junior Commonroom; C.R. Cruttwell, afterwards Principal of Hertford; Bernard; G.Brewis, St Edmund Hall, Lecturer in Logic. Middle row on far right: M.D. Thomas, best man at Bernard's wedding. Back row on far right; Neville Hadcock.

he lived. Throughout his life he worked on this subject, and in 1971 produced, with Father David Knowles, an encyclopaedic book which will always remain the standard work of reference, *Mediaeval Religious Houses: England and Wales*.

In addition to a few British Freshmen a small number of young American officers had been admitted – half a dozen perhaps to Hertford; and although Oxford barely resembled what it had been and therefore gave them little idea of college life, they were themselves an enlivening element, active in study and in playing games. One of them, A. Hoyt, I came to know well and to admire; we were partners in college tennis matches when these were restored and I was able to play again.

There was an arrangement by which those undergraduates who had served during the war could fairly soon take what was called a War Degree, but I preferred to take an ordinary Pass Degree, which seemed more valuable and would still allow time to study for a Diploma in Classical Archaeology afterwards.

For the Pass Degree I attended lectures on Logic by G. Brewis, a Fellow of St Edmund Hall. These were extraordinarily valuable both in clarifying one's own thoughts and detecting the fallacies in other people's; it is a pity that elementary logic is not a common subject at school. I then went on to the Diploma under Percy Gardner and his then young lecturer on Greek vases, John Beazley; and since one of my subjects was Greek coins I first made the acquaintance of the staff in the Medal Room at the British Museum, two of whom, George Hill, the Keeper, and Stanley Robinson who succeeded him, became lifelong friends of both Dorothy and me. Meanwhile the help they gave to the young, their patience in producing tray after tray of coins and in sharing their own profound knowledge, could not be surpassed; it is one aspect of British education probably unique, but seldom recorded.

In April 1919 there happened the most important event of my life; on a visit to Newent I became engaged to Dorothy de Peyer, and we spent an idyllic summer holiday with our respective families in Cornwall.

In the following summer I took the Diploma in Classical Archaeology, was awarded a studentship at the British School at Athens, and later in the year the Craven Fellowship, which allows for two years of travel abroad. In October we were married, and went on our honeymoon to Greece by way of Italy, travelling from Calais to Rome by the famous Train de Luxe, at that time within even

In the garden of Grove Cottage, Wanstead (Bernard's mother's house, near Ilford, Essex), about 1920. From left: Gladys, Elswitha (cousin), Father, Mother, Dorothy and Constance.

Dorothy on her wedding day, Newent, 1920.

modest means, which lived up to its reputation for comfort and good food, a reputation that it lost later on, even before the train itself vanished from the timetables. It ran late; we arrived long after midnight and drove to our hotel in a little carrozza, astounded by the scale and magnificence of the buildings of which we had had only the faintest idea; these were enhanced by the silent, dark and empty streets. Next morning we woke to the sun rising over a view unrivalled anywhere in the world, the panorama of Rome.

We stayed in Rome for a few days and paid only a brief visit to the British School with which we were to become more closely associated later on. From there to Naples where, unaware of its sinister reputation, we wandered round the docks in the evening after dinner and found that we were being surreptitiously followed, but managed to elude our pursuer without discovering whether his intentions were murderous, which, we later heard, was allegedly common at that time. Two or three days later we embarked on a Rumanian ship, and after a very rough crossing landed at Piraeus.

The British School at Athens, for which we were bound, had been founded in 1885 on the initiative of the Prince of Wales and Mr Gladstone; F. C. Penrose, the architect who first discovered the subtleties of the Parthenon, was its first Director. It catered only for archaeologists and classical scholars, and shared a large garden with the more recently founded American School of Classical Studies. For the British School there were two buildings, the Director's House, and the Students' Hostel incorporating the Library. Students were normally graduates and were expected to be single, or, if married, to live outside the School.

The Director was Alan Wace, his Assistant Director Stanley Casson. Wace was a leading expert of Greek prehistory, and also on Greek embroidery, so expert that on his retirement from the post of Director he became Head of the Department of Textiles in the Victoria and Albert Museum. Though good with stu-

The British School at Athens, 1937.

dents, he was not an easy character; he seemed to take a delight in academic and other feuds and was at loggerheads with Sir Arthur Evans on archaeological matters, with his managing committee in London, and with his Assistant Director. He was also involved in Greek politics, being anti-royalist and a strong partisan of Venizelos. As a matter of principle it is clearly unwise for the Director of a foreign institute to take part in local politics, since it affects not only the individual but the welfare of his institution and leads to awkward situations as, for instance, in that which was just developing and leading to the return of King Constantine.

We stayed at first in an hotel in Athens, and then found lodgings with a Greek family on the coast at Phaleron; this involved an easy tram journey into the city. Athens, incredible though it now seems, had little motor traffic, and the first taxis – three of them – made their appearance on one of the two main squares, Constitution Square. Travelling in the country was either by train, horse, mule, donkey or on foot. For long journeys we favoured horse or mule for luggage and occasional riding; donkeys were apt to be rather slow, and it often seemed unfair to ride anything so small. We carried rucksacks, but also my plate camera, usually two or three dozen glass plates, and a heavy wooden tripod.

Towards the end of November the Greek elections were to take place; Venizelos was in power and King Constantine in exile. There were demonstrations by both parties, and it seemed as if Venizelos would be returned by a vast majority; but he was heavily defeated and soon after left for France on a British destroyer.

The first indication we had of this was when our tram from Phaleron was halted outside the city because the driver refused to go further, and when we left it to walk in we were halted by an armed sentry who indicated that it would be unhealthy to proceed. What was happening was that Royalists and Venizelists were exchanging shots with each other from the buildings each occupied, and their supporters were wandering about the streets discharging their revolvers, true mostly in the air, but not all that careful where the shots went. The British Minister decided that all students should be moved into the British School in case they had to leave the country at short notice, and this set the precedent, followed since, for wives to reside with their husbands in the School.

Bernard, about 1920.

Partly because of the war there were not many students, but those there were most congenial: Winifred Lamb from Cambridge, working on Greek bronzes; May Herford on Greek vases; and Miriam Chandler, the Sachs Student, whose statutory duty was to lay a wreath on the grave of the Founder's husband, no easy task since no-one knew precisely where the grave was. We also had some foreign students whose countries at that time had no Institute in Athens: G. A. Snijder, Dr and Mrs Hondius, all from Holland, and Axel Boethius from Sweden who later became a great friend. There were also occasional visitors, for instance F. L. Lucas, the Cambridge Don and author, and Leonard Woolley, the excavator. Another kind and helpful resident was F. B. Welch, British Passport Controller, who had a wide knowledge of the country and the people, often led us all on Sunday walks, and advised us on wider expeditions.

One of our early shorter expeditions was to Methana, a volcanic peninsula not far from Aegina, but reached only by steamer at rare intervals. We wanted to find out whether there was a source, other than the best-known one at Melos, where the Greeks could have obtained obsidian, the volcanic glass widely used in prehistoric times for making implements. The weather was rainy and the extinct volcano we had hoped to explore – two and a half thousand feet high – was covered with mist, so that we could not climb it. Whilst we were waiting by the sulphur-spring that the volcano still produces, we were approached by a friendly Greek who invited us to visit his house on the far side of the peninsula; and we walked with him the two or three miles to what must then have been, though not particularly remote, one of the least accessible spots in Greece. He asked us in, and there on the wall of the little living-room was a picture-postcard of Chigwell, not far from my family home in Essex; surely the oddest coincidence.

We made several long expeditions to places now well-known and easily accessible, but some of them then remote; the walled city of Aegosthena on the Gulf of Corinth; Lycosoura with its shrine and colossal statues; the great monastery of Megaspeleon half-buried in the mountain-side and swathed in mist when we were there; as well as famous sites like Corinth, Olympia and Delphi. Delphi has changed more than most. Then it seemed to cling to the cliff face; the modern tarmac roads and broad car-parks have robbed it of this feeling of almost hanging in the air, but they have not spoilt its wonderful view of the sea of olives that stretches down to the Corinthian Gulf, or the romance of the distant fires kindled by shepherds on hills across the valley of the Pleistos.

'Confrontation with the housekeeper' (British School at Athens), 1920. From left to right: F. B. Welch, Dorothy Ashmole, Bernard Ashmole, May Herford, Miriam Chandler. Drawing by Winifred Lamb.

We made the stiff two-and-a-half hours climb further up the valley to Arachova and from there explored the Livadi, the plateau a thousand feet above Delphi itself, with its fine view of Parnassus; but failed to find the famous Korykian cave there, and after spending several hours looking for it were reduced to melting patches of snow to quench our thirst. Some years later we did succeed in finding it, with the help of a guide who knew how; the entrance is near the top of a wooded hill instead of near the bottom as one would expect, and instead of being a single tunnel-like opening is half concealed in a long narrow horizontal fissure. Inside is what appears to be a colossal seated statue, a natural formation, but one which presumably led to the cave being dedicated to Pan.

On that occasion and when, in autumn seven years later, we had again been in Delphi, we were once more struck, as one can hardly fail to be, by the general beauty of the situation, and at that season by the thousand clusters of yellow crocus studding the grey limestone cliffs. But it was an aesthetic pleasure, easily accounted for; we felt no special sense of awe or mystery, nor saw any obvious reason why the shrine should have been established in that particular place. That was to come quite unexpectedly on a third or fourth visit ten years later still. I had been invited by French archaeologists to supper in their excavation-hut near the northern edge of the precinct. Before supper I took a walk to the Castalian

Spring, lingered rather too long, and on my way back thought to save a minute or two by walking diagonally across the site. I was not thinking of the beauty of the situation or indeed of anything connected with Delphi, except to keep my appointment, when quite suddenly I walked into what I can only describe as a wall of peace, almost tangible; outside it was common day, inside this invisible line it was utterly peaceful, as if nothing else mattered. Its boundary seemed to have nothing to do with the ancient precinct, it was nowhere near the temple, indeed there was nothing on the ground to mark it, but it undoubtedly existed, as real as anything felt by any of the five senses. I stood still, wondering what had happened, then walked on, and in the next hundred yards the sensation faded. Only in one other place have Dorothy and I felt anything a little like it, and that is where we live in 1980 at Peebles; here the precinct round the Cross Kirk is pervaded by a stillness and calm which many people feel.

From Delphi we had planned to visit the great monastery of Hosios Loukas, the churches of which have splendid mosaics; it could be reached only on foot, and in Arachova we hired a boy with a mule for our luggage. After some delay, because the boy we had bargained with the night before had allowed the animal to go off to the vineyards to work, we started off, and descending many hundred feet on the way reached the great enclosed valley which the monastery overlooks. It was the week before Easter and the monks were still observing Lenten fast, but they received us hospitably, with apologies for the meagre fare, which in contrast to their own was not meagre at all. Our fellow guests were a friendly and helpful

Group at British School at Athens, 1921. From left: Miriam Chandler, F. B. Welch, Winifred Lamb, May Herford, Stanley Casson, Leonard Woolley, Bernard Ashmole, and F. L. Lucas.

Greek doctor and his sister (in Greece one did not normally travel with one's wife), our mule-boy, and a poor countryman who was destitute because his house had fallen down on him. He had taken refuge in the monastery and was being treated for his injuries, but he was care-free and an amusing companion, guiding us the next day to Chaeronea and the colossal lion celebrating Philip of Macedon's victory; although the going was pretty rough he very sensibly carried his shoes under his arm to save wear.

The monastery has a wonderful position commanding a view over the valley to Mount Helikon, and Parnassus, always impressive, not a great distance away. In antiquity Helikon was the haunt of the Muses, and it is still haunted by them, as was shown by a quite unexpected thrilling experience. In the evening, after supper, as we sat on the balcony of the guest-house overhanging the valley, there rose up from it a sound as of singing, of many distant voices blending, and suffusing the whole atmosphere continuously. We were puzzled about its source, and then realised that it must be produced by the overtones of the hundreds of sheep-bells from the flocks in the valley far below. We had never heard anything like it, nor have we ever heard its like since; the nearest approach is perhaps in the falls at Tivoli near Rome, where sometimes one hears a kind of singing noise from the overtones of the falling water, but not nearly so persistent or pervasive as this.

We also went to several of the islands, and once set out for Santorin, but the weather was so rough that when the ship reached Paros we gave up and looked for a room there. When we got into it we saw bugs on the walls in broad daylight: this is so unusual – they usually only come out in the dark – that we feared what the night might bring forth, and decided to camp out on the sea-shore instead.

We hired a horse to carry our luggage, walked with it some way along the coast, found a secluded bay, and laid out our kit. It was a crescent-shaped bay on the far corner of which was a little house; soon the whole family came across to us and invited us to spend the night there. This was embarrassing, for we did not like to refuse such charming hospitality; but we explained that we had deliberately chosen to sleep in the open and they reluctantly went away. Half an hour later a small child arrived with a flask of fresh water, a little plate of tiny fishes and a bunch of flowers. I don't think we have ever been more touched by a gift, so appealing in itself and so sweetly offered. We woke in the morning to see the rowing-boat we had ordered gently rocking by our camp, waiting to take us back to join the steamer.

Our last expedition in the Peloponnese was to the temple of Apollo at Bassae in Arcadia. One climbs up from Andritsaena, which we reached after the wettest day we ever had in Greece. We lodged there in a little house where there lived a mother and her two daughters. The husband was dead and the only brother had been killed in Asia Minor. In a Greek family this means, or meant then, that neither girl would ever marry, because neither would have a dowry which the father, or failing him the brother, would have provided. Thus both girls were intensely interested in what Dorothy's dowry had been. Had it been a large one? Had her camera been part of it? And so on.

In Andritsaena we hired a boy with a little horse to guide us first to Bassae, and reached the temple in rather less than the three hours it was supposed to take. Our plan had been to make our way southwards until we struck the railway where there would be a train to Kalamata, and spend the night there. Our boy lost his way, and after walking for three hours we found ourselves at a spot which was said in Baedeker to be only an hour and a half from the temple. It was a rugged track with many steep climbs both up and down, and it involved crossing the steep ravine of the River Neda, and the river itself, a fierce little torrent in spate because of the heavy rain the day before. Even had we not lost our way the walk from the temple to the railway was said to take seven hours, and it was late in the evening when we struck a station on the railway. The only train had gone. The place was aptly named Diavolitzi. The cafe near the station was not used to lodging strangers, but the people were friendly and gave us a room which looked quite clean; in the next room was a hen with eleven chicks, a cat or two, a handloom, and three children sleeping under a rug. About one o'clock I woke with a bite on my forehead and lighted a candle. We each had a little mosquito-net; the candle revealed that both our nets were swarming with bugs, Dorothy's twenty or thirty and mine rather fewer. Only the small ones could get through the mesh, but the very sight of them at that time was intimidating; for half an hour we tried to exterminate them and finally got to sleep again, fitfully, being careful to keep the candle alight, which they didn't like. Quite soon after we were awoken again by a fairly severe earthquake shock; the room fairly staggered, but nothing fell, and no-one in the village was hurt, though many were alarmed, since the Peloponnese was, and always has been, prone to heavy earthquakes.

Next morning we caught a train but got off at a station a few miles short of Kalamata, and from there climbed Mount Ithome. The wild flowers were wonderful, rather different from Attica and even from other parts of the Peloponnese, chiefly wild lavender, asphodel, and numberless bushes of broom completely covered with blossom and contrasting splendidly with the many Judas trees and their deep purple flowers. There were many lizards too, some brightly coloured; and huge tortoises. The view from the top has often been described and it certainly is spectacular: Mount Taygetos, almost equal in splendour to Parnassus; the whole of Messenia, including the Messenian Gulf to the south; to the west the sea again – the Ionian sea; many miles of country inland, including the hills we had crossed the day before; and just below, the city walls of ancient Messene and the two great circular stone enclosures of its Arcadian and Laconian gates.

We reached Kalamata the same evening; I did not see the town again for twenty years, and then in circumstances which, even with the liveliest imagination, I could not possibly have foretold.

In that summer of 1921 we came back from Greece by way of Italy, and being in Rome for a week or two, again visited the British School. This was of a different character from that in Athens. In 1911 there had been an International Exhibition in the Valle Giulia, a mile or so outside the walls of Rome, and the British Pavilion, designed by Lutyens, imitating the upper storey of the façade of

St' Paul's Cathedral in London and consisting simply of a long façade, had so much appealed to Italian taste that the site was offered to the British Government for an artistic Academy, on the condition that the Exhibition building should be reproduced to the same design in permanent materials. This was done, with the addition, by the time we joined it, of a dining-hall, a library, a Director's wing and studio wing; and the Commissioners of the Great Exhibition of 1851 founded a series of scholarships on the model of the much older French Academy at the Villa Medici and its scholarships known as the Prix de Rome. Ours, similarly, were to be held by practising artists called Rome Scholars; they were regarded as renewable annually for three years in all, were awarded in Painting, Sculpture, Architecture and Engraving, and were each administered by appropriate Faculty Committees in London, co-ordinated by an Honorary General Secretary. To this institution an older-established British School of Archaeology in Rome itself had been invited to accede, and it was agreed that the Director of the amalgamated body should be an archaeologist. It thus came about that the new school in the Valle Giulia was normally inhabited by up to three each of painters, sculptors, architects and engravers, all Rome Scholars, and by an unspecified number of archaeologists and classical students. This was not always an easy mix, for in those days university students, much rarer than they are now, were sometimes apt to give themselves airs, and the artists, who were commonly not from universities, naturally resented it. Not always so; if properly associated the two could often be of use to each other, and many friendships were formed, but it was a delicate balance.

The Director of the School was now Dr Thomas Ashby, a leading authority on Italian topography, with Mrs Arthur Strong, an expert on Greek and Roman sculpture, as Assistant Director. Mrs Strong asked me if I would take in hand the manuscript of the projected catalogue of the sculptures of the Palazzo dei Conservatori on the Capitol, which belonged to the Municipality of Rome. The School had already produced a catalogue of the sister museum, the Museo Capitolino on the other side of the Piazza del Campidoglio; it was on the model of the German Institute's catalogue of the sculptures of the Vatican, and though useful, was not entirely satisfactory – illustrations tended to be too small (a fault it shared with the German catalogue) and the descriptions were of uneven quality. The projected Conservatori Catalogue – a great mass of typescript – looked like having some of the same shortcomings, but the photographs (these already taken) were larger and better. The project was under the editorship of Professor Stuart Jones at Oxford, who, although not himself an expert on sculpture, as a previous Director of the School was named as author of the volume.

On our return to Rome next year, I soon began work on this pleasant assignment, and the Director of the Museum, Signor Settimo Bocconi, was extremely helpful. Although well educated, he was in the awkward position of not being a highly trained archaeologist but primarily an administrator, thus at the mercy of scholars – of a type not unknown in Rome – anxious to display their superior knowledge. I think he liked working with people with whom his relationship was on a human as distinct from an academic plane, and we became firm friends with him and his charming Canadian wife.

The Palazzo dei Conservatori is a fine building, and the large collection of sculpture was of high quality and less patched and restored than in some of the older collections. The thousand-year spread of period from Etruscan through to late Roman was a good test of one's judgement, and meant learning things outside one's ordinary beat. It included some famous pieces, each with its own problems of style and date, such as the bronze Wolf, the boy taking a thorn from his foot (*Il Spinario*), and the Esquiline Venus. In the typescript catalogue which I was handed some of the descriptions, which had been written by several different people, were perfect or needed only a little retouching; some needed re-writing and bringing up to date; and there were some sculptures of which no description had been written. One of the weakest features was the identification of the kinds of marble of which the statues were made, including such terms as "grechetto", which can have been intelligible only to Italian stonemasons. This is a difficult task anyhow, and scientists and archaeologists are still, fifty years later, arguing about how to identify marble.

Dorothy and I used to arrive early and spend the whole morning either checking the descriptions against the statues or studying the uncatalogued sculptures and writing new descriptions, often a lengthy business. In mid-morning we used to take a bun or the local equivalent and eat it in the little garden of the Palazzo, beside its gentle fountain.

Working long hours in a museum leads one to consider some of its problems – the placing and lighting of its sculptures, the help it can give to visitors, and the behaviour of the visitors themselves. Only too often a visitor would enter a room which held a sculpture starred in Baedeker, identify it, tick it off either literally or mentally, and pass on with barely another look. Of course there were others less superficial, but the modern tendency to encourage this approach suggests another problem – whether it is really worth while to transport a masterpiece across the oceans in order that ten thousand people may stand in front of it for a few seconds each. In my time as a museum Keeper I have always tried to provide plenty of seats so that visitors can sit and look for as long as they like, but the modern tendency, even, almost unbelievably, on railway-stations as well, is to clear everything away, so that the public can be more conveniently herded.

We were staying at the Hotel Hassler, which we had used on our first visit. This is now a luxury hotel, but at that time it was of a good second class, still having the original furnishings of its first Swiss proprietors, with much red plush and in one room an ingenious picture of a Swiss town square, with a clock-tower in which there was a real clock. The hotel, now standardised, then had some unusual features, partly because its plan was not rectangular – the northern corner, the only one visible, was less than a right angle, and this always gives a building a theatrical quality by diminishing its apparent solidity. One room was shaped like a spoon, the handle being an entrance passage and the room itself oval; the room we had now was known as "Il teatro" because the bedroom, windowless, was divided from the sitting-room by a curtain. It was warm too, because it was immediately over the hotel kitchen, but this was not without its drawbacks; it was swarming with mice, and when we set a trap we caught more than twenty of them in succession. They had however already been investigating the chest of drawers in which I kept my trousers, and had neatly consumed all the buttons (in those days made of casein) leaving only a little disc in the middle round the thread.

But the outstanding merit of the hotel was its superb position; set at the top of the Spanish Steps it commanded a magnificent westerly view over the city, with the dome of St Peter's in the centre, the view we had seen on our first morning in Rome. A few yards up the hill to the north west was the Villa Medici of the French School, with its little quiet piazza, a complete roof of ilexes over a single great fountain basin with a low hesitant jet. When we visited it some forty years later it was so tightly packed with parked cars that it was difficult to find one's way across – just one example of what has happened almost everywhere, a fine lay-out ruined by the motor-car.

In the middle of 1922 we came back to England and I began to work for my B.Litt. in Oxford. We looked about for a house, and had plans for purchasing the Trout Inn, a couple of miles up the river at Godstow. At that time this was hardly an inn, merely a humble public-house at which one could get a scratch breakfast or a lunch of bread and cheese; but it was built of stone, the position was exquisite and we were very keen. The price was not excessive, but the possession of a licence, which we could not utilize, enhanced it by a thousand pounds – quite a sum in those days – and put it beyond our means. Since then it has been transformed into one of the most fashionable resorts near Oxford. We then negotiated and eventually decided to rent 64 High Street, opposite Magdalen, and belonging to the College. This was a fine house, with a façade in stone towards the High embellished with carved stone medallions in Sheraton style, from which one guessed that its date might be around 1800; but at the back it had been extended in gimcrack fashion on a narrow plan and with walls of lath and plaster. Magdalen had just acquired this, the last house in a block of five or six which at that time they intended to rebuild; they had paid a high price and were unwilling to spend anything on repairs. When we had been there a year the back wall fell away so that the laths and wallpaper were our only protection from the weather. When we finally returned to Oxford in 1956 the house seemed even more neglected, and Dorothy, who happened to be sitting next to the Estate Bursar of Magdalen at lunch, mentioned that it looked as if it hadn't been touched since we lived there thirty years before. To this he retorted, plaintively, that it had been repainted, once.

It was at 64 High Street, Oxford on February 23rd 1923 that our first child, a daughter, Stella Muriel (the second name that of my sister who had died in 1917) was born.

I took my B.Litt. in 1923, my examiners being Arthur Smith, Keeper of Greek and Roman Antiquities at the British Museum, and John Beazley. Our three careers were in the future to be curiously inter-related; Arthur Smith, on his retirement from the British Museum, succeeded me as Director of the British School at Rome, and ten years later I succeeded to his post at the British Museum, whilst twenty years later still I succeeded John Beazley as Professor at Oxford.

At the suggestion of Professor Percy Gardner a post of Assistant Curator of Coins was created in the newly formed Coin Room at the Ashmolean, and I was appointed to it. J. G. Milne, a retired Civil Servant and an authority on Roman coinage was the Honorary Keeper, and E. T. Leeds the Keeper of Antiquities. In the new Coin Room he and I worked together for several years. At that time the various odd collections of coins from the Bodleian Library and from colleges were being incorporated as the University Collection at the Ashmolean. Some had been arranged in cabinets before, but some had not, and after we had done some preliminary arrangement we were left with a mass of unidentified ancient coins, mostly Greek bronze of Roman period, many of them extremely worn and corroded. I owe Leeds a great debt in that he showed me how, by working away at these day after day and never giving up one was able to identify coins that any layman would have considered quite unidentifiable. It often turned on the deciphering of a single letter in order to discover the "ethnic" of any one coin (i.e. the name of the city striking the coin); it was amazing to me how a quite unreadable word one day could on the next be read, simply by coming at it again or by some subtle change in the lighting.

The lesson was "never give up, even if it seems hopeless". This has been valuable to me throughout my career as an archaeologist, and had a striking application nearly fifty years later when Paul Getty was offered a small Roman bust in bronze. This was a portrait that has been argued about for many years because although many replicas were known, none was inscribed, and although most people believed it represented Menander, there were many who strongly urged it must be Virgil. When the dealer first showed me the little bronze I naturally hoped that it would turn out to bear an inscription, as many such small portrait bronzes do, but he said that it did not, and after it had been sent to be cleaned the technician still maintained that it was uninscribed. I spent half an hour at the dealer's going over every inch of the surface with a magnifying glass and eventually discovered one letter. I then knew that a word must be there and that I could, sooner or later, trace some at least of the other letters; I did in fact finally recapture traces of every letter except two in the word Menandros, thus settling the controversy once and for all.

The Honorary Curator of Coins was F. Pierrepont Barnard, an aged honorary Fellow of Pembroke College, whose memory went back to the time when on guest-nights it was customary, so he said, for Fellows to drink themselves under the table. When they were insensible it was the tradition that each College servant should come and collect his own Don and put him to bed; for this service he was allowed to appropriate the loose change in his master's pockets, but not any of the golden sovereigns or half-sovereigns.

Barnard had formed the finest collection of eighteenth-century tokens in the world. These were little coins, of copper or base metal, struck unofficially by private traders to serve as small change, because of the shortage of official copper coins; they were plentiful and most varied in the designs they bore. Since he proposed to bequeath the collection to the Ashmolean it was suggested that I should go up to his home in Lincolnshire to take particulars of it; and Dorothy and I were invited to stay there. It was at Bilsby, then a remote part of Lincolnshire, where Barnard and his gentle and retiring wife lived in some seclusion, partly, I suspect, because he was rather a prickly neighbour, and partly because he had married his deceased wife's sister before it was legal.

The importance of his second name, Pierrepont, soon became clear; he claimed descent from one of the nobles who had come over with William the Conqueror, and one wall of the dining-room was covered with a genealogical tree demonstrating this fact. It was a nice old house of medium size, in which an air of old-time formality was maintained; we were served at dinner by footmen whose white gloves concealed the fact that during the day they performed other duties. There were no bathrooms, and when Dorothy was offered a bath before dinner it turned out to be a large saucer-bath in the bedroom into which several cans of scalding water had been poured. The maid retired, and since there was no cold water Dorothy ran the risk of either being boiled alive or late for dinner. But altogether it was a pleasant visit.

We had now made friends with John Johnson, Printer to the University, who had progressive ideas on publishing, and he and I together experimented with illustrations, using pictures of original material from excavations and elsewhere which had not so far been exploited. The older Greek history books, for instance, were illustrated mainly with engravings of coins, but they were only line engravings, usually without explanation, and lacked the feeling of reality that a good illustration should give. We used enlarged pictures of casts of coins which illustrated particular points in the text, pictures on vases, pictures of original sculpture, of architecture and of archaeological sites. The little book we started on was an elementary history book called "Greece" by M. A. Hamilton, and we packed it full of pictures, making it more useful and certainly more interesting for schools. We then did something similar to the Bishop of Derby's Text and Commentary, for the Oxford University Press, of the Epistle to the Galatians. These would no doubt look fairly primitive now, but they were genuine pioneers.

At this time too I began, at Percy Gardner's suggestion (to which he had been prompted by Mrs Strong) a Catalogue of the Greek and Roman Marbles at Ince Blundell Hall near Liverpool. This was the largest collection of ancient sculptures in Britain, over four hundred pieces, and it needed a catalogue because the major book on the many British private collections, by the German Adolf Michaelis, published in 1882 – an excellent work – was compiled before adequate photographic illustration was practicable; although Michaelis's descriptions were thorough, no description by itself can be a substitute for good pictures. My aim was to illustrate everything with my own photographs, limiting my descriptions to the restorations of the piece and its exact condition, or to details which the photographs could not make clear. The Weld-Blundell family, like many at the

Ince Blundell Hall and the Pantheon (façades), 1959. The sculptures were given to the City of Liverpool in 1959 by Sir Joseph Weld. The buildings were sold to a nursing order of nuns for use as a convalescent home.

time, had a tragic history, their only two sons having been killed in the war; but one of the daughters had married a naval officer, Commander Montague, who had adopted the name Weld-Blundell so that the family should persist. He was a fine person who made me welcome, and by the work he had already done on cleaning and labelling the marbles with the numbers given them by Michaelis, made my task much easier. I set to work with a couple of cameras, quarter-plate and half-plate, and photographed everything. It was not altogether easy, for the lighting in the Pantheon at Ince (imitating on a smaller scale the Pantheon in Rome and lighted like it by a single circular hole in the roof) produced very heavy shadows and harsh contrasts. These I mitigated by reflecting light into the shadows, a process I don't like much, and I also found that I could move the heads and smaller busts bodily; I even learned actually to turn some of the full-size statues, so as to improve the lighting, by rocking them gently.

Although the results are clearly not perfect, I did succeed in illustrating everything, and with the help of John Johnson at the Oxford Press, which had undertaken the publication, my pictures were reproduced in collotype, a process now very rare, which depends for success on accurate temperature and humidity, and

Ince Blundell Hall, the Pantheon (interior), 1959.

does not allow (except by re-photographing the photograph) for reduction or enlargement of the picture when printing the gelatine negative from which the final impression is taken. It has however the advantage that the finished picture can be studied with a magnifying glass, whereas the so-called half-tone merely becomes a series of dots when magnified. George Hill suggested an artist who would produce a good block, and we were thus able to have a bold impression of the Blundell crest in gold on the black cover of the book, which still seems to me rather a handsome volume, easy to read and handle, and useful in an unpretentious way. I did a good deal of the work on both pictures and text in 1922 and the next two years, when also I took some pictures for a proposed catalogue of the Melchett Collection (afterwards published by Mrs Strong), but my book did not appear until 1929, for a quite unexpected reason.

Chapter IV

The British School at Rome

IN THE SUMMER OF 1924 we had a surprise visit from John Forsdyke, Secretary of the Archaeological Faculty of the British School at Rome. He explained that, owing to persistent quarrelling between Dr Ashby, the Director, his newly-married wife, and Mrs Arthur Strong, the Assistant Director, the Managing Committee had decided to dismiss both of them and that the post of Director would therefore be vacant. Would I like to consider accepting it? This was a startling proposal and we asked for a little time to think it over. Soon after, Arnie Lawrence, who had read with me for the Diploma in Archaeology, and his wife, Barbara, both of whom had been students at the School, came to see us and described its deplorable state and the discomfort of living there. In addition to the physical discomfort he described the whole place as "something of a bear-garden". This finally decided us and I agreed to accept.

We left for Rome in the autumn of 1925 with Stella, now aged three. It was an extraordinarily awkward situation there because both Dr Ashby and Mrs Strong were still living in Rome and there was naturally a good deal of sympathy with them, not to say open and covert hostility to their successor. On the other hand many others knew how extremely unsatisfactory the set-up had been, and we were cordially welcomed by some of the foreign Schools, especially by Dr Amelung, head of the German Institute. We were also welcomed by an old fellow-student of the British School at Athens, Axel Boethius, who was on the point of establishing a Swedish Institute in Rome, and by Dr van Buren, Librarian of the American Academy, and his wife who was English and an archaeologist.

In these circumstances the obvious thing was to concentrate on the internal problems of the School, which were numerous. First came the food. Breakfast served to the students consisted of bread and butter, tea or coffee. The amounts were limited and soon ran out, and if more tea was needed the pot was simply filled up with water; there was often no more coffee to be had. I calculated that from what the students were paying, they should be entitled to a definite amount of coffee, milk, bread and butter, and I introduced pots and jugs holding this amount, to be served on individual trays with the appropriate amount of bread and butter. I let it be known that this was their entitlement and if they didn't get it they should complain. On this basis I was able to reckon that, on breakfast and teas alone, the cook had been making well over £100 a year in addition to his regular wages. Main meals, which were deplorable, were a more difficult problem. For instance, inferior meat was being bought in the market, and superior charged for. This practice was checked and the cook replaced; but as everyone who has kept house in Italy knows, there is only one remedy for this particular trouble, eternal vigilance. At this time there were still in Rome many Russian refugees, some from noble families or their dependants, or dependants of the Court, seeking to make their living in any reasonable way they could. Our new cook had been Conductor of the Band on the Czar's yacht, but had taken a cook's training in Paris; and he was a very good cook indeed. But he had a way with him and unluckily paid some attention to a girl who was engaged to a local man; it ended when the cook was pursued round the kitchen by the Italian suitor with a knife. The School servants were supervised by the butler, Armando, middle-aged and benevolent but inefficient; when he retired I appointed in his place the young Bruno Bonelli, his assistant, who was later made School Secretary. He was an outstanding success; his good sense and easy manner made him agreeable to the students, and he became, by his personality and efficiency, the keystone of the whole set-up for many years, including those critical ones of the German domination of Rome during the Second War, when it was unsafe to set foot outside the School.

Twenty years after we had left Rome and after the end of the Second War, we invited Professor Zanotti-Bianco, who as head of the Italian Red Cross was on a visit to Britain, to deliver a lecture at University College on his excavations in

The British School at Rome, about 1925.

South Italy: he was also a leading archaeologist who had specialised there. He had afterwards invited me to lunch, and, on the day, I rang at the majestic door of the Italian Embassy in Belgrave Square. It was opened by Alfredo, who had been our hall-porter at the British School; in a charming Italian way he came near to embracing me at the unexpected meeting, which was explained by his having been taken prisoner in North Africa and brought to England, where, after the fall of Mussolini, Italian prisoners of war were allowed virtual freedom. It was a heart-warming moment, for we had always been on the best of terms with all the staff at the School, and they were indeed old friends, down to the little hall-boy Annibale, now proprietor of a fashionable Roman restaurant.

When the cold weather came, not only did the central heating not work properly, but nobody was able to get more than a tepid bath, although we were spending £400 (a considerable sum then) on coke every year. I then discovered that because of the extreme hardness of the water (the Aqua Marcia which deposits vast quantities of travertine) the main flow-pipe from the top of the boiler had become completely furred up. This had happened four years after the original installation, as could be seen by the successive "rings" formed when the plant was

The British School at Rome, Entrance Hall, 1925.

unused during the summer. The blockage extended for about six feet and the result was that all of the so-called hot supply was flowing from a pipe at the bottom of the boiler where the water was coolest. I had the blocked section replaced and six inches of it sawn off and forwarded to the London Committee.

In a mixed community like the British School, consisting of archaeologists on the one hand and artists on the other, there is always a danger of a rift between the two, and this had become acute because of the inept way in which it had been handled. There was also the difficulty because, owing to the war, students tended to be older, some of them were married, and nominally wives were not allowed to reside in the School. The result was that some tried to keep the rule, with inadequate means to do it in squalid lodgings, whilst others broke it. I persuaded the Committee that wives must be allowed to live in and this had happy results. We had several nice couples, Tom and Winifred Monnington, the Robert Lyons, the Jacots, John Skeaping and Barbara Hepworth, and the Evanses; which led to a more humane atmosphere generally. This was much assisted by the young Canadian, Jimmy Dobbs, who was studying singing in Rome, and whom we employed as chauffeur. He was everybody's friend and a most cheerful, lively character. He later married Marjorie Charlton, Dorothy's old school friend, who acted as children's nurse. Our little open Fiat car was much used for expeditions into the Campagna and helped to break up the feeling of seclusion that was apt to descend on the community.

The British School at Rome, Cortile, 1925, showing some of the cypresses and mimosa trees which Bernard and Dorothy planted.

The car was, however, the focus of a startling incident. It was kept at first in an old garden shed, a large, somewhat decrepit structure. I decided that we must have a proper garage, and sited it alongside the shed, but, for ease of access, at an angle to it. The result was an unfinished brick building, not quite parallel with the shed but set at a slight angle to it, leaving a wedge-shaped gap between the two of about three feet in front, narrowing to less than a foot at the back where the corners of the two buildings came nearest to each other. The School employed a night-watchman, Cesare, who patrolled the garden during the night armed with a heavy Service revolver, relic, no doubt, of the First World War. One night a thief removed a plank from the back of the shed, crept in through the opening, stole a fur rug that was kept in the car, and escaped over the garden fence. Exactly a month later the same thing happened again; but this time the thief was removing the spare wheel when the night-watchman heard him and raised the alarm. The man fled, but as he was crawling through the hole he had made in the back of the shed, the watchman, who had come down the gap between the old building and the new, reached through and seized him by the braces; but being of a substantial build he could not pass through the ten-inch gap to secure his victim. He therefore drew his revolver and tried to shoot the man. By the mercy of Heaven not one of the cartridges (being no doubt also of War vintage) went off, and by the time the last had been tried the braces had broken and the man was away.

Next morning I expostulated with the night-watchman, explaining that one was not allowed to shoot people. "Not the first time," he said, "but this was the second". "But how did you know that it was the same man?" He was a simple creature, and the thought had not occurred to him. But he was the centre of attraction among the staff, and whilst re-enacting the scene to an admiring circle the revolver did go off, fortunately whilst pointed at the ground.

Crises of one sort and another were always occurring. One evening a maid-servant in the School had made an assignation with her lover in an unfinished house nearby, where they had screened the windows and lighted a brazier for warmth. In the morning they were both discovered, fortunately not dead from the fumes, but only just alive.

Towards the end of October the students had the idea of making a Guy to burn on November 5th, and the sculptors constructed a splendid seated figure more than fourteen feet high. All was set for the bonfire, but that very day a woman made a half-hearted attempt on Mussolini's life, brandishing but not discharging a small pistol. At first it was thought that she was English, and we considered it prudent not to show ourselves in Rome for a while, but she proved to be Irish, and anyhow the excitement soon died down. The School servants, however, were horrified at the idea of any celebration, and we consulted the Embassy who had already sent some protection for us. They advised that in the circumstances it might be misinterpreted; sadly therefore the noble image was dismantled.

'Guy' made by the sculptors D. Evans (Rome Scholar in Sculpture 1923), J. A. Woodford (Rome Scholar in Sculpture 1927) and H. Wilson Parker for Guy Fawkes celebrations at British School at Rome, 1925.

Virgil celebration at Mantua, 1927.

The two thousandth anniversary of the birth of Virgil approached and his native city of Mantua staged a celebration. The Municipality invited representatives from universities and learned bodies everywhere, and entertained them splendidly with a civic luncheon and a reception at which addresses were made and gifts presented. Since I was on the spot, the University of Oxford invited me to represent them: they prepared a printed address in Latin, and a beautifully bound copy of the Oxford edition of Virgil's poems. I read my address with a strong Italian accent hoping to make it more intelligible. We walked in procession through the streets, drove round in cars labelled "For the magnificent Rectors of Universities", and my sober black silk gown, dark hood and mortar-board were much admired among the somewhat gaudy Continental gowns and pork-pie hats; but all was of the friendliest nature, and the city displayed that pleasant Mediterranean blend of ceremonial and festivity.

Virgil's birthday was also the occasion of the one embarrassing legacy left by my predecessor Dr Ashby. He had invited, or perhaps agreed to accept, at the British School a lecture from Professor R. S. Conway, Professor of Latin at Manchester, on the discovery he had made that an inscription with Virgil's name found on a site near Mantua seemed to fix the spot where he had been born. It was a modest discovery and could have been published adequately in a ten-minute paper: Conway had expanded it into an hour's lecture. We entertained him the night before and it became clear that his Italian was elementary, which did not augur well for the next afternoon. It was worse than we feared. The lecture had been written in English and designed for an average English audience, beginning for instance with a slide of oxen ploughing in the Campagna, which was not calculated to stir a distinguished audience of international scholars to most of whom the Campagna was more familiar than to the lecturer. Not only had the lecture been written in English, it had seemingly been translated into Italian by someone else; well translated, but ill-co-ordinated with the slides. Conway would read a section, press the button for the next slide, read on without looking up, then press the button again. The result was that at one stage, when he did look up, the slide on the screen manifestly failed to illustrate the point he was making, the proper slide by now having passed on. He then tried to get the proper slide back again, and addressed the operator in his own unintelligible Italian; after ten seconds of unavailing pantomime I had to step forward and inform him that the operator was English.

As a general rule, to which there are many exceptions, it is better for a visiting lecturer to speak in his own language (with a typed summary in that of his host), for it sometimes happens that his pronunciation of the native tongue cannot be understood by the natives; and I remember Professor Franz Cumont of the Belgian Institute in Rome, when lecturing to the American Academy there, apologising for speaking in French "Because," he said, "When I speak in English, I say not what I wish, but what I can".

For anyone living abroad language is always a problem. Dorothy and I spoke some Italian from living in Rome in 1923, and from many weeks of a course of gramophone records; and after I had become Director we took regular lessons with an Italian teacher; but it was a severe handicap in the early days not to have anyone who could write an ordinary letter, formal or informal, in Italian. Dr Ashby spoke Italian fluently, as did Mrs Strong. Ashby was a fine scholar and his Italian was strongly influenced by Latin: it was amusing to hear him instructing – or rebuking – a servant in splendid classical cadences; and his Italian colleagues laughed in a kindly way at what they called his "lingua Asbeiana". The difficulties were not on one side only, for Italians cannot easily manage an aspirate in the middle of a word, and "Ashby" itself was literally a shibboleth. It was hard on them when "Ashmole" posed the same problem; and oddly enough a Dr Ashburner was at that time Director of the British Institute in Florence. Yet such names do not seem particularly common in Britain.

When we had first lived in Rome Professor Beazley had given us an introduction to John and Mary Marshall. Marshall had been one of a trio who under the auspices of E. P. Warren, an American, had set up a kind of monastic establishment at Lewes House in Sussex for the study of ancient art. It was financed by Warren who was able to buy antiquities, chiefly in Rome, and bring them to Lewes for study. Warren was an Oxford graduate, first class in classics, Fothergill something of an eccentric but an acute critic; he wrote an excellent article on "Drawing" in the eleventh edition of the *Encyclopaedia Britannica*, replaced in later editions by a superficial and comparatively worthless essay. He afterwards became the host of the Spread Eagle Inn at Thame, celebrated for its good food and capricious treatment of guests. John Marshall, also a first class in classics and perhaps disappointed at not being appointed to an academic post, was the most human of the three. He shattered the ideals of Lewes House by marrying, and what made it worse from Warren's point of view was that his bride was Warren's own cousin. Mary Marshall was the gentlest of people, but full of character and of independent interests. They lived in a flat literally overhanging the Spanish Steps and spent there many happy years. They were less than a stone's throw away from us at the Hassler and were kind and welcoming friends. Marshall, as Beazley had told me, really did know something about Greek art, and he taught me much also about the market in antiquities and the wiles of dealers.

About the time that we were going to take up the post in Rome, the British Museum was being offered, by its owner Lord Yarborough, the charming classical Greek grave-relief at Brocklesby in Lincolnshire, of a girl saying goodbye to her doves. The price, I heard afterwards, was not high – I did not know exactly what, nor did I know about the offer – but the Museum said that they could not afford it, without apparently making any great effort. It was then offered to the Metropolitan Museum in New York, for which John Marshall was acting as agent. Now it so happened that not long before I had visited Brocklesby independently and had studied among their other marbles the Girl with Doves, which was their chief treasure. Marshall asked me about it, and I told him all I knew, although I did not realise that the Metropolitan was actually negotiating. When they finally made the purchase Marshall proposed that they should make me some sort of return for the information I had given; I said this was quite impossible, but that if he liked a gift could be made to the School. In this way it was possible to pay for a new fountain-basin in the middle of the courtyard, four travertine seats set about it, and a fountain in the centre consisting of a square basin resting on a large rectangular block of travertine, on which I asked John Skeaping to carve reliefs.

Now a widower, Marshall was living by himself not far from the School, and was joined there occasionally by his old friend E. P. Warren. He sometimes asked us to lunch, was most warm-hearted and a delightful host, with his stories of Italy and the ways of Italian antique-dealers, how some of them tried to pass off forgeries by skilful patination – rolling them in the gutter of the Via del Babuino or burying them under the vines at Orvieto. He would often tell me when he had a new marble sculpture on offer and I would go round and see it. In this way I first saw and photographed the statue of Protesilaus now in the Metropolitan Museum in New York, whilst it was still in pieces. Although he did not much

Dorothy and Bernard beside the fountain designed by J. R. Skeaping, Rome Scholar in Sculpture, 1926.

care for it, Marshall had bought for the Metropolitan a small marble statue of a girl in archaic Greek style, but discovered soon after that it was almost certainly false and made by the now celebrated forger Alceo Dossena. Partly because of this deception, Marshall was on the alert and thought it his duty to expose any other forgeries from the same source. Accordingly, when he was offered fragments of an alleged archaic Greek group of which he recognised the style, he not only rejected it but warned others against it. Meanwhile, however, it had been acquired by the famous international dealer Jacob Hirsch, and was deposited in Munich for study and possible purchase, where it met with the approval of Franz Studniczka. Studniczka was a well-known German professor, an expert on sculpture, whom we had met and liked in 1921 in Athens. Like Marshall, I thought the group detestable; but Hirsch, having paid forty thousand pounds, naturally believed in it, as did Studniczka, together with a friend of his, a practising sculptor, Professor George.

Marshall proposed that there should be a conference in Munich between himself, Professor J. D. Beazley from Oxford, myself and the two German professors. This was arranged and the five of us held an inquest on the group. Studniczka and the German sculptor were strongly in its favour, Marshall and I equally strongly against. Beazley reserved judgement; he did not like it, but felt that he had not evidence enough to condemn it out of hand. I had the opportunity to give some hours to studying it and taking a series of detailed photographs, and thus was able later on to demonstrate, in an article in the *Journal of Hellenic Studies*, that it was false, not only on its style, but also on its technique and the condition of its surface.

In the early summer of 1926 towards the end of our first session at the School, Dorothy was expecting another baby, and we thought it was wise that she should return to England early. The journey was all arranged, and seats booked on the train from Rome to Calais. As the time drew near the General Strike in Britain was threatening and had actually started when her journey began, with a nurse who had succeeded Marjorie Charlton to take care of the three-year-old Stella. At Roman parties there were horror-stories of the condition of Britain – how the General Strike would lead to riots and even a revolution, and how dangerous it would be to travel – stories not calculated to reassure an intending

John Marshall, classical scholar and godfather to Stella, about 1925.

traveller. All went well as far as Paris, but there the train no longer went through to Calais, and as soon as we discovered this I had telephoned from Rome booking accommodation for the night. Next day they eventually boarded a train for Calais and from there embarked, naturally very anxious about their reception at Dover, how they would get off the boat with their luggage and the child, Dorothy being seven months pregnant. As soon as the ship docked a band of youthful students leapt enthusiastically onto the ship and quickly handled the baggage ashore, relating the while their stories of how helpful the strikers had been in teaching them their various jobs, even how to drive a train. Dorothy's mother and her chauffeur were soon found waiting to drive them to her home in Eastbourne, where, a few weeks later, our second daughter, Silvia was born.

My sister Gladys had been staying with us, and at the end of the School sessions, as soon as I was free, Jimmy Dobbs drove us both back to England in the Fiat. We came as fast as possible, using the pass over the Alps at Mont Cenis. Arriving in Paris, Jimmy and I, wearing boiler-suits, dirty and unshaven, suffered the humiliation of being firmly refused admission to a very modest hotel on the Left Bank. Another was less fussy: we made our cross-Channel journey next day, and so to Eastbourne.

One of the delightful features of the School was the whole-heartedness with which the students would enter into any celebration, especially the Christmas dances; one year the dining-hall was elaborately transformed into the semblance of a London street, the street-scenes being painted on the walls and a replica of a lamp-standard set up in the middle. For one of these parties Dorothy made herself exquisite as Artemis, with a dark blue silk chiton bordered with silver tissue and a silver headdress to match; also a silver bow, really of polished steel and made by Mr Pavey our invaluable factotum. I went as the British lion, with scarlet skin, a fine papier-maché head with electric flashing eyes, and a crown; my tail was a long piece of hose-pipe securely fastened to a belt around my waist,

Fancy dress dance at the German Academy in Rome, 1926. Bernard as British lion, Dorothy as Artemis beside him, on right.

since I foresaw, correctly, that it was sure to be pulled. We wore the costumes also to a dance at the German Institute when Amelung made the charming remark "Dear Mrs Ashmole, so pretty and so true" – some compensation for being identified by others as Cupid. In some Greek myths Artemis is not the virgin huntress but the universal mother, which was appropriate enough since Dorothy had to leave the party at ten o'clock in order to suckle her baby Silvia. We also gave a children's party at which the red lion was a great success, Stella leading me by the paw and explaining "It's only my Daddy."

In 1927 Dr D. G. Hogarth, the Keeper of the Ashmolean, died, and John Johnson was among those who urged me to allow my name to go forward as a possible successor. I was unwilling, partly because I was too junior, but chiefly because the other obvious candidate – apart

Dorothy and Bernard in fancy dress dance at British School at Rome, 1925

possibly from Charles Bell, Keeper of Fine Arts, who was very frail – would be E. T. Leeds, under whom I had worked happily for a couple of years, and the idea of supplanting him was most distasteful; although the appointment of a third party, from outside, would have pleased neither of us. I made it clear that I was not in the field and Leeds was eventually appointed. It had not been a foregone conclusion because he had a reputation, not entirely undeserved, as a xenophobe, hardly a qualification for the head of an institution constantly visited by foreign scholars. He was in the event a great success.

Not long afterwards I had a letter from the Provost of University College, London, asking if I would allow my name to go forward as a candidate for the Yates Chair of Archaeology there. This was held at the time by Ernest Gardner (brother of Percy Gardner, my professor at Oxford) who was nearing the age of retirement. It was an attractive proposal, not so much because the professorship was one of the three or four main Chairs for this subject in Britain, but chiefly because of the nearness of the British Museum with its unrivalled collection of sculpture and other antiquities, and of the so-called "Bloomsbury Square Mile" with its specialist libraries, reputedly the greatest concentration of the means of knowledge in existence. Eventually I accepted, with the proviso that Ernest

Terracotta bust of Bernard by H. Wilson Parker, Rome Scholar in Sculpture, 1927–29.

Gardner should stay on for a year, thus enabling us to do a year's travelling before taking up the post.

When the time had come to leave the School, the farewell party given us was most elaborate and showed a warmth of feeling that touched us deeply. It was a Country Fair: a stage and booths had been erected; there was a coconut-shy, a hoop-la, a boxing match, a melodrama specially written, and finally a dinner in the portico, for which an amusing menu that we still possess had been drawn by Rex Whistler, then a visitor.

We left with deep regret and gratitude for all the kindness we had met from everyone in the School, British and Italian; an ample reward for what we had tried to do for their well-being.

A small epilogue. The year before, I had had to attend a meeting of the Managing Committee of the School in London, mainly to defend the work of some of the art students, which was too modern for some members of the Faculties; and to save time I decided to fly from Paris. These were the early days of passenger-travel by air and the aircraft was primitive; since there was no pressurizing we flew low and the day being stormy it was very rough. Worst was the noise: no insulation against it, the fuselage quite thin and the engines near. I was deaf for a fortnight afterwards.

Whilst I was away, John Skeaping asked Dorothy if he could carve a head of her. Unfortunately, a few hours before, Dorothy had accepted a similar invitation from David Evans, the other Rome Scholar in sculpture, to model her portrait in clay. Now Evans, although a worthy man (he later carved a tolerable head of Arthur Evans for the Coin Room of the Ashmolean) was a realistic sculptor of pedestrian talent, and Dorothy's portrait was lifeless; Evans modelled it in clay, then had it cast in plaster and finally in bronze. The plaster he gave to us, and we kept it in our flat until the time now came for us to leave the School for good. Neither of us liked it, and we decided that since a bronze existed there would be no moral objection to destroying it. One evening therefore at dusk we carried it to a far corner of the garden where there was some hard paving, the intention being that I should throw it as high as possible into the air, when it would fall and shatter into a thousand pieces. We did not know that the plaster had been reinforced with hessian, and the head, instead of shattering, fell with a

Ian Richmond (left) and Rex Whistler at the Farewell Dinner for Bernard and Dorothy in 1928.
'At the farewell party for Professor Ashmole and his wife, one photograph shows Rex in a blond wig as Nero's wife Poppaea. Later that night, comically made up under a sombrero, he sang with considerable style "In a little Spanish town", a recent popular song that he had to be coached in, burlesquing it – with Ian Richmond (afterwards Professor of Archaeology [at Oxford] as the girl behind the grille.'
From The Laughter and the Urn: The Life of Rex Whistler *by Lawrence Whistler (1985).*

dull thud still in one piece. I then took a spade and, whilst it seemed to be looking at me reproachfully and more like Dorothy than before, battered it into a shapeless mass which we then interred, both feeling curiously like murderers.

The year we now had free we aimed to spend partly in studying the collections of sculpture on the Continent; the children were left with Mrs de Peyer at Eastbourne in charge of Marjorie Charlton. We travelled in company with George Hill direct to Greece by the Orient Express, which at that time ran without change from Paris to Athens. There George Hill stayed at the British School whilst Dorothy and I were guests of Rhys Carpenter, the Director of the American School. I had agreed to take photographs for his publication of the sculptured reliefs from the bastion of the temple of Athena Nike on the Acropolis. These date from the generation after Pheidias, and depict a procession of Victories bringing offerings to Athena as the Goddess of Victory: the best known is a Victory who has paused to tie her sandal. Carpenter had made a close and discerning study of the reliefs, allotting the various slabs to their sculptors and demonstrating convincingly the way in which each one carved the marble: his conclusions, published in a small but important book next year, have been generally accepted since.

Rex Whistler's menu for the Farewell Dinner.

George Hill (classical scholar and later Director of the British Museum), about 1928.

Carpenter was a charming host and a most unusual person. He was educated at Columbia University in New York and, as a Rhodes Scholar, at Balliol College in Oxford, shortly before the First War. Before specialising in classical archaeology he had written poetry and books on travel, and his horizon was always wide, embracing history, geography, mythology, language and literature, epigraphy and aesthetics; and to each he brought an original mind. He loved being or playing the heretic, and would put forward the most unlikely theories with an impish delight and a command of English which entranced even when it did not enlighten his hearers or readers. Always there was a germ of plausibility in his theories however fanciful: sometimes he proved to be completely right, and often partially. The danger of his approach was that one often did not know when he was quite serious, and a certain type of pupil might accept as gospel what may have been intended in the first place simply to stimulate discussion: but this was far outweighed by the merit it had of forcing everyone to re-examine their ideas. We clashed several times subsequently in friendly controversy on archaeological matters, but never with any ill-will on either side.

After Athens we sailed to Istanbul; thence to Budapest, where we called on Alfoldi, the Roman historian. These were hard times in Europe and we were distressed by the austerity in which he and his family were living. From there to Vienna, where we were welcomed by the epigraphist, Professor Wilhelm: he recalled with gratitude the hospitality he had had in England in the grim days after the First War, and it made one realise the profound and lasting effects of such acts of kindness.

In Vienna George Hill had to leave us for England, and we went on alone to Berlin, where were able to study the sculptures, including those from Pergamon, which are now in East Germany: then home, in time for Christmas.

Chapter V

'High and Over', 1929 and the Thirties

WE NOW DISCUSSED where we might live: both of us wanted the country, but it was essential to be within easy reach of University College. Eventually we decided that somewhere on the Metropolitan Line to Wendover would be best, since many of the trains, instead of finishing at Baker Street, continued on the Inner Circle, stopping at Gower Street, which was within a few hundred yards of the College.

At that time a large part of the Shardeloes Estate at Amersham, twenty-five miles from London, came on the market, and Dorothy was able to buy some twelve acres of land half a mile to the north-east of the village. It was on high ground, completely bare of trees, sloping gently down towards the south, with splendid views over the valley of the little river Misbourne.

We naturally knew well the architectural students of the British School at Rome, and admired particularly the work of Amyas Connell, the senior Rome Scholar, a New Zealander who had been trained in the Bartlett School at University College. His special study in Rome was the lay-out and buildings of the Capitol by Michelangelo: he had made a series of exquisite drawings of them, and understood their subtleties perhaps more thoroughly than anyone before, except their creator. He was also deeply interested in modern architecture, and clearly had a talent for planning. Dorothy and I agreed that we would employ him on his return from Rome to build us a house in modern style; his views on modern architecture were sensible: he had studied the work of Le Corbusier and of modern German and Dutch architects, but dissented from the extreme view that a house was simply a machine for living in, unless beauty is considered as a part of living, and unless the house reflects in some degree the tastes and even the character of the client. He once said "I want anyone to be able to see that this is the Ashmoles' house".

As soon as possible Connell and I went together to the site at Amersham. In preliminary discussions he and Dorothy and I had provisionally agreed on what might be called an Elizabethan plan, E-shaped, the two projecting wings forming a courtyard which would be open to the south; and the whole building designed and orientated to take advantage of the sun and the views. We were also agreed on our general requirements, and were able to give him approximate measurements for sitting-rooms and bedrooms; if we had been able to foresee the future these would doubtless have been more modest.

We studied the site carefully and decided that the best position would be to-

The site at Amersham before building started on 'High and Over' in 1929.

wards its southern end, where the ground fell rather more steeply and where there was a hollow, probably formed by an old chalk-pit long abandoned and ploughed over. This was the ideal spot, but as we sat on the edge of it and talked, it seemed that a building of the plan we had in mind did not suit the site particularly well, and I asked Connell whether it would not be possible to set off the side wings of the house at an angle of 120 degrees instead of at right angles, in order to make it fit the contours more comfortably. He said that it would be quite possible for the exterior design, but would be likely to cause difficult problems in planning the interior; however he would think it over. It was a mark of what almost amounted to genius that when we parted he set to, and within a few days produced in all essentials the plan and elevations of High and Over, the house that was eventually built. (The name, suggested by Dorothy, was taken from a hillside near Alfriston.)

Briefly, it was to consist of a central hexagon rising to three storeys and providing an entrance hall at ground level, a landing on the first floor, and a nursery at the top. In the centre of the hall was to be a fountain with a single jet, consisting of a shallow glass bowl let into the floor, which could be softly lighted from beneath. When building began, the peg marking the position of this jet was the central point from which the whole plan was laid out. The three wings of the house were set at an angle of a hundred and twenty degrees to this central hexagon, one wing being the sitting-room, another the study, and a third the dining-room, with kitchen beyond it. These main rooms opened with folding doors on to the hall, so that if necessary the whole ground floor except the kitchen could be thrown into one, giving vistas in several directions of more than sixty feet, although each room was itself of fairly modest dimensions. On the first floor the hexagon was a landing giving access to bedrooms and bathroom and on the top floor it was a nursery, but here only one wing was occupied, the other two being flat roofs, for playing or sleeping out, with hoods over them against the weather.

The dominating motive, suggested by the angle of a hundred and twenty degrees, was the hexagon – more interesting and accommodating, as the bees long ago discovered, than pentagon or octagon. It was introduced where reasonable throughout; in addition to the central hexagon, which was paved with equilateral triangular tiles forming hexagons, the plan of the main staircase was a half-hexagon, there were hexagonal stools in the nursery, and even the window-handles were hexagonal in section. This was not a mere fancy, but a harmonising element which entailed nothing but some extra thought and care.

As for orientation, we went on the principle, well known in antiquity, that a building facing south gains heat when the sun is low, in spring, autumn and winter, yet is partially shaded inside when the sun is at its highest in summer. Accordingly, on the north side of the house there were to be few windows, but on the south-east and south-west large windows arranged in a continuous band, so as to give the finest views. The total area of glass was no greater than, for

'High and Over' from the south west, 1935.

'High and Over', summer 1993.

instance, in late Georgian houses, although differently disposed, and the gain of heat from the sun would exceed its loss through the glass. Outside, the shape of the house was planned to yield similar advantages, and we recorded, a year or two later, sitting for an hour or so in the open on the south when a bitter north-easter was blowing.

All this, however, was in the future, and we now faced the practical problems of getting the house built.

We submitted the plans to the local authority, with whom we had already had some disagreement over water-supply. We had had in mind not only a small fountain indoors, but also a swimming-pool outside, and asked if the authority could supply water for them, on a meter if necessary. The request was refused, and the water-company offered to lay, at our expense, a half-inch pipe; nothing more. Here we made a questionable decision; we said that if they could not do better than that we would sink an artesian well. Looking back, it is possible to guess that we might still have had such a well but could have done without the water-tower, fifty feet high, which we now proposed. The local council made it quite clear that they disliked the plan for the house, but because there was nothing about it to which they could legally object, they passed it, "though with the greatest reluctance". The water-tower was a different matter; here their technical objection was that it was not an "out-office", in other words a necessary adjunct to the house, and for this reason they turned down the whole scheme. We were at a deadlock, and it was agreed to hold an inquiry under the Ministry of Health, who sent down an Inspector to Amersham for the purpose. The decision went against us. We then submitted the same plans to the Council again, showing the water-tower six inches lower, and made it clear that we were prepared to go on doing so an indefinite number of times; it was perhaps an unworthy device, but it proved effective. We sank the well and, as we had expected, at just over two hundred feet struck an underground stream in the chalk sufficient for all possible needs; and when the engine-room was built and an electric motor installed we were able not only to supply the house but to fill the swimming pool with twenty-five thousand gallons for a few shilling's worth of electricity. The whole set-up was more elaborate than it would be nowadays, when the motor would have been installed at the bottom of the well instead of at the top.

We planned to build in reinforced concrete, partly in order to demonstrate that this was an economical method of construction and had a great future. But a comparatively small project like this did not interest any of the few large firms who were pioneering the material, and those asked to tender quoted excessive prices. Eventually we accepted the tender of a firm which had recently built the grandstand at Epsom in this material, thinking, wrongly, that they would be expert and their technique sophisticated. It turned out that they had hardly heard of re-usable metal shuttering – admittedly rare then, even abroad – and in effect the whole structure had to be built first in wood, forming moulds into which concrete was poured. For the many technical difficulties we encountered one cannot do better than read H. B. Creswell's *Honeywood File*, which is a light-hearted account of similar difficulties through the use of untried materials – although in a more conventional building. Just one of our own may be described. We had intended originally to make a monolithic concrete construction with an external surface that would need only painting; but because of practical difficulties Connell decided instead to build the house as a concrete frame, filling the walls with brick. This meant that the external surface had to be covered with a rendering of some sort of hard plaster to form a uniform surface over both materials. For this it was decided to use a new material called Astroplax. There were two unfortunate snags; one was that concrete and brick expand differently under changes of temperature, so that the rendering was apt to crack. The other was even more serious. The Astroplax looked marvellous; since it was slightly translucent the general appearance was like ivory. But unfortunately it contained gypsum, and since gypsum is soluble in water, after heavy rain the rendering started to disintegrate, and eventually large patches had to be replaced in another material. I notice that in almost all modern buildings with flat roofs, even some built more than twenty years after High and Over, a related trouble recurs; the upper edge of the wall becomes discoloured and damp, frost penetrates and serious damage may follow.

There were many other difficulties, some due to the use of untried materials, some to the builder's incompetence or lack of experience, and it would be tiresome to recount them. At the time they loomed large, and the mastoid abscess I then had was certainly brought on partly by worry. When a minor operation on the ear had failed to clear it, I underwent the normal major operation in London, by Philip Jury of St George's Hospital, whose care and skill could not have been bettered; the operation was completely successful, and so delicate were his hands that the subsequent dressing of the wound, usually considered an ordeal, was almost painless. Throughout we had the advice of Reginald Hilton, whose acquaintance we had made through George Hill.

Reg Hilton was a consultant at St Thomas's Hospital, a physician of the highest skill, an enthusiastic musician, with a most lively and well-informed mind. He had married Gwendolen, George Hill's niece, and sister of Roderic and Geoffrey Hill with whom I was closely associated later. She had a fine intellect and a lovable personality, was highly qualified medically, and a pioneer of Radiology at University College Hospital, where she was head of the Department. Reg and Gwen Hilton had come with her uncle to Rome when we were in charge of the British School, and became firm friends of our family from then onwards, giving wise advice on every medical problem. We were deeply attached to both of them and were glad to make some return when, after the outbreak of war in 1939, their little daughter Clare came with her nurse out of the danger in London to stay at High and Over for many periods. One of our happiest memories is a supper in the garden at Amersham on the day in late August 1945 when Paris was relieved; for Reg, who spoke French like a native, loved France, with which he had many ties, and his joy was complete.

As one might have expected, the people with clear heads and few prejudices, from whatever walk of life, appreciated what we were trying to do, and the result

Bernard and Stella (eldest daughter) in the Hollow at 'High and Over', about 1934.

High and Over: those with imagination could see that, startling though it looked at first in a bare field, it would fit into the landscape eventually, and the growth of trees round it would act as a foil and enhance the general effect. Objectors were those who hated anything new, among architects, those who were making a success of repeating conventional designs. There was a good deal of controversy, and when Howard Marshall, a popular broadcaster, attacked 'High and Over' without mentioning its name, I wrote a letter to the *Listener* deriding his whole standard of values. On the other hand Augustus Daniel, Director of the National Gallery and a distinguished art critic, wrote "You have a real thoroughbred of a new kind" and the architectural critic of *The Times* praised the whole concept and answered some of the sillier criticisms. Our friend George Hill described it as the nicest house to live in that he had known.

It has been published several times; one of the most balanced publications was by Christopher Hussey in *Country Life* for 19th September 1931, where the garden is still at an early stage and the house naturally looks stark. T*he Architect and Building News* supported us from the outset, and exposed the inconsistency of those, including members of the local planning committee, who were prepared to pass the plans of speculative builders for mean houses of no merit – and even a factory in Amersham itself where corrugated iron was a prominent material – whilst refusing permission for a new building of high quality simply because they had seen nothing like it, and did not try to understand it.

From our own point of view the house was a great success; we and our children loved it – its airiness, its lightness and spaciousness – and of course its superb setting. In view of what happened in the next twenty years it was too large; but we had not the gift of prophecy.

When we first moved into High and Over we needed someone to look after our two daughters, Stella and Silvia. I consulted Professor Stefan, a colleague at University College, and he, to our lasting gratitude, introduced from Vienna Gretl Ullmann, who came at first for some months as an *au pair* girl, but returned on two subsequent occasions and became a lifelong friend of us all.

In 1933, after a good deal of thought we agreed to invite Margaret Pearson, daughter of friends of my parents, a graduate of the University of London, an admirable person and an excellent teacher, to form a little school at High and Over for the two children, to which we invited a neighbouring family to send their two daughters of about the same age.

Margaret had a dramatic reception at High and Over. Our third child was due in a week or two, but on that day, in walking round outside the house, Dorothy struck her head against some scaffolding, and the shock apparently hastened the birth, for she was in labour in the early hours of the night. She was under the charge of Gladys Hill, a school friend who had become gynaecological consultant at the Royal Free Hospital in London, and although we telephoned at once, by the time she arrived (having collected a nurse on the way) our son had been born, to our great delight. The local doctor made Dorothy comfortable until Gladys arrived. This was on 11th January, 1934. Three days later there was a tremendous gale which flung down the timbers on top of the pillars of a pergola which was just being built. The force of the gale can be judged by the fact that the structure at the top of each group of pillars (there were five of such structures) consisted of two beams of timber twelve inches by four, twenty feet long; all were lifted bodily from the pillars, some of which they demolished. Despite this impetuous arrival and this spectacular accompaniment, our son Philip turned out to possess a calmer temperament than any of us.

Dorothy was finding the running of the household and nursing of Philip too exacting, and she advertised in a magazine for someone to help her during the school holidays. A Miss Goff, an elementary school teacher, replied, and although she had other offers, accepted Dorothy's because the duties were clearly stated; when she came, as she did for many periods over the years afterwards, there was no duty to which she did not turn her hand, particularly during the War years, endearing herself as a friend to the whole family.

We had been looking around for a gardener, and I approached George Sibley, the friendly porter of the Ashmolean and secretary of the local British Legion, for some names; he gave me that of George Marlow, who came to the Ashmolean for a talk. I took to him and offered him the post, but a few days later he accepted another to which he was already half committed. However, shortly after, I had a letter from him saying that he and his wife were not happy where they were and would like to change their minds and come to us. Thus began a friendship with them both which has lasted ever since – more than fifty years. They were a completely admirable couple, and we installed them in the newly-built lodge.

George was the eldest of a family of five whose father, a college scout, had died young, leaving his mother, a splendid woman, to bring up the family and support them by going out as a cook. All of them turned out well. George was a tremendous worker who kept steadily at any job he undertook; he had become a gardener of skill and experience, and was not without other interests, for he taught himself to play the violin and built up a large collection of gramophone records of classical music. He must have had a sound education at the village school, for he wrote in a firm clear hand and lively English, showing an inquiring mind, a countryman's philosophical outlook and a wry sense of humour. He was seldom outwardly cheerful except perhaps when things were not going well, but loyal and steadfast to a degree.

May, his wife, was a less complex character but equally admirable; cheerful whatever the circumstances, full of commonsense, and with a sense of humour that showed itself when Amyas Connell lunched with the Marlows at the lodge whilst he was supervising the building of High and Over. It was April 1st, and May had prepared pancakes, but the one she gave Connell was no ordinary specimen; she had cut a circle of thin flannel, dipped it in the batter and fried it. Connell was more interested in conversation than in his food, and it was some seconds after he had attacked it with spoon and fork before he looked down to see what was amiss; and even then it was hardly detectable. Both George and May were as honest as it is possible to imagine, and shining examples of Victorian morality at its best.

To create a garden from the five acres of bare field we had set apart for it was an immense task. The soil was of clay and flints, about half-and-half, lying above a subsoil of chalk; the clay was mostly two or three feet thick, but in places had been removed or eroded, particularly near the old chalk-pit which we called the Hollow, where the chalk was on the surface. It proved eventually to be a marvellous soil for fruit, and when mature we had abundance of apples, pears, cherries, plums, peaches and figs, all growing out in the open.

In a year George had dug more than half of it to the depth of a garden fork, taking out the flints to form a basis for paths; had planted dozens of fruit trees, had laid out and planted a large kitchen garden, and had sown with grass the Broad Walk. This was about thirty feet wide and over a hundred yards long; it began at the water-tower (where we made an oblong pool eighteen feet by six) and sloped gently down towards the south, with a splendid view across the valley to a field called Velvet Lawn, which gave us continual pleasure when it was under grass or wheat, ploughed or harvested. George also constructed the rose-garden, a series of terraces rising in steps on a triangular plan, fifty feet wide at its base, to the east of the house. He and I together cast several thousand feet of deep concrete edges for the beds, and several thousand square feet of cement paving for the paths.

Bernard in the uniform of a Pilot Officer RAFVR at 'High and Over' with Philip (only son), 1939.

In the middle of 1934 George and I embarked on the swimming pool. Modifying Connell's plan, which put it elsewhere, I had sited this at the lowest point of the Hollow, south-west of the house to which it was linked by a long flight of steps – also home-made – conforming exactly to the slope of the ground. Dorothy and I wanted a pool that would give us a swim, and we felt that a circular pool was better than a rectangular one because you can swim round and round it continuously instead of going from one end to the other and then turning back. It was Dorothy's idea to make it shallow round the edges for safety, so we made the bottom saucer-shaped, giving a depth of three feet all round the edge, sloping to six feet in the middle; in this way it would be reasonably safe for a dive. George and I dug a circular pit thirty-three feet in diameter, wheeling the spoil out to the western edge of the Hollow and spreading it there to heighten and improve the general shape; we also dug a trench there to take a drainage pipe. It was solid chalk mixed with flints, and we found that we could manage sixty barrow-loads a day; after that efficiency fell off. George then built of timber a circular wall of shuttering, three feet high, a foot inside the edge of the pit, and the cavity thus formed (with a labourer to help him) he filled with concrete, using no reinforcement but a plentiful aggregate of our own flints; the floor was six inches thick, again without reinforcement, the chalk being such an excellent basis that subsequent cracking or settlement was trifling. He then rendered the whole surface with fine cement, working continuously while it was wet so that there should be no joints.

The pool was an immense success and gave pleasure to dozens of people for many years. The water of our well being from the chalk was an exquisite pale blue, which, however, we had to intensify with copper sulphate against the growth of algae.

A couple of years later there was a disaster. Dorothy happened to be in London for the day. George Marlow and I had the Hollow in tolerable condition, with a promising growth of grass, but it needed rolling and mowing. Answering a newspaper advertisement, I had bought a second-hand motor-mower; it turned out to be a large hand-mower converted by fitting a motor-cycle engine and connecting it to drive the mowing cylinder by a cycle chain. We saw that to convert it into a roller, which we then needed, one removed the cycle chain; what we did not observe was that this left unprotected a large sprocket-wheel, like that on a push-bicycle, but revolving at a high speed. We had successfully rolled a great part of the Hollow when the sprocket-wheel caught in the trousers of George's overall, tore its way into his trousers, then into his leg, and severed the main artery. I guessed what had happened, but even had I known the correct pressure-point, doubt if I could have applied enough pressure in the correct place to stop the violent flow of blood, from which, as the doctor told us later, George would have died in about six minutes. What I did was to rush down to the garage and seize the first thing that came to hand, which was a bundle of electric flex; with this I made a double tourniquet high up around the thigh, and using the starting-handle of the mower as a lever, twisted it as tightly round the leg as I could. I ran to telephone the doctor; unfortunately there was a meet of the local fox-hounds in the village, and he was delayed for what seemed an hour – it may have been half-an-hour – in getting through. It was Dr Johns who came; to him and his partner, Dr Strang, we are still grateful. They had George taken to the Cottage Hospital in Chesham, amputated the leg below the knee although the wound was above it, and attended him faithfully until it was healed. The saving of the knee, though surgically admirable, turned out to be a disadvantage, because the knee became rigid and prevented the fixing of an artificial leg with a flexible knee-joint. George never came to terms with the artificial leg that was fitted, was happiest when not wearing it, got about well and dug well when on crutches, and always sat on the ground without the leg when doing a gardening job like sowing or transplanting seedlings.

This terrible blow did not prevent him helping us faithfully afterwards, and almost as efficiently as ever. He was particularly helpful to Dorothy when I was away at the War; and he and May continued to work for us at Amersham, and later in Oxford, except for a period when we were in London and he took a job in a small local factory polishing cigarette lighters. It is a commentary on the modern production-line that whereas George could polish X number of lighters, all perfect, in a given time, his fellow workers could polish X plus ten; but ten of these had to be sent back to be repolished completely.

There was one curious after-effect. Poor George had nearly been killed, and had suffered not only the shock of the accident but that of the major operation. I had suffered nothing physically, but for the first two or three weeks afterwards the nervous shock manifested itself in a peculiar way; I became frightened of the dark, and when I went down to the furnace-room under the house to stoke up at night, found myself looking fearfully over my shoulder.

Chapter VI

University College; Interlude at Denham; The British Museum

I HAVE WORKED IN SEVERAL universities and know well the merits of the college system, as well as its tendency to create small societies of narrow outlook. The friendly and lively community at University College, London, was no ordinary college: it was unique in its comprehensiveness and unique in its organization. Its Senior Common Room was used by members of every Faculty, and it was possible to obtain first-hand and first-class information on any subject in the world, except theology, simply by sitting next to the appropriate professor or specialist at lunch or in the smoking-room. It is difficult to select for mention any of my colleagues there – so many were friends – but I now remember particularly Norman Baynes the Byzantine historian, who had been largely responsible for my appointment; R. W. Chambers, professor of English, author of a noble biography of Thomas More; Edward Salisbury (universally known as "Sarum") the botanist, always ready with a fund of information; D. M. S. Watson the zoologist, an expert also on Chinese bronzes, keenly interested in the techniques of every kind of art and craft; and G. B. Jeffery the mathematician, who made me see, although not understand, how mathematics in its higher ranges is not a dry text-book study but a creative art.

Another great advantage, at least for the Faculty of Arts, was the plan of the College building, virtually that devised at its foundation in 1826. The dome, with the façade in front of it, struck the dominant note in the design; under the dome was a circular gallery giving access to the main library immediately behind it, and to other parts of the building, the most important being a long extension on the south consisting of a broad passage with a series of rooms on each side of it which housed specialist libraries – French, Italian, Classics, Archaeology, and so on. This enabled teaching to take place in these small libraries using the collections of specialised books, and when a more general book was needed it could be fetched from the central library only a few steps away. This arrangement compares favourably with, for instance, Yale, where the specialised archaeological library, unevenly developed, was half a mile from the main library; whilst the main library was far more comprehensive, even in archaeological books, yet had no space for teaching. Thus, in taking a seminar on some aspect of ancient art, where, naturally, adequate illustrations were essential, one had to plan in advance exactly which books would be needed and carry some of them half a mile to the specialist library, no easy task when several of them might be of folio size weighing anything up to twenty pounds apiece. This is a common dilemma in university libraries, especially where money is scarce and duplication of books deprecated.

The administrative drawback of the College was that, being so large and powerful, its members inevitably occupied many places on the committees of the University a few hundred yards away. The decisions its own committees took were apt to be sent on to the University for confirmation by similar committees manned by many of the same people, a grave waste of time for academic staff who, with a few exceptions, would rather have been employed on their own teaching and research; and on a lower level, for clerical staff who produced agenda and minutes virtually repeating those of the College committees. Many people believed that University College should itself have been a university, as its founders had intended.

The Provost of University College, Allan Mawer, was an admirable Chairman, and the main College Committee, being large and potentially explosive, needed one. The agenda was apt to be long, some items were complicated, and as everyone of experience knows, such meetings can continue for hours, until members are exhausted or have gone away in boredom or disgust. Mawer had no particular charm of appearance or manner, but he had studied the agenda fully, and managed the meeting with firmness, equable temper, readiness to hear different points of view if they were not too long-winded or contentious; and by reasonably quick decisions, usually managed to get his own way without appearing to be either prejudiced or dictatorial. Chairmanship is an art, and this was a lesson in it.

My Inaugural Lecture sought to demonstrate the value of a gallery of plastercasts, not primarily as a substitute for marble sculpture, but to give students the opportunity of making comparisons between pieces in widely separated places, and of taking the preliminary look at statues which might be at the other side of the world, but which they might hope to see eventually. The lecture was fully reported in *The Times* and this made it easier for us to take over from the British Museum, with the willing co-operation of the Trustees, their collection of two or three hundred casts which had accumulated there over the years. This compared poorly with the great collection at the Beaux Arts in Paris which – like that at the Victoria and Albert in London – covered every period of European art, or with those in Berlin, Cambridge or Oxford; but it would make a reasonable working collection.

The problem of where to house it was readily solved. Adjacent to University College on the south in Malet Place there stood empty a large warehouse of William Whiteley, the prototype of all great Department Stores. Whiteleys had begun with a great flourish in the nineteenth century, styling themselves the Universal Providers, so that would-be wits, it was said, had asked to be provided with such things as an elephant or a pint of fleas. They were now reduced to a less ambitious scale and their warehouses came on the market. University College, cramped for space, had long had an eye on them, since they were ideal for conversion, being solidly built in yellow and blue brick, unattractive, but durable, and constructed internally with cast-iron supporting columns in order to give the maximum uninterrupted space for storage; they could thus be converted simply by using light internal partitions. Nor were they only warehouses, for Whiteleys, before the days of the motor-car, had kept there no fewer than six hundred draught-horses and a great number of vans. With practical logic the horses had been lodged on the first floor, which they could reach under their own power, whilst the vans remained on the ground; and on the first floor, which was served by a ramp, there were fully equipped stables, with loose-boxes, and floors made of granite setts, sloped for drainage on to a central channel. The lighting was by long skylights, and this was excellent, although many photographers even today have not realised that a dominant top-light is ideal for sculpture; the BBC in particular (which photographs living creatures superbly) prefers to floodlight sculpture from the front, thus losing most details of features and muscles in statues and effectively killing the modelling of reliefs.

University College had acquired all the Whiteley buildings; we set about converting this part of them, and by inserting a staircase over the ramp and decking over the sloping granite setts with a level hardwood floor, made a pleasant little cast-gallery, the only memory of its earlier use being a pervasive smell. Our entrance passage was planned to be about ten feet wide with shallow corridors on either side, and in the passage we constructed a small lecture theatre with half a dozen seats and three lanterns. Lanterns, screen and seats were all on castors, and after use disappeared neatly back into the wall. The special purpose of the three lanterns was to enable us to make comparisons between Greek sculptures, Greek vases and Greek coins, in an attempt to fix their relative dates. This was a study of particular interest to Stanley Robinson, then assistant Keeper in the Department of Coins at the British Museum, to me, and to Father Claude Heithaus.

Claude Heithaus was an American Jesuit who had come over to work in my Department on Roman coins, with the aim of acquiring a London doctorate; but owing to eye-strain he was later obliged to abandon the close study of coins and changed his subject to the Roman temples of Syria. He made a number of journeys to remote corners of the Near East, discovered the remains of more than twenty hitherto unknown temples, and sent back lengthy reports full of archaeological details, but containing also the most entertaining accounts of his adventures among the natives. He eventually stayed six years in the Department, taking his doctorate just before returning to America on the outbreak of war. He was a remarkable character, visited us often at home and became our firm friend, deeply influencing us and our children by his finely trained mind, his moral and intellectual integrity, and his affectionate nature. He had a keen and dry sense of humour, and his comments on the Near East and on his home university of St Louis after his return there, are of absorbing interest and extremely amusing.

Not all lectures were uneventful. A series of seven had been arranged, each by a different lecturer, the whole being given the title of "The Works of Man". I had been allotted the subject of "Man as an Artist". The lectures were to take place in a converted chapel, a spacious hall from which the religious symbols had been removed, except a golden aureole in relief over the podium, which possibly struck the note for what happened later. I began by speaking of the essential difference between the hand of a human being and that of even the most advanced primate, in the opposable thumb. After I had been speaking for some ten minutes, the lantern broke down; whereupon a man stood up towards the back of the hall and called out "Do you know that God is on the earth?" Dumbfounded by this unexpected query, I murmured that I thought I did, whereupon he replied "Would you like me to tell you all about it?" By then I had collected my senses, and said that perhaps this was not quite the moment to do it: perhaps he would come round and see me afterwards. "Well," said he, "I am God". At that moment the lantern went on again, and the man, whether satisfied with this apparent display of power, or because the audience around him grew restive, sat down again and was heard no more. When I told Tom Kendrick of the British Museum about this episode, he at once said "I can easily cap that. I was on top of a bus in a traffic jam at Hyde Park Corner. A woman stood up and said loudly 'I am the Queen of England: all kneel'. Passengers looked anxiously at one another wondering (a) whether they ought to comply or appear to do so, and (b) whether it was physically possible, when mercifully the bus went on and she subsided."

In the early thirties I became involved in a bitter archaeological controversy. In 1931 I had delivered an uncontroversial lecture to the British Academy on Greek art in Sicily and South Italy, a subject I had worked at for several years. This was intended to show that although little major sculpture had been found in these western colonies of Greece, it ought to be possible to form an idea of what distinguished their art from that of their parent cities by studying the smaller works of art, especially coins and terracottas, at least some of which must have been produced locally. I tried to show, within the limits of an hour's lecture, that not only were there distinctive western styles, but also some connections with the art of the parent cities.

The publication of this in the *Proceedings of the British Academy* happened to coincide with a publication being prepared by G. E. Rizzo, an Italian professor, on the coinages of the western colonies, for which he had employed a fine photographer and written a discursive essay. He turned out to be almost pathologically jealous, and instead of regarding a fellow scholar as a worker in the same field, which archaeologists generally do, chose to regard it as a trespass on his preserves. His attack was ill-tempered, and contained a number of inaccurate quotations from my lecture. This gave me many weeks of unhappiness, until eventually I wrote a counter-attack in the *Journal of Hellenic Studies* called "Manners and Methods in Archaeology", which was devoted mainly to correcting his mis-quotations but also deploring the personal attack. To this he replied later with an abusive pamphlet, and there the matter ended; except that, fifty years later I was awarded the Cassano Medal, as a pioneer of Western studies, by an archaeological Conference in South Italy. It was an unpleasant experience, and a discouraging side-light on the world of Italian archaeology, which at that time was – with happy exceptions – something of a cock-pit.

A year or two after I had taken up my professorship there came an unexpected diversion. An historian, Ross-Williamson, asked me if I would work with him as technical adviser for the film of "I, Claudius" which the Kordas were preparing to make at Denham. I liked Ross-Williamson and accepted, with the proviso that my name should not appear anywhere: this was thought sheer folly, but was agreed. At Denham I found that we were working as advisers to Vincent Korda, who was Artistic Director for the film. Charles Laughton, who had had a great success as Henry VIII in the film, had now been cast for the title role, and the whole cast was strong – Merle Oberon as Messalina, Flora Robson as Livia and Emlyn Williams as Caligula: the whole set-up is described in Michael Korda's book *Charmed Lives*. Charles Laughton had insisted that he should have Josef von Sternberg to produce the film; but as time went on it became clear that they were at odds, particularly on how the character of Claudius should be presented.

My job was to provide information about everything Roman, from the organisation of the Roman Empire down to the details of daily life. I had a drawing-pad and a black pencil, and when, for instance, I was asked what an ancient plough looked like, I simply sketched it on the pad, explained the mechanism, and the plough was then produced in the workshop, which was highly efficient, especially in its plaster-casting. Similarly with the armour which soldiers and officers wore; this was fairly easy, because there are many sculptured reliefs of the Roman army and the details of equipment can be copied. Other details are not so easy; for instance, exactly how does a soldier salute his officer? And so with domestic affairs, the details of which ancient writers have often omitted to describe. How does one lay out a banquet for thirty people? They recline at meals and thus take up more room than if seated. That is all right for a party of two or three, but how exactly is a really large dinner party arranged? At long tables? – if so, of what shape? – or groups of small tables?

We had formed a little working library at Denham and I was able to find the answers to most of the problems. I was listened to with the greatest respect by Vincent Korda, with whom I was on most friendly terms, and by others; the trouble was that if what I had said didn't happen to agree with what they wanted, they went straight ahead and took not the slightest notice of it.

One of the major conflicts was over the Vestal Virgins. "I, Claudius" being somewhat lacking in sex appeal, von Sternberg believed that this was the way to introduce it, envisaging troupes of lovely girls who could be manoeuvred seductively. He was taken aback when I explained that there were only six of them and that their ages might range from six upwards. We argued about this, for although my name would not be openly associated with any gross solecisms that might be committed, I felt that here was a factual point that anyone could verify and which really could not be ignored. In the end we compromised for eight, von Sternberg thinking in terms of four pairs.

In order not to interfere with my work in College I came to Denham only at weekends, and when I went away on that Sunday evening I thought the matter was settled; but when I returned to Denham on the following Saturday and reported to Vincent Korda, he seemed embarrassed, and asked if I had been along to studio 4, which was the largest set, laid out in a building the size of an aircraft hangar.

What I saw there was partly connected with another problem, one of the many queries about dress. It was this: did the Romans use net as a dress material? I really hadn't the faintest idea, but since net is a fairly primitive kind of fabric used in various ways, I thought that it might reasonably have been used in that way too, and said so. I had no inkling of what the results would be, but in studio 4 I was soon to see. Everything everywhere was swathed in a fine net; even the sculptured busts, with which film producers love to decorate their sets, had lengths of net looped round them. But the major provision of net was for the Vestal Virgins, and here there had been a transformation; on the Monday von Sternberg, dissatisfied with our compromise, had suddenly said "We must have more Vestal Virgins: we'll have forty of them".

In those days it was always possible to engage supers, happy to walk on for a guinea a day and all found; and the extra thirty-odd needed had readily presented themselves. They had each been given six yards torn from a wide roll of net, and instructed to strip and swathe themselves in it becomingly. In studio 4 the scene to be shot was the deification of Augustus, and what it looked like I told Dorothy when I got home "a very large first Communion in St Peter's, staged in the manner of the Folies Bergères". Amid clouds of incense, the forty Vestal Virgins, draped in their six yards of net, were waving palm branches round the base of a

Vestal Virgins in Michael Korda's film 'I Claudius' shot at Denham near London, 1931.

colossal statue, of which the inscription on its pedestal, its feet, and its legs up to the knee could be seen. The net had a second and altogether unexpected effect on the proceedings. It is beloved by film photographers because it photographs beautifully: but it is also feared because it is so inflammable, and insurance companies insist that it shall be fire-proofed. The fire-proofing here had consisted in dipping the whole roll in a fire-resisting solution; this had dried out, and when the girls each tore off their six yards it went up in the form of powder which they inhaled. The powder formed a powerful laxative, and the ceremony was thus punctuated by hurried departures elsewhere.

The presence of the colossal statue was simulated by a pretty technical device. Only the lower part of the legs was of full size; but at the other end of the studio was the model of a basilica about six feet long, in one of the side niches of which was a complete statuette of Augustus. First the camera was focused through this model building to coincide with the legs and the procession a hundred feet or more away. Then the scene would switch to a close-up of the procession itself, and the illusion was complete.

On another occasion I went with Vincent Korda to a studio where all the staff and the cameras were in position and the lights on for photographing, but the set appeared to be empty. I asked him what was up and he pointed to the far right-hand corner of the set where a substantial body lay on its face on the ground. It was Charles Laughton literally biting the carpet. Until this time I had always understood this action to be a metaphor only, but here it was taking place before my very eyes, and it was certainly astonishing. Things were obviously wrong somewhere, and it wasn't difficult to see where. The carpet-biting was simply a visible sign of the complete deadlock between Charles Laughton and von Sternberg. This was sad, because it had the makings of a fine film, as is shown by the two or three sequences since seen on television. Fortunately for Denham, at this moment Merle Oberon, playing a key part as Messalina, suffered injuries in a motor accident; and, as everyone knows, this writes off the production automatically.

I said good-bye to Denham with some regrets: it was a glimpse into the world of films, a world as utterly different from my own almost as that of Claudius himself. I was thankful too. I had succeeded in producing, without major errors, and with the aid of the moulders' shop, one or two long formal inscriptions for the bases of statues, and I had prevented Vincent from decorating the sets with busts of people who had not been born until Claudius and his contemporaries had long been dead. The chorus of Vestal Virgins, had they ever appeared publicly, would not only have been a fatal blot on my name as a scholar, but would have proved beyond doubt the uselessness – not quite total perhaps – of employing a technical adviser.

In 1937 I had been awarded the Florence Bursary of the Royal Institute of British Architects, which enabled me to travel in Greece for some weeks the following year. On my first visit to the British Museum after returning, some of the metopes of the Parthenon, a part of the Elgin Marbles, were on exhibition. They had been cleaned in preparation for their move to the new gallery presented by Lord Duveen, the picture-dealer. They were at eye-level, but railed off so that a close view was impossible, but they did look unnaturally white; I ought to have realised that something was wrong, but didn't.

Not long afterwards John Forsdyke, who had succeeded Sir George Hill as Director of the British Museum, made an alarming revelation. It was that Duveen had in effect bribed the chief mason, who happened to be a drinker and therefore not all that trustworthy, to clean a number of the marbles drastically so as to make them more showy for his new gallery; the mason had removed the patina, which is that change, mainly in colour, of the surface which tends to occur with age, especially in Pentelic marble. The crisis had arisen through a combination of unfortunate circumstances. It was a tradition that Keepers of Departments in the Museum were independent, and were normally advised rather than directed by the Director. This meant that apart from occasional visits by the Director or a Trustee and an annual meeting at which the Keeper presented his report to the Trustees, a Department was left to itself. The then Keeper of the Greek and Roman Department was seriously ill and had been away for some time; his senior Assistant Keeper, though a fine scholar, preferred to read books in the Departmental Library rather than make a round of inspection that would include the masons' shop. The result was that the mason carried on his evil work undetected.

The British Museum, Elgin Room, about 1920.

The British Museum, Duveen Gallery: J. Russell Pope's modified design, dated 4 February 1932.

Forsdyke explained that the Keeper had retired and his senior assistant had resigned. Would I become Honorary Keeper and hold the fort with the only remaining member of staff, the junior assistant Keeper? He pointed out that some stone-walling would be necessary against journalists, questions in Parliament and ordinary enquiries – in fact "holding the fort" about covered it. This seemed a job that, however tiresome, looked as if it needed doing, and I accepted, after receiving permission from the College.

I was to have executive control of the Department and of my two assistant Keepers, one remaining from the crisis and another, a promising young archaeologist, transferred from the Victoria and Albert Museum. The junior staff, called then the "clerical grade", I already knew, having been a frequent visitor to the Department. At the head of them was Albert Keyte who had worked his way up from a boy through the grades of the Civil Service. He was at heart a most worthy man, but had absorbed the jargon, and partly because of this had an extraordinarily complicated way of saying the simplest things. One of his finest remarks, verging on the metaphysical, was overheard when he was on the telephone to someone wanting to purchase a plaster-cast (the moulders' shop was run by our Department): "Yes sir" he said, "We have four hundred objects, or, if you like to look at it in that way, subjects". I got on well enough with him, much put out when I did; in the peculiar circumstances I often had to and, as an outsider, was reasonably immune to the consequences.

I had understood that the appointment was to be an honorary one, and was surprised to find that I was to be paid the equivalent of about half my College salary; this enabled me to relinquish that half and give my time to the Museum with a clear conscience. It proved to be no sinecure: apart from searching enquiries from the public, the international scene became more threatening, and elaborate arrangements had to be made for the packing and disposal of our treasures, by the provision of standardised wooden cases for the lighter objects (collapsible, for storage meanwhile), sandbags and other materials for the preliminary protection of the larger, and by arrangement for safe depositories in the country and elsewhere.

Crates of sculpture from the British Museum stored in the Aldwych underground station with sand bags, 1939.

CHAPTER VI

The shadow of war was over most of the thirties, and as they went on we had the Labour Government steadily refusing to introduce conscription or to spend enough money on defence; those well-meaning dupes the Peace-Pledge Union; the irresponsible jesters of the Oxford Union, with their debate on King and Country; the pro-Nazis; the Communists and crypto-Communists, including even a so-called historian or two, helping Germany through Russia (her booty to be half of Poland); plus a plentiful sprinkling of traitors; all these combined in reducing to impotence anyone who had to deal with Hitler, so, when Neville Chamberlain went to Munich, he was at a hopeless disadvantage, negotiating from utter weakness against the massive strength that Hitler had built up. He was bound to compromise; he claimed it as a victory for peace. It is true that he was deceived, but the fact remains that in 1938 war with Germany would have meant defeat for Britain.

Seldom has there been a better example of the creation of a scapegoat, and of its convenience for masking one's own culpability; heap the blame on someone else, and then destroy him. Those who had been so active in making inevitable some kind of appeasement, although they did not call it so, now united in condemning as appeasement a conclusion they themselves had brought about. Munich became a term of reproach, and those who had more to hide and were more guilty, were then, and still are, those most ready to use it.

We were now given explicit instructions to begin packing. This naturally meant long hours and I arranged to save time by staying, at Father Claude Heithaus'

Sculpture from the British Museum (a block from the Temple of Athena Polias at Priene) in the Aldwych underground station, 1939.

invitation, in the Jesuit Hostel in Hampstead. Everyone in the Department was wonderfully helpful, and day after day we all packed, making an inventory, case by case, of the thousands of objects. Particularly tricky were those in the Gold Room, many of them small and extremely delicate. Every one had to be detached from its setting in the show-case, listed, laid in cottonwool, and then packed in such a way that it would not be crushed. Also packed up were such things as the exhibits in the room of Greek and Roman Life, the best of the ancient glass, and all the more important Greek vases. The less important sculptures and hundreds of the less important vases were moved into the extensive basements of the Museum, most of them vaulted in brick and therefore some protection against light bombing or fire. The Elgin Marbles were, as a preliminary measure, taken from their pedestals, set as close to the wall of their gallery as possible, and then roofed over with heavy timbers and sandbagged in.

In 1936 the Olympic Games had been held in Berlin. This had been a blatant piece of political propaganda, and I looked with suspicion on an International Congress of the German Archaeological Institute planned for 1939; though not so spectacular, it had much the same taint. We were invited to attend, but I declined and asked an Assistant Keeper to go instead. This was wiser than I knew; the Congress broke up on the eve of the war and some of our delegates, hurrying homewards, felt themselves lucky not to be interned.

Chapter VII

The Second War

AFTER PACKING UP and shutting down my department at the British Museum I worked, mainly at home in Amersham, on transliterating into English the place-names on the map of Greece, in preparation for a new map to be issued by the General Staff. The work was under the auspices of the Royal Geographical Society, and our friend Sir George Hill, just retired from the Directorship of the British Museum, came to live with us at Amersham so that we could work on it together. It was a curious compilation, because the quality of the sources we had to use varied extremely according to the area of country concerned. For many parts, especially on the northern frontiers we had Greek Staff maps, which were excellent; but for some places – remote islands, for instance – we had to rely on tourist guides only or even on maps published by the local stationer.

In mid-1940, after the fall of France and the retreat from Dunkirk, I volunteered for the Local Defence Volunteers (afterwards called the Home Guard) and we kept watch from the top of our water-tower at Amersham for possible German parachutists, with one rifle and the few rounds of ammunition that the force possessed. One of the great needs at that time was for ground-defence officers on airfields, and anyone who had served in the First War and had some knowledge of firearms was of value. One of George Hill's nephews, Geoffrey, was a colleague of mine as Professor of Engineering at University College; his brother Roderic was an Air Vice-Marshal. With these introductions, and after a medical examination, I was commissioned as a Pilot Officer in the RAFVR. (The rank is misleading; there is an Administrative and Special Duties Branch which does not fly, but the ranks are the same as in the General Duties Branch, which does.)

I was at once posted to a station in the West Country where Geoffrey Hill had been entrusted by the Air Ministry with the task of devising methods of defending airfields from attack. He was instructed by the Government that he was to make no demands on any material that could be used in producing munitions for offensive warfare – he must as far as possible use materials that already existed. One of his more ingenious devices was a rocket-barrage composed of coastguard rescue-rockets, of which there was a plentiful supply. These were powerful rockets each attached to a length (perhaps two or three hundred feet) of steel cable, their original purpose having been to fire at ships in distress so that a lifeline could be attached. Geoffrey Hill's plan was to set a long line of these, mounted twenty feet or so apart, pointing vertically upwards and connected by an electrical circuit; by pressing a button the whole line could be ignited, and thus for ten or twenty seconds a steel fence was created which then subsided groundwards; the idea being that if it was set off at the right moment a low-flying aircraft would crash into it. Knowledge that such a barrier existed might even act as a deterrent.

After training in the mechanism of this I was posted to the RAF Station at Sumburgh at the southern point of Shetland, as a Ground-Defence Officer with the special job of supervising the operation of several of these rocket-barrages at vulnerable points. Weaponry after Dunkirk was otherwise sparse and apart from a few rifles we had only two Bofors anti-aircraft guns, and an exquisite little cannon from the Museum of the Coventry Ordnance Works (naturally soon christened the Cow-gun). This might well have been a relic of the Boer War and was called a quick-firer – perhaps six shots a minute; it could not of course have been used against aircraft in the air, but might have been effective on the ground. The shells weighed two or three pounds, the range was about a thousand yards and the drop at that distance very great; indeed the velocity was so low that one could actually see the shell in mid-air. Nevertheless we were glad to have it and admired its beautiful workmanship; fit, as they used to say of the old GWR engines, to go on a lady's watch chain.

Life at Sumburgh was strenuous but fascinating; we patrolled the perimeter of the airfield and camp continuously day and night and became so weatherbeaten as to be hardly recognisable. It was rewarding too because one was working among fighter-pilots and other airmen who were hourly risking their lives over the North Sea, and one hoped, if opportunity offered, to be able to do something in return. Everyone lent a hand in strengthening our ground defences, chiefly by excavating and filling sandbags, for since we were the part of Britain nearest to German-occupied Norway, it was thought that we might be first on the list for attack. Many of the ground crews were survivors from Dunkirk and they had astonishing tales to tell of their experiences.

One described how a woman parachutist (not a disguised man) fell from the sky at his very feet; another, how they had been on the beaches so long being strafed that they no longer cared whether they were hit or not, then they got on to a little ship and saw the cliffs of Dover – the loveliest sight of their lives – but what really broke them down was the welcome they got on landing.

The wild life on Shetland was marvellous; many gulls, and Arctic terns – the most exquisite thing on wings. The gulls were very bold and one kind had learnt a trick of carrying up young rabbits into the air, then dropping them so as to kill and eat them. One day a gull tried this on a kitten belonging to the Infantry cookhouse next door to us, but being a cat it survived the treatment. There were also seals which came out on to the beach to look at us when we were checking the defences, and the occasional whale.

Also on the airfield was a company of Argyll and Sutherland Highlanders – a Pioneer Company of elderly reservists. They were helping to excavate for and erect Nissen Huts against the winter, since living under canvas, as we now were, would become impossible then. There was a NAAFI, a village shop and Post Office, and a small Public House. When at night this closed at the appropriate hour, dozens of these elderly Scotsmen would be disgorged on to the edge of the airfield (at that time a vast featureless plain, with no clearly defined airstrips) and would have the task of finding their way home in the total blackout. It was alleged, possibly with truth, that some were still to be found wandering there at dawn. Fortunately, the nights in summer were never pitch-black, and dawn came early. In October the northern lights began and continued on and off; not the coloured kind, but as if the whole sky were covered with brilliant white shafts of light, scintillating like ice, which I think they are.

In December I was posted to the Middle East and left Shetland with the distinction – said to be unique – of never having set off one of the rocket-barrages by mistake. I spent a last leave with Dorothy at an hotel in Bournemouth, where she had been living with her sister Hilda, and where Stella was at school. Round Christmas the hotel gave a party. Each guest, as he or she entered the room, drew a number (for making partners at games etc.); mine was thirteen. Midway through the party there was a 'lucky dip' for which everyone drew from another series of numbers quite independent of the first; mine was again thirteen. This might have seemed an ill omen, but I did not feel alarmed and the sequel showed that there must be something wrong with the superstition.

My posting was to Greece, but the Mediterranean was impassable then because of attacks by air, and the way we reached it almost incredibly devious. No ships could sail with safety from the southern ports of England, so our train took us to Liverpool. Liverpool had just had an air-raid and the railway station was ankle-deep in glass; but calm, heroic women of the Salvation Army and the YWCA were serving tea to us all. At Liverpool we embarked on the SS Abosso of the Elder Dempster Line and sailed almost north, nearly to Iceland; then westerly; and at some point in the neighbourhood of Greenland, must have turned south and eventually landed at Takoradi on the Gold Coast six thousand miles or so away, but with a third of the journey – across Africa – yet to do. This would have been about mid-January, for on January 8th I wrote that after a preliminary tossing about and freezing, which made us all feel low, it was now just warm enough to sit on deck and in another day or two would probably be too hot.

My companions were Wally Hammond, the cricketer, and Philip Kerr the Herald, Croix Rouge I think; both were most congenial. Takoradi made a pleasant impression; the natives were friendly and smiling and those working at the RAF Depot efficient. Otherwise things in general seemed happy-go-lucky, and I remember the comment of a foreign observer contrasting the colonial regimes of Africa and saying that in those under the British he was struck by the number of people lying about and doing nothing. In that climate, provided everyone is happy, there is much to be said for this. What a contrast to the Belgian Congo, to which we were flown next! The huts for the natives were model dwellings, there was a fine little Catholic Church for them and every amenity. Yet I felt that they were a captive people, cared for like prize cattle for what they could yield; and only there did I see a colonist strike a native – not cruelly, but as if it were a matter of course, the recipient seemed to take it as such. Unthinkable in Takoradi.

Before starting we stayed a night in Lagos in a disreputable hotel, with a cabaret going on in the roof-garden outside, and meals served on a long balcony near the top of the building, this being the only way of getting any coolness. The humidity in these places is the trouble (on unpacking we found our clothes quite damp and even beginning to be mildewed), but it also means that one simply cannot get cool even at night, and streams with perspiration most of the time. Next morning we emerged from the hotel with virtue unsullied, and later in the day had tea with the British Education Officer, a most enlightened person with a beautiful garden near one of the lagoons (you can take a motor-boat from his landing-stage and go six hundred miles through practically unexplored waterways); it was full of interesting flowers. Everyone stationed there seems sooner or later to have a bout of fever, the great difficulty of eliminating mosquitoes being the land-crabs, which live in burrows that fill with water at the bottom and so make a breeding-ground for them.

Flying as we were at a fairly low altitude, probably about eight thousand feet, Africa looked very much what one would expect – hundreds of miles of the densest jungle, terrible-looking swamps of all colours, little lost villages miles from each other almost hidden in jungle, and in the Congo area enormous muddy rivers meandering about, splitting into lakes and lagoons because of the extreme flatness. Our first stop was in Belgian territory and our bungalow here was on the bank of a huge and not too muddy river, presumably the Congo itself, with dense jungle on the other side. Next, also in Belgian territory, Stanleyville, where we were received in a friendly fashion by a "Belgian Ladies' Committee for helping the Allies" and were taken to see the local sights: the Stanley Falls (not the major ones which were too far away); African elephants – the most difficult to train – being washed after work; and lately-captured okapis, then one of the rarest of animals. This was our hottest night, and all of us found that our pyjamas were simply soaked with sweat; but even so everyone got a good deal of sleep and the heat wasn't oppressive, it was simply like being in a Turkish bath all the time.

The next day the country changed, there were some hills, then the trees got rarer and there were bare grassy spaces, many of them covered with a dense network formed by the tracks of animals, often leading to muddy drinking pools; but we saw very few of the animals themselves – some elephants so far below us that they really might have been goats, and in the rivers an occasional crocodile. On the whole that was fierce rocky country, but there was still some greenery, and some marshes near the uppermost reaches of the White Nile; then the Nile became broader and broader until finally the Blue and the White joined. Down it to Khartoum. There I was able to call on Dorothy's sister Christine, who was headmistress of the Unity Girls' High School. She entertained Philip Kerr and me perfectly to dinner and cabled Dorothy of my arrival. Sadly I learned later that Kerr, to whom I had become much attached, had died of cerebral malaria, presumably from a mosquito-bite in Takoradi or Lagos.

Thinking back to the austerity of war-time Britain I found Cairo, where we arrived on February 2nd, in general over-prosperous, fat and rich, yet displaying painful contrasts between wealth and extreme poverty. Of course there were many admirable people there less in evidence, and among them Ibrahim Noshy, who had worked in my department at University College ten years before, had produced an excellent archaeological thesis and had been a welcome guest at High and Over. I now went to call on him, received the kindest of welcomes, and we went to the Pyramids together.

GREECE

On February 18th I left Cairo for Greece. The military position there then was that the Greeks regarded Italy as their first enemy, and on the Italians invading them in October 1940 had allowed us to bring in five squadrons of aircraft, of which 84 Blenheim Squadron was one. These had operated successfully against Italian supply-ports and lines of communications, but the Greeks did not until the last moment – namely February 1941, when it was clear that the Germans were about to intervene – give us permission to land any other troops, for fear of provocation. As early as April 1939 Britain had given a pledge to Greece to guarantee her independence. There now arose the difficult question whether this pledge should be honoured. Not everyone agreed: 'Strategicus', for instance, in his *Short History of the Second World War* writes "By intervention she gained nothing". To those on the spot the choice seemed absolutely clear, and the event, although at first not obviously, certainly justified it, not only on the ground of honour but also on that of morale and therefore – in the end – strategy. These things are imponderable, but it is impossible to maintain that the immediate military loss was not counterbalanced by the moral gain which that example gave. The parallel of Thermopylae has been quoted; and who can say that the Spartan decision to stay and die was not ultimately justified?

In Greece I was posted to the ex-civilian airport of Tatoi, renamed for military use Menidi. This was held by 84 Blenheim Squadron, which had at its disposal good offices and the use of a KLM Airline Bus, which was extremely useful for trips down to Athens. When I first arrived I was made Adjutant of the Station; but the Adjutant of 84 Squadron had finished his tour of duty and I was soon appointed in his place – a very happy post with most congenial fellow-officers and men. The Squadron had its full complement

A Blenheim in flight to the Far East about 1940.

of airmen and ground staff; it also had a number of recruits from Palestine, enlisted as ordinary airmen, but untrained, and organised rather differently. They were known as Palestinians, and were a very mixed lot; some highly educated – a young architect, for instance, was among them; some very rough countrymen; all anxious to help, but not all qualified to do so. Several of course were employed as clerks in the Orderly Room or equipment stores, others in the cookhouse and Officers' Mess. I had one as a batman, a very good and well-meaning but primitive fellow. In the little guest-house that we had taken over as Officers' quarters I was sleeping on a camp bed; my batman, with the best of intentions, had found his way into the basement and discovered there a real bedstead which he brought up and erected in my room. From past experience of Greece I ought to have guessed that all was not as it seemed, for in the middle of the night I was fiercely attacked by what has been charmingly described as the "terror of the Balkans"; they were not in the bedstead, which was of iron, nor the mattress, which was of wire, but in the wooden stretchers to which it was attached. On our journeys in Greece in the twenties Dorothy and I had learnt that the presence of these creatures is not due to an accumulation of dirt, but almost always to old wood.

There was naturally a good deal of harmless joking about the doings of the Palestinians, and one story was told (perhaps from an over-lively imagination) that the Medical Officer, who was President of the Officers' Mess and thus responsible for our meals, had often had complaints that the food was sodden and lacking in crispness. He carried out an inspection of the kitchen equipment, accompanied by the Officers' cook, a stalwart, elderly Englishman from the West Country, and after looking at it said "What you really want here is a griller". The cook looked at him for a moment in a puzzled way and then replied "I've got enough to do looking after them there Palestinians; I don't want one of those hairy brutes about."

A few miles away from us at Kephissia was a large Australian Medical Unit, staffed by delightful officers with whom we often exchanged Mess parties. We were particularly friendly with the Colonel and his Second-in-Command, a Major who had lost a leg in the First War. His star turn was usually deferred until about midnight, when he would stand against the bar and raise his artificial leg (so good that no-one had suspected its existence) until the instep rested on top of his head. On the less abstemious the effect was noteworthy.

We had a fair amount of spare time, and I was able to go down to Athens and call on Gerard Young, Director of the British School, who had with him at that time as a guest Alan Wace, who had been Director when Dorothy and I lived at the School in the twenties. Wace later worked in Alexandria for the British Government, and Young I was to meet again eighteen months later in India.

I also paid a visit to Shoe Lane, an old haunt of Dorothy's and mine, where there are not only shoe shops but antique shops; and I went into one we had known. Looking round it was Erich Boehringer, a German numismatist who had often been a visitor to the Coin Room at the Ashmolean when I was Assistant Keeper there. I went up to him with hand outstretched; he took it, but with what seemed some embarrassment. I assumed that, like several German archaeologists who were not enthusiastic Nazis, he had sought refuge in one of the German foreign Institutes, in order to avoid breaking entirely with the regime without actively helping it. Later that afternoon I went to tea with Dr and Mrs Karouzos. He was Director of the National Museum and his wife an Assistant Keeper; both were old friends and strongly Anglophile. I described the meeting with Boehringer and what I imagined was his status. They were amazed at my misunderstanding: "He is not at the German Institute at all", they said, "but is Third Secretary at the German Embassy". By now it was clear that Germany was threatening to invade Greece from the north; in his position he must be privy to their invasion plans, and it seemed to me a gross betrayal of classical scholarship that an archaeologist who, as a student, had been a guest in the country, should use his knowledge of it thus acquired in order to make sure that she should literally be stabbed in the back – Italy was already attacking her from the west. In fairness it should be added that during the occupation of Greece by Germany later on, Boehringer did all that he could to alleviate the hardships the Greeks suffered.

The Squadron did an ample share of raids and reconnaissance; on the airfield itself life was very placid. We had there an ancient aircraft – I think a Vickers Vimy – looking to modern eyes not unlike a box-kite, and lacking a tail-plane. Air Headquarters had decided that, old though it was, it would be worth repairing and spare parts having been located and flown in, repairs were carried out. Alas! A few days later a German fighter ground-strafed the airfield, and the Vimy was destroyed. This was a sure sign, if indeed we needed it, that the Germans were now uncomfortably close, and there began the sad arrival of several Yugoslav aircraft flown by pilots who had no intention of surrendering to the Germans; sad because their loyalties were so divided. The aircraft were marked with a black cross, and at first being mistaken for German – the Germans bore a black swastika – were fired on by our ground-crews, fortunately without casualties.

We were kept well-informed about the news from the north; the collapse of the Olympus and then the Thermopylae lines and, on April 20th, the surrender of the Greek army, already exhausted by months of fighting the Italians, where sixteen of their divisions had pinned down in Albania no less than twenty-seven Italian divisions. On the 22nd the general evacuation of the British and Commonwealth forces was ordered.

We received our orders from Air Headquarters, I think about mid-day on April 24th, to leave Menidi and embark at Nauplia. There was a good deal of packing-up to be done, but the move was orderly and unhurried, and the column of lorries passed safely over the bridge spanning the Corinth Canal (to be captured early on the 26th by German paratroops, but not before it had been heroically demolished by Captain Phillips and Lieutenant J. T. Tyson). (See: C. Buckley *Greece and Crete* 1941, p. 123.) We halted in the early morning in the plain of Argos, between five and ten miles from Nauplia. We must in all have been five or six hundred in number – the ground-staff of our own Squadron and of a Fighter Squadron and Air Stores Park who had been stationed at Hassani near the coast in Attica – and were under the command of an Air Commodore, whose name escapes me, but he had been a pleasant, very quiet guest in our Mess some weeks earlier. He had brought with him one of the heavy felted woollen capes with a pointed hood that Greek shepherds wear; being a small man when he put it on he was completely enveloped and became the quintessential gnome, and equally inscrutable.

A curious little incident whilst we bivouacked in the Argive plain: there had been in my office at Menidi a fine large safe, most useful for confidential documents, cash etc. When we left the Station I considered what would be the most tiresome condition for the next occupant, presumably a German officer, in which to find the safe – short of sheer destruction – and decided that completely locked and its three keys lost would be the most frustrating; so I locked it thoroughly and put the keys in my pocket. When we halted on the plain of Argos we backed onto a ploughed field, and I thought that the best way to lose the keys for ever would be to throw them as far as I could into the plough. This I did, but within half an hour they were brought back to me by an airman who had been relieving himself there and was naturally puzzled where they had come from.

The trouble about Nauplia as a port of embarkation – apart, it seemed, from a lack of shipping – was that a munitions ship the *Ulster Prince*, had been hit by German dive-bombers, beached, and lay burning steadily right at the entrance to the harbour. (See: C. Buckley *Greece and Crete 1941*, p. 117 – "she was an ordinary ship which had run aground accidentally": but she was certainly burning when we saw her and she certainly blew up.) The hours went by with nothing happening, and it seemed as if we were trapped there for good; so in the afternoon I went to the Air Commodore and said that if we were really intending to leave Greece, as our orders were, it was useless to stay there since Nauplia was unusable.

I happened to know that part of the Peloponnese fairly well, partly because Dorothy and I had travelled over it on foot in the twenties and partly because I had been engaged in transliterating the place-names for the new Staff map of Greece. I explained to the Air Commodore the general lay-out of the southern Peloponnese, with its two bays and two harbours, one at Gythion, small; and the other Kalamata, nearer and a considerable port. I suggested that our best plan would be to take to our lorries again and go over the mountains by way of the pass at Tripolitza and so down to Kalamata, where we might find merchant ships, or, failing that, a number of caiques – Greek fishing boats; embarked there we could slip southwards, keeping close to the east coast, to Cape Matapan, then across to the island of Kythera, thence to Antikythera, and so to Crete, with the minimum of open sea, thus lessening risk of submarine attack. "And," I added, "there is in fact a Greek here who knows the country and who says that there may well be Greek civilians waiting to get away from Kalamata, who would know what the position is." After some discussion, the Air Commodore said "Well, if you think it can be done, you had better go down to Kalamata and arrange it" – just like that. Accordingly, towards the end of the afternoon, I set off in a one-ton Ford truck, driven by this Greek, an admirable driver and a staunch companion, over precipitous mountain roads. As we breasted a ridge and came within sight of the harbour of Nauplia the *Ulster Prince* blew up with a tremendous explosion.

We were soon up in the mountains above Argos which rise from sea level to two thousand feet and it grew dark. Somewhere in the mountains, perhaps near Tripolitza but possibly further west near Megalopolis, we suddenly came upon a road-block; half a dozen wild-looking men with lighted torches came towards us threateningly, but when they discovered who we were let us through with good wishes – evidently the local Resistance preparing for the arrival of the Germans.

We reached Kalamata, something over a hundred miles, between 8 and 9 in the evening, and went straight to an hotel where we had been told that a retired merchant sea-captain had been waiting some days for a ship to Egypt. He was most helpful; but whilst he was explaining the possibilities he strode suddenly to the door of the room and flung it open. I thought this kind of thing occurred only on the stage, but to my amazement there was someone at the keyhole; probably no-one more sinister than a waiter or hall-boy, but as surprised as I was. The captain told us what he believed was available in the way of shipping, but advised me to go and talk to the Harbour Master. Off we went, and again met with extreme kindness.

The Harbour Master said that we could probably get hold of a few caiques, but that there were also two possible larger ships – an empty oil-tanker anchored near the harbour, and an old merchant-ship which had been moved to a deep creek not far away so as to be unobserved and perhaps saved from dive-bombing. This ship, he said, had an ancient wireless transmitter, but he thought that if I wanted to get in touch with the Squadron again it would probably be easier to use the ordinary telephone which was still functioning. He made what turned out to be a most helpful suggestion, although at first it seemed to me fantastic, namely that I should telephone to the Demarch (regional governor) of Argos, and order a special train to bring some of our men from Argos to Kalamata, since a large convoy on the road would almost certainly attract dive-bombers; in fact systematic dive-bombing attacks did not come until about twenty-four hours later since the newly established German landing-grounds were not yet near enough. The idea of being able to order a special train was quite outside my ordinary way of thinking, but perhaps owing to the stunned condition of the country I was able with the Harbour Master's help to get through to the Demarch in a few minutes on the telephone, and in less than half an hour had arranged for a special train to be at Argos station, with steam up, before eight next morning. I am glad to say that I was able eventually to reward the Harbour Master, to his complete surprise, with the gift of a fine estate-car, which I hope, and expect, he quickly disguised by repainting it; the rest of our transport before we left Kalamata we abandoned by driving it over the edge of the quay into the deepest part of the harbour we could reach.

It now remained to make contact with the Squadron and other troops in the plain of Argos and to explain in detail the arrangements I was making for their journey and reception at Kalamata the next day. This again seemed fantastically difficult, but proved to be quite easy; within a quarter of an hour I was speaking to the Air Commodore over the ordinary telephone, which had apparently been extended by a land-line to his HQ in the Argive plain.

The arrangements I proposed were simple: half the force would travel by the special train direct from Argos to Kalamata, as early as possible, and on arrival would find cover of some kind in the town speedily; the remainder, and this included all of 84 Squadron, would come in lorries at long intervals, to avoid giving the appearance from the air of a large organised movement, I would meet each lorry and would, with the help of my driver, direct it into the olive-groves or other cover where it could lie hidden for the rest of the day; in the evening the lorries would come out one by one to the harbour and the men embark on any shipping that could be produced. All this was agreed and the first part of the plan worked perfectly next day; the driver and I discovered enough hiding-places, reasonably dispersed, and the lorries arrived at sufficient intervals to allow us to guide them in.

All seemed set for embarkation in the evening in the empty tanker, said to be capable of taking five hundred people, which, with the Harbour Master's approval, I had commandeered, leaving the old merchant-ship for the other army troops who would almost certainly be arriving later. At this stage Group-Captain Lee, from Air Headquarters, arrived and told me that the whole movement was unauthorised and could not take place until approval had been given by the Air Officer Commanding. We had a heated argument, but I was naturally obliged to give in owing to his much superior rank, and the result was a deferment of all movement for twenty-four hours; this had the effect of delaying the embarkation of large numbers of the army who were now dribbling into the town and I suspect that it also prevented the evacuation of many of them since from the next day onwards there was dive-bombing which otherwise they might well have escaped.

However, the next evening everything did go according to plan. As soon as it was dark men from 84 Squadron and others to the number of about five hundred assembled on the quay; I put them under the command of my Warrant-Officer Stevens, and myself helped each one to board the empty tanker, mostly on deck since the tanks were not usable. The ship got away safely, but the next day, for some reason so far unexplained, put in at Kythera; the men got out, washed, and even bathed. But whilst they were doing so a dive-bomber appeared and sank the ship; no-one was hurt. All this I heard at second-hand, and long afterwards was shown a snap-shot of the ship on fire. The men were later taken off by destroyers; but it was a sad waste of the Navy's time and energies, which might have been used in rescuing others and involved them in journeys now becoming more and more hazardous.

With others, both from the RAF and the Army, I stayed on in Kalamata, and later in the evening an aircraft, believed to be a flying-boat, circled the town; we could only hear, barely see it, and in a few minutes it crashed into the water not far from the beach. Several of us rushed down and someone launched a rowing-boat that happened to be there, all in pitch darkness. Alas! the bung was missing and the boat quickly filled with water. Most of us could only stand helpless on the beach; but somehow or other two of the crew who were on the wing whilst the aircraft was sinking were saved; the others, how many no-one knew, must have drowned; the two we put on make-shift stretchers and carried to the local hospital, not seriously hurt.

The next morning there was a certain amount of bombing, and I remember seeing one or two dead animals, mules or horses, lying about near the harbour. Several RAF officers and a number of airmen from other units were in the town, and a kind of headquarters had been set up with, I think, Group-Captain Lee in charge. He told us that there was an arrangement that that evening all would be taken off by the Navy; and some hours after dark a destroyer arrived. With marvellous seamanship she came into harbour; the method was for her to switch the necessary searchlights on for a few seconds, then off, and work in total darkness. I do not know how many in all were taken on board, but should guess between fifty and a hundred; nor do I know how many were Air Force and how many Army.

The destroyer then drew out of the harbour, using the same method, and steamed what seemed to be some miles out to sea; there we joined a merchant-ship which had been waiting for us. We were at a lower level, and had to scale the side of this ship on a cat-ladder into a small opening about the size of an ordinary doorway. Orders had been given for as little kit as possible to be taken, and most of us had only our shaving-tackle, but naturally some of the Army had more, perhaps a rifle or even a pack, and this was where the organisation of the Navy was so admirable. To get into the opening at all off a cat-ladder was difficult enough, with a pack or any sort of gear extremely so. The Navy had stationed, just inside the opening, a couple of naval ratings, and as each man appeared they leaned out, seized him by the armpits and lifted him bodily inside. I reckoned that this device must have saved perhaps as much as a vital quarter of a minute on each man, and thus a total of half an hour in a perilous operation which had to be completed with the utmost speed.

The ship steamed off, and we soon discovered that it was a quite luxurious regular liner, British India I think, taken out of its ordinary run and complete with its own crew. After the dangers we had gone through – and many had suffered far more than we had – it was an incredible transformation, the unreality of which was heightened by our sitting down to a full English breakfast, together with a menu dated for that day, printed on the ship's own printing-press.

A rude awakening from this dream, however. We were now in convoy, and were within range of German dive-bombers, from which we suffered a pretty sharp attack, with some very near misses. I believe other ships in the convoy were hit, but am not certain, since we had to stay below deck. Oddly enough I – and I think others – found this one of the worst experiences we had been through;

the relief at finding ourselves, as we thought, safe at last was so suddenly reversed as to produce a strong reaction, and we felt really frightened as we had not been before. The ship took us direct to Aboukir, near Alexandria, where we disembarked, and there sorted ourselves out as far as possible into our own units. This must have been on May 1st since I sent a telegram home then and wrote a few days later "'Thank God for the Navy' is everyone's sentiment here"; and they certainly were marvellous. As usual the poor old infantry bore the brunt of it, and there was real heroism of a most moving if unspectacular kind in their steady marching, without air cover, under dive-bombing attacks.

We were then taken through the Sinai Desert by rail, in good old cattle-trucks – quite comfortable – and found ourselves in Palestine, at Aquir – inland, but somewhere near the coast and Jaffa.

Whilst at Aquir I had a letter from Dorothy, having been out of touch for some weeks; this was a marvellous refreshment. Enclosed with it was a letter from the American Institute of Archaeology, saying that Wace, Forsdyke (Director of the British Museum) and I had been elected Honorary Members of the Institute, as a tribute to the stand Britain was making. Our nerves must have been in greater tension than we had realised, since on reading this message from another world – another world in more senses than one – I found myself unexpectedly in tears.

For 84 Squadron there was one unexpected aftermath of the Greek campaign. When Yugoslavia was threatened with invasion by the Germans in February and early March the government there was hopelessly divided. Prince Paul, at its head, was preparing to surrender, but General Simovitch (who later vainly but heroically deposed the Prince and formed a new government) was still loyal to Britain. At this crisis General Pereschitch from Belgrade was sent on March 8th to Athens to find out how much aid Britain might give if Yugoslavia joined Greece and Britain. After fruitless talks 84 Squadron was given the task of flying him back to Yugoslavia. This was done, but on the return journey to Greece the aircraft crashed somewhere near the frontier.

The pilot had a broken arm and the crew of two, navigator and gunner, had minor injuries and were badly shaken. They found their way into a local Yugoslav hospital and the pilot managed a lift back to Athens by road. I reported the two aircrew to Air Headquarters as missing, but the senior Personnel Officer there told me not to submit a formal report at present, since they might find their way back. Accordingly I did nothing. But they did indeed find their way back. Some time after we left Greece one of them walked into the RAF depot at Uxbridge, and the other later also found his way to England; both had been flown out of some Yugoslav harbour in a flying-boat to neutral Lisbon. On receiving the news of their arrival in England Air Headquarters was extremely angry and rang up the Squadron; but I reminded them of their previous instruction, and this was a trump card.

Recovering, as we hoped, from Greece, I was suddenly appointed Adjutant of the airport at Lydda, and for seven hideous days I held, rather than performed, this, the worst job I had ever undertaken. Lydda was a civilian airport now being used with greatly increased traffic and partly by military aircraft; but what kind and how many no-one seemed to know. I knew nothing of the general lay-out of the airport and its buildings, nor of the position of its various offices, none of its staff, military or civil, their rank, status, or function, and no clear idea of what my job really was.

Despite my position I never knew what traffic to expect, and had a wry reminder of an earlier life in recognising, as I came in to breakfast one morning, the tweed coat and flannel trousers – British civilian uniform – of Professor Ronald Syme of Oxford, on his way to Stanboul with a diplomatic mission.

I was allotted fine sleeping-quarters, rather like a glorified ship's cabin, but even this was under a curse, for I awoke in the night with a partly paralysed but very painful lower leg, and at once thought I had been stung by a scorpion. However on searching with a light I saw the tail of an extremely large centipede disappear behind the fancy panelling, and assumed that that was the brute that had attacked me; I had not known that they were poisonous.

This nightmare ended mercifully soon, because of events in Syria and Iraq, of which a brief summary follows.

IRAQ

The German plan (which aimed at seizing in succession the main airfields in Iraq and Persia, thus giving them access to Afghanistan and threatening India) was intended to coincide with a *coup d'état* in Iraq by Rashid Ali, the Prime Minister, who, although bound by treaty to assist Britain, planned to go over to the Germans. He made his move on April 3rd, but, as became clear later, the resistance of the Allied troops to the German airborne invasion of Crete, and the few days' delay thus caused, disrupted the whole scheme.

However, Rashid Ali's move threatened the safety of any British residents in Iraq, and at the end of April British women and children were moved from the capital, Baghdad, to Habbaniya; the next day an Iraqi mechanised force, with some light artillery, occupied the ridge of ground dominating the site. Habbaniya was an extraordinary place, where the Iraqi Air Force had been in training under British instructors for some years. It had been created out of the desert entirely by systematic irrigation near the Euphrates, forty miles or so west of Baghdad. Round the landing-ground had been constructed a very fair imitation of a large English village, with all the features that home-sickness could suggest – gardens, public houses, two churches (each with a synthetic peal of bells), cinema, swimming-pools and other amenities; and here the teaching staff lived in comfort, with access to Lake Habbaniya a few miles away, where there was bathing and a sailing club.

After a while the Iraqis began a desultory shelling, lobbing a shell, probably over open sights, into the enclosure every few hours. Not many casualties were caused, but it was naturally the kind of treatment to produce extreme nervous tension, which it soon did. The Iraqis seem to have realised that, since the whole site lay at a low level, they could, by cutting certain of the irrigation dykes, flood it to a depth of four or five feet and thus make it uninhabitable; they did in fact cut one of the dykes, but the wrong one, running to waste the water that could have done what they wanted.

Meanwhile the defenders had not been idle; the British instructors tied what bombs they had to the wings of their training aircraft and dropped them on the Iraqi positions, despite being overlooked as they took off and landed. At this point 84 Squadron was told to organise a flight of Blenheims to operate from Habbaniya itself – no easy task in view of the casualties and destruction of equipment in the Greek campaign; but they succeeded in flying in.

The Blenheims were of a light-bomber type, not equipped as fighters and therefore hardly usable for ground-strafing, for the machine-guns were mounted near the tail against attack from the rear, and there were few if any bombs. The crews, however, did their best; they actually fitted bull-roarers to their aircraft and flew low over the Iraqi positions, with excellent moral effect. Meanwhile someone in Habbaniya realised that if a breech-block could be fitted to one of the old Turkish field-guns, souvenirs of the First War which decorated Air Headquarters, it could be made serviceable; and someone else knew the whereabouts of the right kind of breech-block and some ammunition. An aircraft flew out to fetch them; the gun was found to work, and one of the first shots scored a direct hit on the Iraqi battery and effectively silenced it.

The flight of 84 Squadron was operating at Habbaniya without its own ground-staff, and about May 27th when Rashid Ali's forces were starting to disperse, orders were given for the whole of the Squadron to reassemble there. The majority would travel in cars and lorries the five hundred miles from near Lydda, through Transjordan and the Syrian Desert.

This was a most interesting journey, extremely hot and dusty, but everyone seemed to enjoy it. Our car was hung round with little canvas bottles containing a pint or two of water, and evaporation kept this wonderfully cool, although sometimes there was so much evaporation that little water was left. We normally started early in the morning when it was apt to be cool with a gentle breeze, but it gradually got hotter and hotter, and sometimes the breeze became a really strong wind which raised the dust (for it was often deep dust rather than sand) and made our fellow-vehicles in the convoy look as if clouds of smoke were pouring from them. Sometimes when the dust was very fine, the whole convoy was enveloped in a thick haze like a mist at sea, and the tops of the cars could be seen just as if they were floating; another kind of wind raised "sand-devils" – columns of sand whirling like waterspouts, and very tiresome when you happened to be in the middle of one. By midday it was usually so hot that it was not possible to touch any of the metal parts of the car, and one got to the stage of staying on a particular part of the seat to keep it cool, for the unshaded parts were blistering. I got a good deal of comfort from sucking a pebble, which kept away thirst tolerably well, only one's lips suffering from the dry heat.

At night we slept in the car with all the doors open, and once I slept on its roof, which was pleasant, though convex and rather noisy, since one's bones made dents in the metal that sprang back on shifting position. There were some forts here and there on the way which were like a scene from "Beau Geste" or "The Four Feathers" except that the whitewash was not quite what it was on the films. In one, which had seen a stiff little fight lately between the Arab Legion and the Iraqi rebels, a few stone cannonballs about gave it a touch of romance. There were, too, all the other romantic accompaniments of desert travel – birds of prey, skeletons of animals that had died on the way, and, when nearer civilisation, vast herds of dromedaries.

Much of the country was not sandy but volcanic and scattered with basaltic rocks, with here and there the cones of extinct volcanoes. Anything more desolate could hardly be imagined. It was as if some giant had decided to pave thousands of square miles – in fact as far as you could see – with gigantic tarmac (but the stones were about a foot cube instead of a couple of inches), and having got to the first stage of laying out the tarred stones, had then abandoned it; a coating of brownish dust had then taken the gloss off the tar, but the general effect was still black, and unbelievably forbidding.

Another stretch of country changed to sand, mirages immediately began, and we saw some very fine ones, rather like the lagoons when you approach Venice, with long, low islands; others with trees, and some seemed so close that it looked as if you had only got to go half a mile for delicious bathing. There was also a splendid mirage of the "lost city" type, with many low buildings and domes, vague at the edges, but looking quite solid and real. It seemed to me that these were not created out of nothing, but caused by outcrops of rock, vastly magnified by the distorting refraction.

Washing and shaving were practically impossible on the last stages of our journey, and we certainly looked pretty odd when we arrived – thickly coated with brown dust everywhere, except where sweat had turned it into mud. Although in good spirits we were very tired, and I had one phase, during a halt, of feeling – as often happens in Chinese fairy-tales – completely detached from the body and floating, fully conscious and peaceful, twenty or thirty feet above. The sensation lasted perhaps for half a minute, and was no illusion but a genuine experience.

Habbaniya itself was delightful – water everywhere, and trees, hundreds of them, swarming with birds. Mosquitoes and other biting insects in plenty too, but no malaria, and everywhere properly wired against them. The Army, with the Arab Legion, had relieved the settlement and finally driven off the rebels only a day or two before, and everyone who had been through the siege was in a state of nerves through the constant shelling; one had to be careful not to bang a door without warning. Before long another friendly military force arrived, this time a brigade of the Indian Army which had disembarked at Basra and marched up the railway from there to Baghdad, clearing the country of the enemy as they went. They had reached Baghdad and had restored normal government under the Regent on June 1st.

I have no record of how long the Squadron stayed in Habbaniya, but should guess it was a matter of days rather than weeks before we flew and drove two hundred miles north up to Mosul, which had been reached by the Army on June 3rd. Mosul had an airfield, and this had been taken over by German engineers in civilian dress, who had since disappeared; they had in fact abandoned a Heinkel there. The airfield had been bombed, and some bombs were said to have fallen in the town, so that when the Squadron moved up bodily we were instructed not to go into the town, since the inhabitants might well be hostile. The mood soon passed and although we lived on the outskirts we afterwards visited the town itself freely.

Mosul is on the banks of the Tigris, and looking across the river to the east one sees what would be taken at first sight for a low range of hills. Then one gradually realizes that it is in fact entirely artificial – the collapsed, or rather eroded city walls, made of mud-brick, surrounding the ancient Nineveh. Nineveh was described by Jonah as "an excellent great city of three days' journey", meaning that it took three days to walk round, and this, from its apparent size now, is not hard to believe; whilst the country round is full of the remains of buildings and canals, evidence of great technical skill and abundant manpower. I was delighted to be there, for as a child one of my favourite books had been Henry Layard's *Nineveh*, and I had been fascinated by his account of his excavations of the great palaces, and of the sculptures, most of which are now in the British Museum.

Our Headquarters were in a delightful old Turkish house built round a courtyard, with many of the rooms half sunk in the ground for coolness in summer and warmth in winter; its only drawback was a resident population of bats in various dark corners. Because of the summer heat – often after sleeping on the roof – we usually started work at about 4 am, and went into retirement at about ten until the late afternoon. Some of our buildings were kept cool by a simple native device, a mattress of camel-thorn (a local shrub) fixed to an open window facing the prevailing wind, and constantly watered gently through a pierced pipe along its top edge. The result was a current of cool, slightly moist air, far more comfortable than mechanical air-conditioning.

The Squadron also owned a small soft-drinks factory, which we operated successfully until the supply of synthetic flavourings ran out.

The evenings were perfect, cool and still, and the Army had constructed a great open-air cinema with musical accompaniment on a gramophone, very loud; "Mexico Bay" was their favourite tune, and I shall always associate with Iraq that and the smell of synthetic rubber from the abandoned Heinkel on the aerodrome.

One of the agreeable features of our daily life was the morning and evening "stand-to" of the company of Gurkhas guarding the landing-ground; the men crouched with drawn kukris – a terrifying, but, as we were on their side, reassuring sight.

Towards the end of July the CO decided that I could do with a day off, and since there was a car going out more or less on duty to a place in the country, I joined the party. We started at 4.30 am, as one has to do when the midday temperature is around 115°, and had a very pleasant run, down beside the Tigris for the most part; this is two or three hundred yards wide, sometimes with low islands covered with small trees on which there are said to be wild pigs. We then came to a stream flowing under a road-bridge like any other stream; but when you came to look at it more closely you saw that it was chalky white in colour with large streaks of oil on the surface, and floating in it from time to time black lumps varying from an inch to a foot across. These were bitumen, and in fact most of the stream was either oil or bitumen, springing out of the soil naturally in such a state that it could be used either to put on the roads or burn in furnaces straight away. Some people believe that this or something similar was the original "burning fiery furnace" as described in the book of Daniel.

We next came upon a building-party who were making mud-bricks. The brick is about eighteen inches square, made in a wooden mould which lies on the ground. The mud consists of soil dug straight out of the ground with stubble in it, which is well soaked and put in a pile; the actual maker takes three balls of this mud and dumps them one after the other into the mould, splashes water on it and forces it down with his hands until the mould is exactly full and level with the top. He always gauged the amount exactly – never anything over – and it was amusing to see how in handling the lumps he used dust and short straw to prevent it sticking to his hands, just as you use flour in making pastry. The mould is whipped off immediately it is full, the brick lies there for a day or two and is then turned on edge, after which it soon seemed ready for use. It is a wonderful material, an excellent insulator against heat and cold.

We then had to do some gazelle-shooting with the local Sheikh; this was necessary in order to provide the men with a change of diet, but there is little to be said for it except that it is merciful – in short one's impulse was to turn vegetarian on the spot after seeing these beautiful animals run down and slaughtered. The meat however is good, rather like a soft rich lamb. We went back to the Sheikh's fortress – you could hardly call it anything else – for dinner. This was most interesting, except that one has read about it almost too often in books of travel. The fortress was, I imagine, an old Turkish one consisting of a huge courtyard formed by a massive wall with heavy buttresses outside and a range of buildings round the inside. The Arabs had made no real effort to inhabit it; they were still simply nomads who happened to possess a building. Nothing had been done to beautify the courtyard, and cooking was done on a shallow hearth scooped out of the soil in an odd corner. But the people themselves were pleasant and friendly. We were entertained in a room cleared for the occasion, which showed evidence of having at some time been used for a stable, and there were still one or two agricultural implements in one corner; but it had been washed out, and indeed there were still pools of water lying on the floor.

We started off in European fashion sitting on chairs at a table (once belonging to the British Army, and evidently a relic of some former campaign). We were given a drink of whey made from sheep's milk which, except for a slightly nauseating smell, was really quite good; biscuits soon followed, and it was interesting to see how, though made in a town in these parts, they still resembled their

English or French prototypes – *Petit beurre*, *Marie* etc. – except that they were all double, sandwich fashion, with sugar icing in between. After a longish time of conversation – fortunately there was a good interpreter and the leader of our party could also speak Arabic – preparations for dinner were made, to which, on a blazing day and with not very good appetites, we looked forward to with some trepidation. First rugs were laid on the floor, then two long kilims side by side, and in the centre of them a leather patchwork rug about six feet across, much tattered and stained, which, seeing its purpose and evidently long use to stand under the main dish at meals, was not surprising. Round this were set four longish cushions on which we sat cross-legged, and these various floor coverings were so effective that we were neither damp (from the floor) nor bitten (by insects which must inevitably have been there) during the meal.

The Sheikh and a brother or cousin sat down with us three, while the rest of the family and dependants (except women), consisting of about twenty men of all ages from ninety down to three, stood round and watched us. The main dish consisted of a pile of rice about eighteen inches high on a dish some three feet across, and against the sides of this mountain was set perhaps half a boiled sheep in fragments. Having been treacherously manoeuvred into a position on the right of the Sheikh, I looked with alarm to see whether the animal's eyes were included; but the dainty he eventually picked out for me was a kidney – I considered myself lucky. As a concession we were supplied plates, forks and spoons, but our hosts fed themselves (and served us) with their hands. The smaller dishes round the central one held little cucumbers, cooked in an incredibly thick, greasy, red gravy (really very delicious and the only possible lubricant for the enormous quantity of rice) and also aubergines cut into slices, which, too, were a great help. We did our best, but it was hard work to keep up with the quantities that continued to be piled on our plates.

Fortunately we knew that it was good manners to leave something to show that we had eaten our fill, but I fear they thought us rather poor trenchermen. As soon as we got up, the next grade of dependants started on our dish, and so in succession until even the lowest and the youngest had something. Meanwhile we were being served with coffee. This was in its way the most unusual thing about the meal. A man brought the coffee – black, very strong and hot – in a metal pot, holding at the same time a number of little china bowls. These he handed to us one by one, putting what was little more than a splash of coffee in the bottom, certainly less than a teaspoonful; this one drank and handed the bowl back, when another splash was put in. It was etiquette to have two splashes, but I think not more, and one indicated this by returning the bowl upside down.

Then came fruit – large pink melon, grapes, tiny apples and pears, nectarines; none of them very fine and the nectarines, like all stone fruit there, picked unripe, but nevertheless very good. So eventually we finished, and left in the extreme heat of the day – about 1 o'clock. The soil was by now roasting, and the air that came off it like that from an oven, and you consequently had the curious effect that the faster you went the hotter you felt.

When we had been going an hour or so we came to something between a stream and a river, not very clear, not very cool, but in the circumstances attractive – and absolutely swarming with fish. This was the Lesser Zab, a tributary of the Tigris, and I suddenly had a strange experience while walking beside it; as a child I had a recurrent dream that I was walking with my father beside a river full of fish, and that I killed them by throwing stones. I may have had the dream two or three times, perhaps forty years before, and had never recalled it since; yet now it suddenly dawned on me that this was, with absolute certainty, the river of my dream. I naturally (and as it turned out wrongly) supposed that this might mark some great moment in my life, and was particularly careful to see that it was not my last – we had rifles with us, and accidents can happen. We had no tackle, and our only way of getting the fish was the unsporting device of shooting them with a rifle; the shock of the bullet striking the water stuns the fish nearby, and you have to pick them out before they recover. In this way we must have got about fifteen pounds of fish – mostly about one pounders – and were able to feed the Mess at supper that evening; they were mostly carp, and what we thought might be trout turned out not to be. In the Tigris itself there are fish called salmon, and not at all bad; some of them run to a hundred pounds or more.

Life in Mosul was comparatively uneventful. As bearer and Mess waiter we had an Assyrian Christian; he had been employed between the wars as bearer to the Air Force operating an embryonic postal service, but when this ceased I believe the Assyrians had a rough time from the Iraqis. He was a gentle, devoted creature whose menus ("means potchek") and laundry lists ("pilakis") were a constant delight; and he embroidered with care and skill the initial B on one of my face towels, a service issue so durable that, with its embroidered initial, I used it steadily until 1979. In our room on the upper floor of our Turkish house it was possible, without any artificial heating, to enjoy a really hot shower in the evening – the water-pipes ran across the roof.

We found the army officers congenial and co-operative, and I made a particular friend of a Medical Officer named Anstie. Both he and I became due for leave in October, and we agreed to go to Jerusalem together; he arranged that we be flown there as passengers in a two-seater light aircraft. A few days before, Anstie developed a bad sore throat; being a doctor he suspected that it might be diphtheria and began taking swabs, which all proved to be negative. Accordingly, though he felt very unwell we decided to go, and, packed into the aircraft at very close quarters, arrived safely in Jerusalem and went to the Scottish Hostel, where we had arranged to stay. On settling in there Anstie took a new swab of his throat; it was positive. I took him off to the Military Hospital, established in a handsome civilian building; arrived there he was put to bed, and, since I had been in such close contact I was given a massive dose of anti-diphtheria serum, and returned to the hostel.

The next day I went to visit Anstie and found him fairly well, so that I was able to sit by his bed and talk to him. After a few minutes the Matron came in and said "It's rather awkward, but the Colonel-in-command is coming to inspect the hospital, and although we know it is in fact all right for you in the circumstances, strictly speaking diphtheria patients are not supposed to have visitors. I wonder whether you would mind if we got you a white overall and I said you were the Chaplain?" Naturally I agreed, the white overall was brought and put on, and I sat down again. Soon I heard behind me the Colonel talking to the Matron as he entered the ward, and the next moment I felt a hand on my shoulder and a voice saying "I thought I knew the back of that head!" It was the delightful Colonel who had commanded the Australian Medical Unit stationed not far from us in Greece six months before. I did not hear the Matron talk herself out of it, but both he and I were happy to meet again, and I dined in their Mess that evening.

I finished my leave in Jerusalem; Anstie was on the mend, though still in hospital, and I flew back to Mosul in a very ancient aircraft, top speed with the wind about a hundred miles an hour. We flew at a few hundred feet with a crosswind; there were occasionally lorries on the road below us and with our crab-like course we hardly seemed to be gaining on them. It was rather bumpy and some sort of hot exhaust-pipe which passed just behind the back of one's neck was another hazard; but all went well and our little party landed with relief.

It was here that the Air Force had the task of handing over some aircraft to the Russians. With innocent enthusiasm we looked forward to this meeting with our new Allies and prepared to welcome them. When the Russian aircraft arrived we found that its crew was divided far more rigidly into officers and men than would be conceivable in any British Squadron. The Captain was accompanied by a political Commissar and they alone were allowed to disembark. The rest of the crew were ordered to stay on board and not to accept the tea we had ready for them; they mostly seemed to be simple, jolly people of country type, not unwilling to be friendly. Far different were the two it was now our task to entertain. The Commissar was a sinister, taciturn individual who kept a constant eye on his companion, who himself was not an endearing character; naturally reserved and without charm, he hardly dared open his mouth. We spent a depressing evening doing our best against impossible odds, and we understood well the complaints heard later in the War of help being brought by our Arctic convoys with the sacrifice of precious lives, and accepted without a word of thanks. Nor was there any difficulty in believing that orders had been given that anyone who left the aircraft to visit Mosul that night would be shot.

But the focus of events was now shifting elsewhere and the Squadron was transferred to Egypt.

THE WESTERN DESERT

In late October and early November a campaign in the Western Desert was developing, and the Squadron moved there somewhat to the East of the Egyptian frontier. We were camped in long tents stretched over hollows of the same size cut two or three feet into the ground; this made them less visible from the air, gave some protection from the wind and dust, and also served to mitigate the sudden drop of temperature from day to night. Most people loved the desert with its dry air, wonderful changes of light, and the feeling of being on one's own, away from civilisation; drawbacks were the so-called desert sores, which some people got after a few weeks, and the dust-storms, sometimes so dense that it was literally impossible to find one's way, and one came into the tent to find all clothes unrecognisable under a blanket of dust. Miraculously, human ears have a mechanism for preventing the sand making a heavy deposit inside. There was also the occasional scorpion.

An official booklet, the *RAF Pocket-book*, contained, in a thousand small pages, a mass of information on every possible subject in the most condensed language, and this included in its medical section instructions on how to deal with snake and scorpion bites. We were laughing one day at the wording, which said that, on being stung "with a sharp knife make a cross-shaped incision, half an inch deep, and rub in crystals of permanganate of potash. This treatment is painful..."; but Nemesis was at hand, for that very evening an officer was leaning against our improvised bar in the Mess Tent, and a scorpion in one of the crevices stung him on the thigh. Everyone knew the correct treatment; it was immediately applied, and was indeed painful, though effective.

About 20th November the camp and airfield at Gambut in Libya between Bardia and Tobruk was occupied by the Allies after the Germans and Italians had retreated, and 84 Squadron was ordered in. I still have the instructions on how to get there, which are interesting as showing the way one did manage to get about in featureless country (the figures are map references).

> Route 75 Talata to Sidi Abel-el-Salam 576324. Thence west along track marked A to junction of Ambulance Track. Thence parallel with Ambulance Track until reaching telephone wires. Thence west to Conference Cairn. Follow track marked with red diamond for 23 miles. Thence follow notices to Sheferzen and Libyan Sheferzen 494345. Thence by compass course to Gambut.

At Gambut we found a delightful establishment. The Italians had made themselves very comfortable by enlarging a series of natural caves in a long cliff not far from the coast. The lay-out was most ingenious, and the various elements of the Headquarters – Officers' mess, Orderly Room etc – were connected with each other by long coloured ribbons fixed to the rock so that with a pocket-torch one could find one's way about at night, despite black-out. There was some evidence, too, that our predecessors had not been without female companionship.

The Officers' Mess was in a dry bed of an underground stream, with sandy floor and the natural stone roof about eight feet high, and was perhaps the same depth below the surface; it was about forty feet long and just wide enough to take a long trestle table and chairs, yet still leave room to pass behind people seated. In the kitchen and store at one end we were delighted to find two huge carboys of wine, one of the so-called Chianti Ble, bright purple in colour, the other

Barolo, more mature and brownish – both excellent. When we left Gambut the only vehicle to take these safely was the Squadron ambulance – we hoped not against the Geneva Convention. We also found an exquisite marquee of the finest linen or cotton, which, when extended, has almost the plan of a cathedral, with long nave and a number of small apsidal chapels down the sides. When we left Gambut we had not the heart to abandon this masterpiece and packed it on to one of our lorries, but on meeting an Infantry Unit coming in to take our place we realised that it might be more useful to them, and made them a present of it.

The Squadron had been supplied with a new and newly-designed mobile Orderly Room, a trailer well equipped as an office, and supposedly most efficient because each wheel was sprung independently on a torque spring. This made for smooth running on uneven ground, but when the Squadron received orders at the beginning of January 1942 to draw back to Heliopolis to be re-equipped before flying to the Far East, one of the springs and consequently its wheel was out of order, and the trailer was useless. I had to transfer to an ordinary lorry, on the assurance that the trailer would be brought back to Heliopolis next day; I therefore took with me the essential Squadron documents and left behind amongst the minor things a fine captured Italian typewriter and the Squadron souvenir known as "Jane's panties". This consisted of that garment and a brassiere which had belonged to a passenger named Jane in a civilian aircraft which (in the early days when the Squadron, before the War, had its home-base at Shaiba, on the Persian Gulf) had force-landed in the desert. The Squadron had mounted a rescue, had located the aircraft, the passengers of which were sheltering from the heat under the wings, minimally clothed, and had brought them back to safety. Only a souvenir was asked in return, and appropriately, the only clothes Jane had been wearing were given. These had been mounted and framed, and a brief account of the whole affair printed below; the frame was always hung in the Officers' Mess and was regarded as a mascot. I had saved this when we fled from Greece, and it was a sad blow when my Orderly Room never returned to Heliopolis. A replacement was obtained from "Jane" many years later and by then married, after a suitable explanation to her husband.

SUMATRA

84 Squadron was being withdrawn from the Western Desert to Heliopolis in order to fly to the Far East; part of the last attempt to prevent the fall of Singapore. It was divided into two parties, the Sea Party and the Air Party. My task, before flying as a passenger in the fourth Flight of the Air Party, was to ensure that the Sea Party embarked safely at Port Tewfik, which is opposite Suez at the Southern end of the Canal. With the aid of the Assistant Adjutant, P. O. Walker, we successfully loaded all the two or three hundred of them, even those who had been celebrating too freely, on to lorries at Heliopolis by nine o'clock in the evening of 16th January, and they embarked on a ship called the Yoma early next morning, with Walker in charge.

CHAPTER VII

The Air Party moved in four Flights between 14th and 18th January, twenty-four aircraft in all, each carrying, in addition to its crew of three, a couple of passengers. There were eleven stages on the journey of six thousand miles: Habbaniya; Bahrain, at the head of the Persian Gulf; Sharjah at its southern end; Karachi; Allahabad; Calcutta; Toungoo, on the Bay of Bengal; Rangoon; Lhoknga, near the northern point of Sumatra; Medan (two hundred miles to the south-east and within striking distance of Singapore); and Palembang, three hundred miles from its southern end. At each stop crews were briefed for the next stage, and on the whole the briefing was sound except for one serious error, the fault apparently of 221 Group who controlled the airfields of Toungoo and Rangoon itself. This error was so disastrous, leading to the loss of two aircraft and the endangering of many others, that it may well have been due to the enemy or fifth column. It was this. The stage from Rangoon to Sumatra was a very long one, only just within the limits of what a Blenheim could fly before it ran out of fuel. The briefing was that pilots should land not at Lhoknga near the northern point of Sumatra, but at another airfield thirty miles away instead. A precise map-reference was given, but this proved to be a rugged spot up in the hills, so that, when an aircraft failed to find it, because of shortage of fuel it could not fly around looking for it or fly back to Lhoknga. An example of the consequences is given in Appendix I.

We left on the 18th; Squadron Leader James, an admirable pilot and companion, flew the aircraft. Three or four incidents on the way are perhaps worth recalling. At Dum-Dum (Calcutta) the airstrip was only eight hundred yards long – beyond it a marsh – whereas a Blenheim with five up needs a thousand yards for take-off. The result was that as we reached the end of the runway the pilot took her off very sharply. In a Blenheim the passenger sits alongside the pilot but about a couple of feet lower, and behind them there is a bulkhead where the hatch-cover fits when closed. Inside this bulkhead there is a convenient shelf on which one could put small oddments, such as a book or the like. We flew with the hatch open, and I had put there my stiff peaked service hat which is awkward to wear on a journey but also awkward to pack. The sharp lift-off caused a fierce little gust of wind in the cockpit, and it whipped out my peaked hat over the side and presumably into the marsh at the end of the runway, now some hundreds of feet below. A minute or two after, when we were safely airborne, the pilot leaned down to me and said "The air-gunner has got your hat; it caught in the guns on the tail" – a chance in a thousand, one would have thought.

A second incident was halfway across the Bay of Bengal. The pilot bent down and said "We have almost reached the point of no-return, but the oil-pressure gauge registers zero and I think we should go back." It wasn't alarming, partly, I think, because the layman mistakenly supposes that the sea is softer to land on than the earth. We turned back, but when the pressure was tested after landing it proved to be the gauge and not the pressure itself that was at fault.

A third incident was after we had landed at Rangoon. A Japanese fighter pilot, running out of fuel, deliberately flew his aircraft at speed into the ground in the hope of writing off one of ours, fortunately without success. In Rangoon that evening there was an air-raid, with a fine display of search-lights and gunfire. As we stood looking up at this I was struck sharply on the throat and thought it must be by shrapnel; it turned out to be a bat, whose built-in sonar system of direction-finding had been upset by the explosions.

On the next flight to Sumatra itself on 28th January James wisely decided to land at Lhoknga as soon as he found it, which was just as well when we heard what had happened to other people. The aircraft needed repairs, so he flew on to another airfield, Paken Baro, where there were facilities. Whilst there it was strafed by Japanese fighters and a bullet went through one of the fuel-tanks. James was doubtful about taking off heavily loaded, so I was taken by road to Kotaradja, the town at the extreme northern point of Sumatra, where I stayed in a hotel. (James and his crew, I am happy to say, were eventually taken off by the Navy, transferred to a Dutch merchant ship and reached Australia safely.) In the hotel at Kotaradja there was a charming Dutch family, Countess van der Feltze with two little daughters; her husband was in charge of all the harbour installations at Sabang, an island a few miles away, and came back from time to time. I became friendly with the family, and the two parents visited us in London after the War; in the interval the mother and children had been prisoners of the Japanese, had been reasonably well treated, but were short of food and managed to supplement it by gathering mushrooms and berries. Since James's aircraft was still unserviceable it was decided that I should fly in a Hudson transport-aircraft down to Palembang, and I arrived there on 12th February. The morning before there had been a severe earthquake shock at Kotaradja; impressive, but fortunately no casualties. What I noticed particularly was not the feeling that the earth is giving way, which is frightening, but the noise everything made: buildings, lamp-standards, even the tram-lines creaked and groaned, and our apprehension was not lessened by the knowledge that we were not all that far from Krakatoa, which a generation before had produced the most tremendous volcanic eruption ever known.

The small town of Palembang (from which I cabled to Dorothy that I had arrived "safe and well") was the rest-centre for 84 Squadron, and I don't want it to seem that what we did there, although it certainly saved lives – including our own – compares in importance with what the aircrews had done before that in the way of harassing the Japanese, often under intense difficulties because of poor servicing and low morale at Singapore. The full details, which are long and complicated, are given in two despatches, one by Wing-Commander Jeudwine, the CO of the Squadron, the other by the officer who later commanded it, Flight-Lieutenant Arthur Gill; and the following account of our own action, though correct as far as it goes, is shortened and simplified.

To make things a little clearer it should be explained that the Squadron operated mainly from two airfields, one called P1 eight miles north of Palembang, the other, P2, forty-five miles to the south. The small town of Palembang is on the north bank of the Moesi River, and if one was at P1 or in Palembang itself, and wanted to get to P2 or to anywhere in the south of Sumatra, one had to cross the river by means of a ferry, which was a small steamer able to carry five vehicles at a time and taking fifteen minutes for the return journey. I arrived on 12th February and found there in the empty girls' school called Maria School which we had for sleeping-quarters, Squadron-Leader Tayler, Flight-Lieutenant Gill, Pilot-Officer Macdonald and Pilot-Officer Maurice, the first three being pilots and Maurice the navigator of Macdonald's aircraft. (The adventures of this aircrew when they force-landed in deep mud at the mouth of a river on 23rd January owing to a briefing which showed the distance to be flown as 419km whereas it was really 619, make a separate and fascinating story – see Appendix I) There were also a number of NCO aircrew and airmen, eighteen or twenty in all.

Our Squadron was no longer operating from P1, having lost three aircraft there by ground-strafing some days before, but from P2; however some of 232 Squadron were still there.

On 14th February about nine o'clock in the morning, we looked out from Maria School and saw that parachutists were being dropped in the direction of P1; numbers have been variously estimated and there looked to be a great many, but between fifty and a hundred and fifty is probable. Maurice, armed with a rifle, had been down to Group Headquarters about this time, and on seeing the parachutists had taken a lorry with some armed men up the road towards P1, but had been turned back by the Dutch. On the strength of a message received from the Dutch Home Guard, Tayler, Gill, Macdonald and four officers of other units, with eight men (mostly unarmed) went down to the ferry to form a bridgehead, and soon after, Maurice, who had now returned, crossed the ferry with a few armed men supplied with Mills' bombs, to guard it against possible attack from Japanese who might come up the river. Air-Commodore Hunter was at the ferry and gave orders that P1 was to be evacuated, unarmed men to move to P2, and those armed to remain for the time to guard the ferry.

Soon after the dropping of the parachutists I went out on foot with a couple of airmen up the road towards P1 to find out exactly what was happening. We soon came to a Dutch road-block, and after consultation with the Dutch officer in charge who explained that the Japanese had blocked the road further up, I went out on a side-track towards the east for a mile or so, to see if there were any parachutists in the neighbourhood. None could be seen, and the little detachment of Dutch native Home Guard whom I found guarding the track said that they too had seen none, so I returned to Maria School at lunch-time to find it empty, the houses round deserted, unfinished meals on the tables, and an uncanny silence everywhere; except apparently down at the ferry where Arthur Gill, who came back soon afterwards in a lorry, reported crowding and confusion.

We discussed what to do. The obvious thing was to try to clear the road to P1 where we knew that some of 232 Squadron were cut off; for this reason we thought the order by Group to leave Palembang was premature. Accordingly we loaded up the lorry with food and water, collected as many men as we could, and set off up the road to P1, Sergeant Hough driving. We were thirteen in all, about half with rifles. We passed several Dutch pickets, and eventually, about six or seven miles up, came to the last, which consisted of two Vickers guns mounted on an open truck. A Dutch officer there told us that about two hundred yards further on, round a bend in the road, an RAF petrol bowser had been overturned; it had been trying to rush through from P1 loaded with men of 232 Squadron, but had been ambushed by Japanese parachutists, who had then set up a roadblock there. We considered firing incendiary bullets and blowing up the bowser, but then learned from two RAF officers there that a dying airman was pinned under it. They also told us that there was a convoy of wounded in motor lorries trying to get through from P1.

We parked our lorry, and those of us with rifles, under Gill and myself, together with some newcomers who were armed, moved cautiously up the road. About a hundred and fifty yards up we had to take to the swampy jungle at the side because of Japanese trench-mortar and machine-gun fire. Native troops under Dutch officers (some of them wounded), together with some RAF airmen, were retreating towards us. Soon after, however, we were able to advance along the road, past two dead Japanese parachutists (one hanging in a tree tangled up in the ropes of his parachute) and reached the petrol bowser. Among the trees were other Japanese dead, and also British dead (including the engineer officer of 232 Squadron) and wounded. These were attended to, and a car sent for to take them away; it arrived about a quarter of an hour later and they were taken into Palembang. We then made contact with a Royal Artillery officer who was trying to clear a Japanese machine-gun post in order to get the convoy of wounded through from P1.

We consulted him and decided that we might try to work round the Japanese post, so Gill went off into the heavy swampy jungle on the left of the road where the original ambush had been, to see if parachutists were still there, and I went off into lightly wooded country on the right to try to work round it. This seems to have been effective – they may have thought there were more of us than there were – for eventually the convoy, consisting of three or four lorries full of wounded, got through, and the road being clear we returned to Palembang at dusk.

Apparently as soon as night fell the Japanese were able to re-establish a roadblock in spite of the Dutch, for the lorry with hot food and ammunition which we sent from Maria School was fired on and its load had to be transferred to a Dutch armoured car which rushed through and delivered it to P1 safely. We slept soundly in Maria School that night; I can't think why we were not more worried, for the next day and night were hectic.

As soon as it was light the next morning (the 15th) we agreed that the time had come to move to P2 as ordered by Group; P2 was forty-five miles away and the other side of the river. Gill went off to refuel the same lorry we had used the day before, an open Ford three-tonner; this proved to be a very lengthy job because of lack of petrol at the various pumps, most of which were either closed or empty. When he finally got back about eight, Macdonald had collected a small civilian van, and the two vehicles set off together with the airmen, all available ammunition, and kit; we were eighteen in all. Arrived at the ferry we found great congestion, the Dutch rightly claiming priority for a number of vehicles loaded with troops destined to deal with the Japanese who were now known to be coming up the river in boats. The Squadron's lorry and van were between thirtieth and fortieth in the queue. Gill, in co-operation with a Dutch Officer, here took charge in regulating the traffic, and thanks to them there was no panic. Odd civilians came to the ferry with young children, many of them in arms, and the most varied belongings, and were helped across it; but for the most part they stayed in their homes. During this wait at the ferry there was a touch of nightmare in that the whole scene was enveloped in dense drifts of black smoke from oil storage tanks set on fire by the Dutch, which had been blazing all night; and by periodic explosions as the wharves were blown up. An official at one of the local banks started giving away bottles of brandy, wine and liqueurs, of which he had an enormous supply, but this was checked and he was made to shatter each bottle with an axe, until the gutters were running with it.

When it seemed possible that our vehicles might not get over at all before the Japanese either started bombing the ferry or arriving by river or road, we agreed to send over our people with their small kit, and if we couldn't get the vehicles across, try to obtain others on the far side. Tayler, Maurice and others were sent across with the kit, I went next, Gill and Macdonald remained with the vehicles. All our people helped with the loading and unloading of the wounded on both sides of the river, and a third motor van was commandeered and also put at the disposal of the wounded.

The Dutch native crew worked their ferry nobly and without panic until, just after midday, the captain announced the last trip. By this time Japanese fighters were flying low over the river, but surprisingly (perhaps thinking their own river-borne troops had reached the ferry) did not open fire. On the last ferry but one came Macdonald with the Ford lorry. On the last boat of all came Gill and Flight-Lieutenant Jackson of 34 Squadron who was driving the commandeered civilian van. We loaded some food on the lorry and also took on board a number of officers from 226 (Fighter) Group, and set off for P2. On the road we picked up one or two others, including a Fleet Air Arm officer on a stretcher, who was supported on the hands and knees of Maurice and others for thirty miles or so. The journey to P2 was otherwise uneventful except that we had to refuse room, owing to extreme overcrowding, to various people on foot, and also to a Chinese member of a crew of a British ship who had been wounded in the foot. None of these, however, should have had difficulty in getting a lift eventually, for there were a number of vehicles running from the railhead at Palembang to P2. We arrived at P2 about 3 o'clock and immediately made contact with the CO; he rang up Group, whose instructions were that we should proceed to transit-camp Oosthaven at the extreme south of the island – our first intimation that complete evacuation of Sumatra was intended.

Those aircrews of the Squadron who had aircraft, and the ground-staff of P2 were to fly to Bandoeng in Java that evening. We therefore added Ellis, Lister,

Sherrott and Pile, who had no aircraft, to our passengers, together with two or three airmen belonging to 226 Group, and having refuelled set off as soon as possible, about four o'clock in the afternoon. It was agreed that we should drive continuously through the night, partly because of the need for speed, partly because we had no protection from the wild animals in the jungle who might have been a nuisance, or from the rain, which falls every twenty-four hours at this time of year. The lorry, though heavily overloaded, ran excellently, Gill and Tayler taking turns at driving it with an airman driver through the night. About midnight torrential rain started; there was no cover and few groundsheets, and everyone got pretty wet, some soaked through. However it was warm, and the wetting seemed to do no-one any harm; but it was a difficult matter to hold up the heavy lorry from skidding on the sodden road-surface on many of the hills, and over what seemed to be numberless bridges, often narrow, over the many torrents, so the average speed was low. We stopped at Batoeradja to refuel and at Partapoera for a snack. Just before dawn Kotabeomi was reached, only fifty miles from our destination, and we felt it was safe to stop for a while, so we kindled a fire and made tea.

We then set off for the harbour, but when we had gone a few miles had a surprising meeting with a decrepit local bus; surprising because the driver was Corporal Burrluck of the mechanical transport of our own Squadron, and he had been one of the Sea Party who had embarked at Port Tewfik a month before. This was the first of the Sea Party that we met, and we learnt from him what had happened; but first, since the bus (full of small-arms ammunition that he was attempting to drive from Oosthaven to P2, a distance of over three hundred miles) had broken down several times already and was obviously unfit to go much further, we told him that P2 was evacuated and he ought to return to Oosthaven. He told us that the Sea Party had arrived at Oosthaven on the 10th but by then the situation was such that instead of sending them, as had been intended, to staff an airfield and perform normal squadron duties, all that could be done was to send such of them as were armed, about two hundred, as infantry to hold Natar, a junction of road, rail and river, about twenty miles north of Oosthaven; and that was where we found them as we passed through on our way to the port.

At the docks Squadron-Leader Tayler, as senior officer, reported to a Group Captain and was ordered to join those members of the Squadron ashore. The remainder of the lorry party were ordered to embark at once, which we did, and found that the ship was actually the Yoma, and that the unarmed members of 84 Squadron, including the Assistant Adjutant, Walker, were still aboard. She sailed at midday for Batavia, near the north west point of Java. She lay off Batavia in the morning of the 17th and when she docked in the afternoon members of the ground-party, including Tayler, were on the quay, and some came aboard the next day; they had re-embarked on a small fast ammunition-ship, and had reached Batavia before us. It was fully expected that we should disembark and re-equip in Java, but we were not allowed off the ship. Preparations were then made for several hundred RAF to embark, and these we expected would be the remainder of our own Squadron; but, instead, a hundred and seventy civilians, mostly wives and children of officers and civilians from Singapore, came aboard, and with them we sailed, but not until midday of the 20th, forming up into a convoy during the afternoon and finally leaving Java at dusk for Ceylon and India. As the Yoma steamed away, one of the airmen, looking back over the stern, declaimed, in the manner of a travelogue, "And so farewell to Sumatra, Pearl of the Southern Seas!"

We arrived at Colombo on the first of March, left next day for Bombay, which we reached on the sixth, and I was able to relieve Dorothy's anxiety with a cable. There we had docked just behind a troopship carrying an army unit, some of whom were refusing to embark again because of the conditions on board. The officer in charge of them came and suggested that I, as Adjutant, should send a detachment of our men to compel them to do so; but I was relieved to be able to tell him (which I hope was true) that the various Services were responsible for their own discipline.

We left Bombay on the 13th, disembarked at Karachi on 17th March 1942, and were lodged under canvas there.

Meanwhile, back in Java, between fifty and a hundred of the remainder of our Squadron, who had in fact reached Java before us, had disembarked at Tjilatzap, a port on the south coast, where it was expected they would be taken off by the Navy. But no ships came, and, with fires now raging in the harbour, they decided to take ships' lifeboats and try to sail away. They secured two, and sailed them round to a secluded cove, but wrecked one of them on landing there. They then decided to concentrate on the other, giving it a crew of twelve. One of these was chosen because he was the only person besides the CO who knew anything about sailing, another because he could handle a sextant; the remainder were picked from Australian air crews, since it was felt that they should be given the chance of returning to their own country. It was then hoped to send back a submarine to pick up the remaining officers and airmen from an agreed spot on the coast. The journey to the nearest point on the west coast of Australia, about a thousand miles, was estimated to take sixteen days, since an atlas in the boat showed (falsely) favourable winds and currents at this time of year. However, double that time was allowed for, and rations and water for thirty days

Bernard in Karachi, 1942.

loaded. There was also a large supply of American canned beer which, carefully rationed, proved to be a godsend. The whole journey, which is described in detail in "The Log of the Scorpion" and which included perilous encounters with a Japanese submarine and a whale, took forty-four days, and covered nearly fifteen hundred miles – one of the greatest open-boat voyages of all time. At the end of it the CO wrote "I would not, if the opportunity again occurred, alter one of my crew. They were magnificent." On arrival in Australia a submarine was briefed for Java, but at the rendez-vous, alas, no-one was there; they had all been captured by the Japanese. The Log is an absorbing narrative, and, although not personally involved, I reproduce it as an Appendix II, so that it shall not be forgotten.

INDIA

In a day or two a staff-officer was sent down from Air Headquarters at Delhi to interview all the officers and decide on their postings. He was Wing-Commander Farrow, DSPSO (Deputy Senior Personnel Staff Officer) brusque and provocative, but with sound commonsense and a fair eye for character; he wasted little time and returned to Delhi within twenty-four hours. Soon came my own posting, and it turned out to be Air HQ, where I joined Org. (Organisation).

Although Org. was very well run – one might say perfectly run – with strict discipline and no talk in the office except shop, I was not particularly happy there, largely because it was hard to judge what effect anything we produced in the way of a policy document was likely to have; the document itself would take what seemed an unconscionable time to produce, and we never seemed to see any tangible result. In contrast to a small and active unit such as a squadron, where everyone was perforce occupied and everything one did was essential, sometimes urgent, and had an obvious and often immediate effect, the mechanism there seemed cumbrous, even unintelligible, and remote from the demands of active service. This was doubtless an unjust conclusion, but natural perhaps in one new to it, who had no means of judging the size and complexity of the Command. Besides, Org., by its very nature, made plans but did not carry them out. However, my fellow officers were congenial, there was no discord, and I was soon to find another post of a very different kind.

The officer who walked into my office to relieve me turned out to be someone I had already met in unusual circumstances on Sumatra. There had been an air-raid alarm on an airfield where I had landed on my way down to Palembang, and I had found myself taking cover in a slit-trench beside an RAF officer rather older than myself, an Australian who had served on Gallipoli in the First War; his name was Dick Davis. He had just been flown out of Singapore with a number of other officers and was distressed by what he had seen of the failure of morale there, and neither of us much liked the company we found ourselves in, because of their defeatism and general slackness. This had been a brief encounter, but when we met again in Delhi we became close friends. A sterling character, he did admirable service not only in India but with Transport Command at a vital period after the War when there had to be some improvisation, and smooth working was essential. He had first-rate practical and executive ability, and made sure that the airmen in every out-of-the-way or emergency station were properly housed and fed. He came to stay with us at Amersham soon after the War, re-visited us several times, and was beloved by our whole family.

Both Dick Davis and I were now lodging with Mr and Mrs Leslie Flatt, and I found that Leslie and I had been at school together thirty years before, and completely out of touch since. In the meantime he had become Manager of the whole elaborate railway system in India, now one of the most valuable legacies of the British; and he was willing to tell us something about his work, including some of the essentials that a layman rarely understands, for instance the system on which the permanent way is laid. It was new to us that rails, together with their sleepers, give a little in their bed of ballast when the train passes, and that without this flexibility the coaches would rapidly shake themselves to pieces. This technical fact has a wider implication; the track needs constant inspection and upkeep, which were possible in India because labour was comparatively cheap. Another factor in the success of the railways there was, at the time anyhow, the absence of any comprehensive alternative system of long-distance travel, and the extraordinary pleasure people found in travelling by rail, of which I was soon to have ample experience.

Leslie Flatt had worked his way up as an apprentice right through the Great Eastern Railway workshops at Stratford, near our home in Essex, and told us of his feelings when soon after his marriage a tap-washer needed replacing and his wife said "We must send for a man." They were charming hosts, and we were sad to move elsewhere when they left. Another friendship renewed was that with Gerard Young, whom I had last seen in Greece just before the German invasion the year before. His life had taken a strange turn. He had risen to the top of the Indian Civil Service and had become, more than ten years ago, Secretary of State for War in the Government of India; he had retired at the age-limit and had returned to Europe. Being a classical scholar he went to stay in Greece, and in Athens worked at the British School, becoming a close friend of the Director, Humfry Payne, who was Professor John Beazley's most brilliant pupil at Oxford and a classical scholar of outstanding merit. Together, Young taking the photographs, they published a splendid book on the archaic sculptures of the Acropolis Museum. After Payne's untimely death in 1936 the managing committee of the School wisely appointed Young to succeed him, a post he was holding when war broke out. Now, ten years later, after having been forced to leave Greece at the German invasion, he had taken up once again his old post of Secretary of State in India. In Delhi he made me feel at home, and we went bicycling together in the country round.

In visiting other departments at HQ I met again W/C Farrow who had first interviewed me in Karachi; he introduced me to the SPSO, Group-Captain Hawtrey, whom in fact I had already met in Iraq, where he had been one of the instructors training the Iraqi Air Force, and had played a leading part in attacking Rashid Ali and his troops when they besieged Habbaniya. It must have been Hawtrey who appointed me to a job in P Staff (Personnel) which was really worth doing. In India the Air Force, because of the Japanese threat, was expanding rapidly, and more than a hundred new airfields were being constructed, mostly towards the northern part of the country, but extending as far as the frontier on the west, and on the east down to Chittagong on the Bay of Bengal, further south still to the romantically named "Cox's Bazaar", and to the wilder country inland. On almost all these there were naturally problems of manning, of finding the right people for the various posts, and my job nominally was to visit the airfields in turn, have talks with their Station Commanders on problems of personnel and then return to AHQ and report directly to Hawtrey. It was worth doing because there were more problems than those of personnel – transport, drainage, water-supply, surface of air-strips, etc. – and I was able to make notes of these also and report them to the relevant departments in AHQ.

It was most interesting too, partly because of the personal contacts and discussions, and the hope that one might be able to help – to say nothing of the interest of the problems themselves – and partly because of the varied methods of constructing the airfields in different parts of the country with materials available locally. For instance, on an airfield on the extreme east, in the jungle behind Chittagong, I found the band of native labourers using only one material for everything – bamboo – of which there seemed to be an inexhaustible supply in the neighbourhood. They also seemed to have only one tool each, a kind of billhook which served to do almost anything to the bamboos of all sizes, some truly enormous. The buildings were supported by a series of large bamboos set vertically with the ends buried in the soil; the floors – raised three feet against the damp – were of bamboos lashed with strips of thin bamboo to these uprights; the walls, and the partitions between the room, were of bamboo strips woven to form heavy matting: bamboo joists supported the roof, and even the tiles were made of the thick divisions between the sections of the largest bamboos, cut in such a way as to form overlapping discs. Nothing was wasted.

In this new assignment I travelled many hundreds of miles, often by train, and this was most enjoyable, because in India the journey is taken in unhurried fashion, both when in motion and when stopping at stations, and the carriages, though mostly without air-conditioning, were roomy and comfortable.

Dick Davis and I were now living in the house of Sir Henry Prior, Home Secretary in the Government of India; it was a pleasant little community there, with people, mainly Army and RAF, of diverse characters and tastes. It was now high summer and we found the heat oppressive; being so far inland and without movement of air it was different from anything I had experienced before – although the temperature may have been no higher – for instance the dry heat of the Western Desert or the intermittent tropical storms of Sumatra. Everything one touched was hot. Our offices, in the great red-sandstone pile of the government building, were cool, but the mass of the building itself absorbed the heat during the day and was like a gigantic radiator. When we bicycled away to our lodging in the evening its warmth could be felt for about half a mile; beyond that the temperature would fall, not much, but quite distinctly. We worked a long day, though with an hour's break in the afternoon, during which we lay flat on our backs and dozed; and when we reached home in the evening were usually too tired to do anything more strenuous than talk.

One evening we started to plan a fictitious museum, whether as a parody of André Malraux's Musée Imaginaire I cannot remember. It began in this way. One of our fellow guests was Simon Elwes, the official painter at Army H.Q., engaged at the time on a portrait of Lord Wavell. He was an ebullient personality, not without a pardonable – because light-hearted – touch of conceit, and full of amusing stories, mainly about himself and his career. One of these was that, staying in the country seat of a Duke in order to paint a family portrait, he penetrated one day to the top floor and opened with some difficulty the door of one of the rooms; as he pushed it open something fell down and rolled across the floor – it was the Ducal coronet, and the room turned out to be the family museum.

We then discussed the kind of things one would expect to find in such a museum – stuffed birds, mementoes of Royal occasions, souvenirs from the Grand Tour, trophies from the East – and so on. From this we proceeded to the creation of such a museum, and in order to tease Simon we began by imagining that one of his paintings had been reduced by age, damp, and decay to a crumpled canvas; and this became our first exhibit, with a suitable label, using the kind of language peculiar to museum labels throughout the world. We then prescribed regulations for forming our museum; anyone might present an object, but he had also to draft a label explaining what it was and connecting it with the history of an imagined family, the Earls of Melksham. Just one example:- our host had a set of Susie Cooper dinner-plates with double fluted rims. The cook had put a large pile of these to heat in the oven, and the pressure of those on top had neatly forced out the centre of the bottom one, leaving a perfect ring with two flutes all round it, one pale blue, one white. This was presented to the Family Museum and registered thus:

> HALO from a terracotta statue of St James the Less by Luca della Robbia; inadvertently removed by the third Earl during a party in the sculptor's studio.
> Note: some doubt exists whether this is not, rather, part of a model of the planet Saturn from the Planetarium of Galileo in the Villa Medici, which was visited by the third Earl later the same evening.

This may in retrospect seem a childish occupation, but as a recreation from the grind of ordinary business, a little more creative than playing games – which anyhow it did not prevent – and of course the whole thing was only a brief diversion; but it served its purpose in bringing us together, and on the occasions when we had guests and were waiting to go in to dinner it served to break the ice.

In a week when I was not travelling we had a day free on Sunday, and our morning diversion was the visit of a dealer in rugs. We used to sit in comfortable chairs on the lawn, and the rugs, mostly Persian, were displayed one by one in a knowing way so as to enhance their sheen and colour. It was delightful because of the leisurely bargaining, at which Dick Davis was adept. The dealer was friendly and congenial, had a keen sense of humour, would react with feigned indignation to a low offer, and was never at a loss for some ingenious form of praise. One such was to extol the weight of the rug and the quality of the wool, but this was a tactical error, for Dick Davis had been a sheep-farmer and there was nothing about wool that he did not know; so that when the weight or staple was praised he would handle the rug expertly and say that it only weighed so many pounds, or that its fibre was too coarse. Many of the rugs were extremely attractive, and each of us, at the end of our tour of duty in India, had bought nine or ten. My batch, a few years afterwards met a sad fate; almost all were stolen from 'High and Over' when we were away in London.

In the middle of the hot season I had an unexpected and welcome invitation from my niece, Elswitha Williams, to spend a week with her and her husband Fred on a house-boat at Srinagar in Kashmir. We had always been on affectionate terms; their daughter Gillian had lived with us in Amersham for some years whilst her parents were abroad, and had become so much part of the family that we called her our third daughter. Fred was in a tea firm in Calcutta, was in the Special Reserve, and had served in the Forces sent from India to the Persian Gulf to quell Rashid Ali's revolt in Iraq. His unit had now returned to India, and he too was due for a short leave. This was a wonderful refreshment; in addition to the peace and beauty of the place, it had several fascinating shops selling local products, and here I bought several trays, each carved from a single piece of wood, which we still, nearly forty years later, use daily; and furs for Dorothy and the children.

The whole military structure in India was now expanding and, on 7th October, Admiral Lord Louis Mountbatten arrived as Supreme Commander, South East Asia, which the Command was now called. Lord Louis' first action was to assemble all the available officers of all the Services, and talk to them. He began diplomatically by saying that when, for instance, one takes on a new bearer one expects to receive a chit giving his qualifications; and he proposed to follow this procedure.

He gave a sketch of his own career both before and during the war, and the circumstances which had led to his present appointment. He then gave a broad account of the set-up in India itself, of the strategic situation in south east Asia, and of the likely developments and dangers. The conference was not long, but it was effective, giving us all an idea of what the general aim was, making everyone feel involved and aware of what his own particular task was likely to be. In short it was a demonstration of clear and determined leadership. The area surveyed was vast, the numbers involved enormous and the machinery complicated, so that in the next few months our Headquarters, though active, had little immediate result to show.

Air Headquarters India had now been transformed into Air Command South East Asia, and P Staff was correspondingly busy. At that time the apparatus for recording the personal particulars of officers and airmen was the comparatively primitive Hollerith machine. This worked on a system of stiff cards which were punched with holes in various places, corresponding to the qualifications of the officer or airman whose card it was. For example an airman might be: a corporal; unmarried; armourer; trained machine-gunner; C of E; ending tour of duty 1945.

Each detail would be represented by a hole punched in the appropriate place on the card. Then, when a post for such an airman was vacant, the cards would be placed in the machine and if all the qualifications on this one were satisfied it would fall right through and the man would in theory be available. If on the other hand he proved to be married, or due for repatriation in 1944 or RC instead of C of E the card would stop on its way through, and the objection examined to see how serious it was. The drawback to the system, which seems to be shared by its modern successor the computer, was that if a card was incorrectly punched the error was extremely hard to trace, unless by chance, and thus might persist for weeks or even months. It was difficult to say how well we worked it, but I had the invaluable help of a Regular Air Force Sergeant, Sergeant Rowswell, who was always at hand to advise, encourage and discuss the drafting of letters, in which he and I saw eye to eye on the use of correct and simple English. Some years after the war I had a letter from a Franciscan friar, Brother Bruno, who turned out to be none other than Sergeant Rowswell; he came to see us, endeared himself to us, and we looked once again at our old problems, how we agreed on the way of handling them, and how efficient, as we hoped, our co-operation had been.

I was still travelling to various airfields, on one occasion in a light aeroplane, when we had the amazing experience of flying straight into the oncoming monsoon. This appeared in the distance as a solid grey wall approaching us, and the experienced pilot, with whom I was now alone, explained that it was better to go on – and anyhow there was nowhere to land. The rain, when we met it, was unbelievably heavy, and it really seemed as if the aircraft would hardly be able to bear the weight of it; we flew at a few hundred feet, and could just see through the haze the bending trees and drenched landscape beneath us.

We landed safely at our destination, and after a stay of two or three days and a full discussion with the Commanding Officer of the Station on his various difficulties, I returned to Delhi to report as usual to my chief, the SPSO G/C Hawtrey.

Hawtrey was by no means a simple person. He was highly intelligent, highly critical of his superiors, and nursed, I fancy, some sort of grievance at lack of promotion. It was said too that he had been handicapped financially for years by having to bring up a niece whose parents had died; but whether true or not we did not know, for he never spoke of it. In short, he was not easy, and had a tendency to bully any subordinate who did not resist. He got on well enough with his DSPSO W/C Farrow, who was of a completely different temperament – unorthodox, outspoken, even violent in his opinions, who stood up to him fearlessly. When W/C Farrow returned to England in the autumn of 1943 I was promoted into his post. The advantage of being a temporary officer is that one need have no hesitation in speaking frankly – one's career is in no danger – and although I had not Farrow's robust manner or command of expletives, Hawtrey appreciated someone who was prepared to say what he thought, even if it was distasteful.

At the end of the year Hawtrey himself was due to return to Britain, and the Air Marshal in charge of Org. asked me if I would be prepared to take over the post of SPSO that Hawtrey was relinquishing. He sounded me in advance because promotions above the rank of Wing Commander (which I now held) were not within the power of India Command and had to be referred to Air Ministry in London.

This was a flattering proposal, but ill-advised, for such an important position, which involved the posting of officers of all categories (though of course subject to higher confirmation) ought surely to be held not only by a Regular Officer but also by one who had first-hand experience of flying. That, however, was not my motive for declining; I felt that I ought not to be any longer away from home, where Dorothy had been coping single-handed with a multitude of problems.

I left Delhi with warm feelings towards those I had worked with there. It had at times seemed something of a backwater by contrast with what had gone on before and what was going on elsewhere; but this was misleading, for although Delhi was far from the front line, the officers at AHQ had mostly seen, or were expecting soon to see, active service, had a real concern for those already in action, and gave powerful backing to them.

Before leaving I enjoyed once more what was called, so Dick told me, "the sailor's pleasure". It consisted of laying out the treasures one had acquired, looking them over, savouring them. In addition to the furs and other things from Kashmir there was, for instance, a length of Chinese silk brought in by a merchant from Tibet, a woollen rug of such fine fabric that it could be drawn through the proverbial wedding-ring, and other little things bought in Delhi itself, some jade bangles and even a pretty Victorian half-hunter lady's watch.

There was one last treasure of a very different kind that I was able to add to these on the journey home. We left Delhi in a Liberator and landed first in Cairo. The Liberator at that time was not a comfortable aircraft, unpressurised and rather cold; but it was more comfortable for me than it was for the Army officer with whom I travelled, who was also returning to Britain after his tour of duty abroad. He was Brigadier Hardy, the largest man in the British Army, no less than seven feet tall; but the noteworthy thing about him was not his height but his size, for unlike most so-called "giants", who tend to look weedy, he was splendidly proportioned and developed, a true giant. He had a fine temperament, was a pleasant companion, and, most remarkable, completely unselfconscious; people would stop in the street and stare at him in amazement, but he seemed quite unaware of it.

I realised then what a handicap such size must be; the seat in the aircraft was much too small, as were most ordinary chairs: beds were far too short, and he had to bend low on entering any door. We next landed in Gibraltar, and had a day to spare before going on. As we walked round Gibraltar – I for the first time – he said "As serving officers we are entitled to go to the Ordnance Depot here and get some sandbags on payment; if we were to buy half a dozen of them we could fill them with oranges and lemons, which are pretty well unobtainable in England." So that was what we did, and when I arrived home I had two sandbags full of these rarities. We landed at Lyneham in Wiltshire; from there to London and Amersham by train, where Dorothy and Philip, just turned eleven, welcomed me on the platform.

Dorothy was now able to tell all that had happened while we had been parted. After I had left for Shetland she housed refugees of one kind or another, but in the autumn (incidentally having spent the first night of the Blitz, 10th September, in George Hill's basement in Regent's Park) sensibly decided it was time to let the house, which she did to a business firm, and spent the winter with her sister Hilda, then living in Bournemouth, where Stella was attending Talbot Heath High School, working up her defective knowledge of scientific subjects as a preliminary to medical training. The tuition there was excellent, she passed the required subjects up to London Matric. standard after one year's work, and First MB in the second. Silvia was then at Cheltenham, and Philip lived with Pat and Camilla Campbell at Gerrards Cross, for the school was there where Pat was Second Master. We all met in Bournemouth at Christmas before I left for Greece.

In the following April, 1941, they all returned to 'High and Over' and remained there for the rest of the war except for short holidays: Philip was now a weekly boarder with the Campbells and went on several holidays with them. Dorothy cared and catered for many guests, naturally often in pretty difficult circumstances since food was scarce and rations strict, although poultry, with plentiful fruit and vegetables from the garden, were a great help. She had Clare Hilton, daughter of Reg and Gwen (George Hill's niece) with her nurse Kennington; George Hill himself; her mother Mrs de Peyer, with her companion Mabel Lidbetter; she also took a girl refugee from London for a couple of terms, and another girl as a companion for her. Such guests, when bombing grew less, tended to return home. My sister Gladys stayed many months, working as a physiotherapist in the local hospital, until, hearing that our wounded in Egypt were being treated by inadequately trained people, she went up to the War Office, told them bluntly what was happening and persuaded them to send her out; her ship actually touched Brazil on the way and then rounded the Cape before reaching Egypt through the Suez Canal.

Dorothy used sometimes to go with Silvia, on holidays from Cheltenham, to blacked-out London for theatre or shopping, and they saw an exquisite ballet performance, including "Les Sylphides", at the New Theatre. It was after this that Silvia decided to train as a ballet dancer; but Dorothy said that she must take her London Matric. first, in case dancing was not a success. This she did, and left Cheltenham for the Ripman School of Dancing in Baker Street in 1942, just after her sixteenth birthday.

Stella was then at the medical school of University College Hospital which had moved to Leatherhead. Whilst there she became engaged to a fellow student Peter Ring, but had to obtain my consent to marry. This was not difficult since I was then in India, and Stella sent a long dispassionate account of Peter to reassure me. They had been married, Dorothy told me, on a lovely summer day in June 1943, with the rose-garden in bloom, and cherries, a speciality of High and Over, hanging on the trees. The families rallied round well, and George Hill gave Stella away in my stead: it had been difficult to get ingredients for the wedding cake and coupons for a sketchy trousseau, but Dorothy managed it, and they went to Cornwall for their honeymoon.

No need to stress how absorbing it was to hear all this and much else, or what joy it gave to be together again.

Chapter VIII

The Air Defence of Great Britain

NOT LONG AFTER returning to England, while waiting for a posting, I met by chance Geoffrey Hill, my erstwhile colleague at University College, who told me that his brother Roderic (whom I knew through meeting him at the house of his uncle, Sir George Hill, at the British Museum) had a Wing Commander's post for a Personal Staff Officer at Fighter Command, and he would tell him that I was available. This was a most attractive idea; I did not demur, and soon after was posted to his Headquarters at Stanmore in Middlesex; thus I could live at High and Over and go daily to my office by train.

Air Marshal Sir Roderic Hill was now Commander-in-Chief of what was no longer called Fighter Command, but Air Defence of Great Britain (ADGB) with all the responsibilities which that implied. He had control of the activities of seven Groups of the Air Force, of the whole Anti-Aircraft Command of Artillery, of the Royal Observer Corps, and of Balloon Command. He was the most conscientious person it would be possible to imagine, not only in the general ordering and conduct of operations, but in all important details. Yet he always found time to consult with his staff and with the Commanders of the other Services under his control, and discussed and weighed their advice sympathetically. How comprehensive yet how meticulous all his plans were can be seen from the Dispatch he submitted to the Secretary of State for Air reporting the operations of his Command in 1944–45, which was published as a supplement to the *London Gazette* on 19th October, 1948. On this the following brief account draws in all essentials, sometimes verbatim.

On personal relations also he had precise ideas. For instance, one of his first tasks on taking over his headquarters at ADGB was to assemble and study photographs of everyone on the staff at Stanmore, beginning with the guard at the entrance, and to memorize their names, so that he could address everyone by name and so set up a personal relationship. This might seem to a sceptic mere artifice, but it had a genuine value, because, even if the relationship went no further, it did show that the Commander-in-Chief had thought it worth while to take this trouble, and thus to show that it was his duty to be as helpful to others as he expected them to be to him. Morale is a curious thing, and it is often impossible to judge what effect even a slight incident or a casual word may have on raising or depressing it.

Similarly on the occasions when he had to present decorations to the Poles and

CHAPTER VIII

Air Marshal Robb presenting decorations to Czech Officers at Stanmore in 1944. From left: Bernard, Air Marshall Robb, Air Marshall Janecek.

Czechs who were serving with us, he would write out a little speech of congratulation, encouragement and friendship. He would then ask a Polish or Czech officer, as the case might be, to come to his office and translate the speech into his own language. Roderic would then go over the script word by word with the officer, getting the correct pronunciation and intonation; and after that would learn it by heart, to deliver when the ceremony took place. Again this might seem simply a device, and the speech may not have sounded quite like their native language, but it demonstrated to these exiles that they were regarded as comrades, and that their Commander-in-Chief cared about their well-being and knew the value of their help and friendship. There was, however, one occasion on which this failed to succeed as it should have done. Some Czechoslovak officers were to be decorated, and Roderic had composed a short speech which ended with the Czech formal cheer; this is divided into two parts like our own - "hip hip", and the response "hurrah". By some mischance Roderic had learnt these two parts in the wrong order, so that when he was reaching the climax - and it was clear what that was to be - the Czech officers could be seen to be drawing themselves up in order to give a hearty response. Alas! when the response came prematurely and by the wrong performer, they were left confused and frustrated. It may have been a failure, but even that was relative, for it naturally became a joke that could be shared at the party afterwards by everyone, whether Czech or British.

There was a wonderful example of the correct procedure when, in 1945, President Masaryk of Czechoslovakia reviewed the two Czech squadrons at Northolt, when they were about to return to their own country. He made his speech, and then gave the trigger formula, which was instantly taken up in one tremendous roar.

My own job as Personal Staff Officer I took to be that of seeing that the Commander-in-Chief's office ran smoothly, with the help of his admirable Personal Assistant, WAAF Squadron-Leader Pitts, and of relieving him as far as possible from little worries, trivial perhaps in themselves, but adding to his whole massive burden; occasionally too of scrutinizing a draft letter or draft order to make sure that its meaning was absolutely clear – and here an intelligent layman can have some value.

Roderic's preoccupation at this time, in addition to countering orthodox bombing raids, was the "Revenge" attacks known to be hatching in Germany with new weapons, mainly against London but also against Bristol. Of these new weapons the existence of one, the flying bomb, had been established with certainty, and of another, the long-distance rocket, with probability. A third, the multi-barrelled gun, was stifled at birth by attacks on the emplacements, which were fairly near the coast in France. Then too the invasion of France was imminent, and it was essential to protect the many places on the south coast where preparations were being made. On 5th June, the day before invasion started, the Air Officer in charge of Administration of ADGB made a tour of the various assembly points, and I was able to accompany him. The concentration was almost incredible, and one could well understand the joke then current that Britain was tilting downwards because of the weight of troops and armour round its southern edge.

Meanwhile the defence waited. A new deployment of its various elements, differing somewhat from that against ordinary bombers (and now diminished in numbers because of the demands of the invasion forces in Normandy) had been planned against the attack of the flying bomb, of which Air Ministry had estimated there might be a month's warning, and the new deployment was planned to take eighteen days. In the event, the attack started without any warning at all, at about 4.00 am on 13th June, with four flying bombs, which were immediately identified as such by the Royal Observer Corps on the coast. One exploded near Gravesend, another two in Kent and Sussex, and the fourth in Bethnal Green, east London, where six people were killed.

There was a lull of two days, and then, at 2.30 pm on the 15th the main attack began. In the next twenty-four hours more than two hundred bombs were launched. One hundred and forty-four crossed the coast, and seventy-three reached greater London; thirty-three were destroyed by the defences as then deployed against normal aircraft.

The weapon had many names – originally "pilotless aircraft" or "flying bombs"; officially V1; known by all units of the defence, in code, as "Diver"; by the public as "doodle-bug", with other more pungent epithets.

The appearance and behaviour of the bombs will still be remembered; the effect that they had in London was unnerving because the attacks, though not concentrated, were continual and unpredictable. The earlier attacks by bombers, terrible though they were, had been limited to night-time, and there was a respite during the day. Now there was no respite, and the casualties in crowded streets could obviously be disastrous. I remember particularly one which fell outside the Air Ministry, although I was there only on the day after; and many remember that which destroyed the Guards Chapel during a Sunday service, with hundreds of casualties.

The noise the bomb made, like that of a defective car firing on one cylinder only, was frightening, although it had an element of comedy when people plunged under beds or grand pianos when it was in the offing; if it passed overhead all was well, but if the engine cut out it would dive to earth and explode within seconds. The general result was that the streets of London were almost devoid of traffic, and I remember being able to walk down the middle of the road in the Strand in the middle of the day. Nevertheless people who had to be in London carried on heroically, and there was one example of a theatre giving a regular performance, although behind stage everything had been destroyed.

Roderic immediately ordered the planned re-deployment, and this was accomplished in five days instead of the minimum eighteen that had been estimated. It was, broadly speaking, as follows:- there were fighters patrolling the coast between Beachy Head and Dover about twenty miles out; another fighter belt over the coastline between Newhaven and Dover; and a third between Haywards Heath and Ashford. The anti-aircraft guns, light and heavy, eventually over eight hundred in all, were concentrated on the North Downs as the main defence of London, backed by the balloon barrage; but there was also a narrow belt of them along the coast.

Roderic followed every detail of the operations with the closest attention, and in order to understand all the problems at first hand soon decided to share in the fighter operations as a pilot, using various aircraft in turn; he was thus able to discuss matters with all the pilots on equal terms. A fighter could destroy a bomb in two ways, either by shooting it down – but not at a range closer than two hundred yards, since the explosion might destroy the attacker – or alternatively by lying in wait for it, then flying beside it and overturning it by tilting it over with a wing-tip. This second method, naturally admired by pilots for its daring, could only be used by pilots flying either a Spitfire XIV or a Tempest, and then only if – at Roderic's suggestion – the aircraft had been modified to use fuel of a higher octane, had been stripped of paint, the surfaces polished and the guns removed; this could increase the speed by as much as 30 mph, giving it a slight margin over the bomb. (It had been demonstrated to Hitler that none of our aircraft was capable of overtaking the bomb; the demonstration was using a captured Spitfire of earlier type.)

The re-deployment was not so successful as had been hoped, largely because the Germans had, without our discovering it, reduced the height at which the flying bombs were to fly. It is possible that they were actually unable to reach the height estimated by the Air Ministry, 6000–7000 feet; but whether this was so or not, the change made them more difficult to destroy. Had they been flying at 6000 feet or so they could have been located and attacked more easily by the heavy AA guns; but arriving as they did at 2000 feet or less they were too high and went too fast for the light AA guns, but were too low and crossed the field of vision too swiftly for Radar and predictors to be used and the heavy guns laid by hand. A second difficulty was that they flew faster than had been predicted; it was 200 mph at launching, increasing, as they used fuel and became lighter, to 350–400 mph. There was one further handicap. Before the attack started some of the launching sites had been located and bombed, but this had had the unforeseen effect of causing the Germans to invent and use mobile launching pads – over two hundred of them – which were more difficult to destroy because they were not only less conspicuous but often changed their positions.

The instructions for guns and fighters were complex, because they varied according to the varying weather. In good weather fighters were much more successful than the guns; but when the weather was bad, poor visibility hampered the fighters and the guns were more effective. Roderic therefore arranged that in very good weather guns should not fire at all, in order to give the fighters complete freedom of action; in bad weather guns would have freedom and no fighters would be used. In middling weather, however, fighters would operate in front of the gun-belt and enter it only when pursuing a flying bomb; the guns would then cease fire. But in some circumstances there was bound to be interference of one arm with the other and one afternoon I had a striking example of it. I rang up a rest-station for aircrews which, before the advent of the flying bomb, had been established in the very heart of what came later to be called "Bomb Alley" – roughly the whole south-east corner of England. I spoke to the Commandant, who said "You wouldn't believe what is going on overhead; there is a flying bomb, and two fighters are chasing it, each trying to overturn it. At the same time it is being engaged by AA fire – quite an entertainment for us all."

The difficulties are clearly explained in Roderic's Dispatch:

> "It was sometimes hard for a pilot," he wrote, "to realise that he was approaching the gun belt in time to avoid infringing the rule against entering it. Conversely, gunners in the belt who were engaging a flying bomb did not always realise in time that a pilot was legitimately entering the belt in pursuit of this or another missile, and would go on firing, to the peril of the pilot's life. The crews of the guns on the coast and elsewhere outside the gun belt were in a still more difficult position, for except in bad weather they always bore the onus of ensuring that no fighters were about before they could open fire. In the excitement of the moment, when the attention of the gunners was concentrated on their targets, it was only too easy for a fighter, travelling at six miles a minute, to slip unnoticed into the field of fire. Consequently numerous infringements of the gun belt by fighters were reported by the guns, especially in the middling weather when guns and fighters were simultaneously in operation. Charges and counter-charges mounted; and with deep misgiving I began to sense a rising feeling of mutual distrust between pilots and gunners."

Even so about half the bombs launched were being brought down, and the performance of the defences had improved continuously since the beginning of the attack; but Roderic concluded that the limit of improvement had been reached, and that a slow decline was more likely than further progress. The solution he believed would be to give guns and fighters each freedom of action within their own sphere, and prohibit any overlapping. When this was discussed with General Pile, commanding the guns, he pointed out that the obvious corollary was to move all the guns into the main belt and so provide fighters and gunners with clearly defined spheres of operation.

With this in mind Roderic instructed Air Commodore Ambler, his DSASO (Deputy Senior Air Staff Officer) to prepare an explanation of any changes, which could be handed out to lower formations. A/Cdre Ambler in fact drew up a formal appreciation of the whole situation and presented it to Roderic on the morning of 13th July. Ambler agreed with the two proposed decisions to banish fighters from the gun belt and to put all the guns in one place; but he went a step further and argued that the guns ought to be put in the place where they could function best, and that was not on the North Downs but on the coast – they had originally been sited on the North Downs to avoid the jamming of their vital Radar; but because of our selective bombing of German Radar and Wireless stations that threat had now receded. On the coast the gunners would get a better view of their target; the hampering effect of ground echoes on their Radar-sets would be minimised; and they would be able to use shells fitted with "proximity fuses", which could not be used inland because they were dangerous to life and property. Further, there was the important point that if the guns were on the coast most of the bombs they brought down would fall harmlessly into the sea.

On paper the proposed changes may look simple; in practical and administrative terms they were far from it. The guns were part of a complex defensive system which also included fighters, searchlights and balloons. Hundreds of guns with all their equipment were now in position on the Downs. Great reserves of ammunition had been collected and stored there. Thousands of miles of telephone cables had been laid over a period of six months. Accommodation had been found or improvised for the gunners. The best positions available for the guns themselves and their equipment had been selected and commandeered, and for the last two weeks men had been busy building permanent emplacements for the guns among the apple-orchards and on the slopes of the chalk hills in Kent and Surrey. In short a small city was spread out between Redhill and the Thames; the proposal was that this should be picked up bodily and transported thirty or forty miles further south, and during that move, for three days or so, the defences, although not completely interrupted, would obviously be much weakened.

Nevertheless Roderic was convinced that the tactical theory behind moving all the guns to the coast was sound, and he had learned that Sir Robert Watson-Watt, scientific adviser on telecommunications to the Air Ministry, had reached substantially the same conclusion. Sir Robert's opinion was the more weighty since better conditions for the Radar equipment of the guns was one of the main advantages claimed for the proposed change.

He therefore decided that he would think the matter over during the day and hold a conference late that afternoon, primarily for discussion with General Pile, to whom he gave an advance copy of the proposals. Sir Robert was also asked to attend, as well as a representative of the Air Commander-in-Chief. Air Vice-Marshal Sanders, the AOC No. 11 Fighter Group also attended; he was in command of the all-important fighters.

Roderic opened the conference by outlining the situation. He then asked General Pile whether he supported the proposal to move all the guns to the coast, leaving the balloons where they were and creating two areas for fighters, one between the balloons and the new gun belt, and the other in front of the gun belt over the sea. General Pile replied that he was in full agreement, that the merits of siting the guns along the coast had been considered by his Command for some time, and he proposed that they should be deployed all the way from Dover to Beachy Head and be given freedom of action on a strip extending 10,000 yards out to sea and 5,000 yards inland.

Air Vice-Marshal Sanders, who might have been expected to demur, since this threw a barrier across the area on which his fighters operated, on the contrary welcomed the proposal; Sir Robert also spoke in favour, and undertook to produce improved Radar equipment for controlling the fighters over the sea.

The consensus was remarkable, and Roderic decided that the change must be made. But he now faced a dilemma. He might maintain that the move was tactical – a re-arrangement of the forces already allotted to him for the defence of London against flying bombs – or, alternatively, since no move so great had ever been made on tactical grounds before, he might refer the matter for approval to higher authority. Knowing how such things go, and that if he submitted the plans to higher authority so many controversial questions might arise, and so many further authorities might claim to be consulted that he could not count on a decision before it was too late, he decided to go ahead on his own responsibility.

After the conference the Air Commander-in-Chief was informed: he asked whether it would not be possible to make a trial deployment on a small stretch of the coast: Roderic replied that this would be worse than useless. The Air C-in-C did not question his judgement, and made no further comment.

The move began that very evening, 13th July, and by dawn on the 17th the heavy guns were all in action in their new positions, to be joined by the light guns two days later. During the week, vehicles of AA Command had travelled two and three-quarter million miles; stores and ammunition weighing as much as two battleships had been transported, in addition to the guns themselves; 23,000 men and women had been moved to new quarters, and enough telephone cable had been laid to stretch from London to New York.

Without waiting to judge the results, Air Ministry informed Roderic that the Air Staff considered he ought not to have made the move without prior reference to themselves, and left him in no doubt that he would be held personally responsible for the outcome, and that any blame or credit would be laid on his head. (Later, when the plan had succeeded, they sent a message of congratulation.)

In this context it is worth noting that Duncan Sandys, who acted as informal liaison officer between the Prime Minister and ADGB, was not in evidence during the decisive period, but that when, a generation later and long after Roderic's death, that excellent programme "The Secret War" appeared on television, Lord Sandys (as he had now become) conveyed the impression that it was he who had initiated the vital move. I felt it my duty to write and remind him of the facts; the suave reply disclaimed any intention to mislead.

The first anxious week after the change promised well, and between sunset on 20th July and sunset on the 21st sixty bombs were brought down, well above the average; and the rate continued to improve.

But it was characteristic of Roderic that he now considered it his duty to see that every one of the units under his command was thoroughly familiar with its part in the new plan; and it was also characteristic that he decided that he must undertake this himself. The Staffs of many of the formations were so fully occupied, especially in connection with the operations in Normandy, that they had no time for this additional task, whilst the formation of a special Task Force and the appointment and briefing – even training – of an officer of Air rank to operate it and to report back to HQ would have taken precious time, and would have demanded resources of man-power which he did not possess and had no chance of obtaining. Accordingly he decided on giving a direct lead himself to all Station, Squadron and Battery Commanders concerned with flying bombs. In his own words:

> Here my practice of sharing actively and frequently in the fighter operations stood me in good stead. Trying to shoot down a missile travelling at six miles a minute while flying at the same speed at a height of perhaps a thousand feet across a narrow belt of undulating country bounded by balloons and guns was a business whose subtleties were not readily appreciable from an office chair. I found that a practical acquaintance with this business had its uses. Not only did it help me to acquire a fund of tactical knowledge that I could hardly have gained in any other way; above all it enabled me to talk on a basis of common understanding and endeavour with the pilots whose devotion it was my task to foster.

The changes had brought two incidental advantages. One was that the removal of the guns gave the searchlights, which remained, more scope to assist night-fighters; the second was that the move had brought the Headquarters of AA batteries and the bases from which the fighters operated closer together, and thus Station Commanders and local Battery Commanders could meet and discuss their difficulties. Again one must quote:

> The hint was taken. The consequences were profound and striking. As a result of these meetings between Station and Battery Commanders, the first requisite of understanding between two parties whose interests must occasionally conflict – was attained. The mists of suspicion whose gatherings had troubled me so much were dispersed almost overnight. On subsequent visits to the same Stations I was again shown aircraft that had suffered minor damage from anti-

aircraft fire. But this time, instead of having to listen to grievances against the gunners, I was told of pilots who had flouted discipline and good sense by venturing too near the guns. In short, pilots and gunners were beginning to understand one another's problems and work together. Unity was restored. The process reached its climax towards the close of the main attack. Flying towards the south coast on 28th August, I could see over Romney Marsh a wall of black smoke marking the position of the 'Diver' barrage. From time to time a fresh salvo would be added to repair the slow erosion of the wind. On the far side of the barrage fighters were shooting down flying bombs into the Channel; on the nearer side more fighters waited on its fringe to pounce on the occasional bomb that got so far. The whole was as fine a spectacle of co-operation as any Commander could wish to see. That day ninety-seven bombs approached these shores. The defences brought down ninety, and only four reached London.

At the beginning of September, the capture of the launching areas by the Allied armies ended the main attack.

Roderic still had other problems, although none of this magnitude. One was the launching of flying bombs from aircraft instead of from the ground, so that they came in from unpredictable directions and sometimes at very low altitudes.

To another problem there seemed no obvious solution, that of V2, the long-distance rocket. These began in mid-September. Launched from well inside Holland or Germany and arriving in Britain on a lofty trajectory at a speed greater than that of sound, the conventional defences of guns and fighter aircraft were virtually useless. The only sound plan seemed to be to track the missiles, and to locate and then bomb the firing and storage points with fighters and fighter-bombers, heavy bombers being fully engaged elsewhere; and this was systematically followed. The attack was far less intense than with the flying bomb – an average of three a day – and less frightening, since the rocket arrived without sound or warning. Eventually the sites were over-run; but as was remarked at the time, whereas the flying bomb had had its day, the rocket was the weapon of the future – a prediction now amply fulfilled.

Chapter IX

After the Second War

It is surprising that so few people seem to have recognised the reason for the return of a Labour Government in 1945; yet it must be evident to anyone who served in the Forces. At the end of the European War there was a strange lull in Britain. Everything was strictly rationed, including materials for rebuilding, and many hundred thousand service men were still with their units, either at home or abroad. In any war nowadays where at least half the servicemen in democratic countries are civilians in uniform, many of them conscripted, their one desire is to shed the uniform and get back into civilian life. But demobilization is a complicated business, and above all slow. Whilst many units were far from the Front, bored and impatient with little to do, a system of Discussion Groups had been devised, the idea being that an officer or senior NCO should open a discussion on some subject of general interest, and that this should then be debated in an informal way. Leaflets were then printed to summarize each subject and to suggest points for discussion. These leaflets were printed and must to some extent have been prepared by Allen Lane, publisher of Penguin Books and a strong Labour supporter; they were reasonable and moderate, but had a distinctly leftish bias. The Germans surrendered in May, but the election was not until July, so that many thousands of servicemen fretting for weeks at the slow rate of demobilization, blaming the Government for it and well primed with socialist ideas, naturally cast their votes in favour of Attlee, who had done an admirable job in the Churchill Government.

I was demobilized reasonably early and returned to civilian life. Because of the events of the late thirties I still held two posts half-time, one as a Professor at University College, the other as the Keeper of a Department in the British Museum. Both buildings had suffered heavy damage. On 18th September, 1940, a landmine carried away the Great Hall in College, destroyed the Physics laboratory, and did extensive damage to other parts. Only a few days later a number of incendiary bombs were dropped, and some of them, finding their way through the battered roofs, caused a vast fire which destroyed many of the specialized libraries. The loss of books was comparatively small, since the Library Committee had decided before the war to send all the most precious single volumes to the National Library in Aberystwyth, and to move most of the other books to the ground floor of the College and cover them with sandbags and galvanized iron. My own office near the main portico of the College was destroyed, but the cast Gallery in Malet Place, together with a small office there, had suffered little, so that my department was still in being, and my efficient secretary, a trained archaeologist, Alice Lodge, soon returned. On the other hand for some months there were no students, soon only a few, and none needing individual tuition. Thus I could easily keep the College Department going and devote much of my time to working in the British Museum, where there was much to be done, since neither of my Assistant Keepers had yet been demobilized. The destruction there had been great, not so much to the structure perhaps as in University College, but extensively to roofs and windows and to the galleries on the top floor; here again fire had been a great destroyer.

The large glass-roofed hall containing the Exhibition of Greek and Roman Life – empty of course – was gutted, and the roof had collapsed. The four long galleries leading from it, which originally contained the whole collection of Greek vases, were damaged but reparable. The whole of the Department of Coins and Medals, by the side of the Greek and Roman Life Room, had gone, but at the south end of the Life Room a stout oak door, charred through, had finally resisted the flames, and in doing so had preserved not only the whole of the large Gold Room, but also our little laboratory, our library with its fittings, and all our Departmental Offices. This proved to be an inestimable blessing, for not only were we able to restore our offices to normal, but were able to make over

British Museum, the Greek and Roman Life Room after its destruction by incendiaries in 1941. This view looks east.

the Gold Room to the Department of Coins; it offered them much less space than in their old quarters, but enabled them to bring back a great number of the coin cabinets, and to work there happily for several years.

There remained the problem of making the destroyed rooms reasonably weather-proof, for they were open to the sky and the wooden floors permeable. When I returned from the war I found that the Office of Works had given all these floors a heavy coating of asphalt, thus converting them into roofs. They had sunk a little after having been made good, and water tended to lie in shallow pools, but stepping-stones overcame this difficulty. To the wall was affixed a large painted notice saying "Not suitable for wheeled traffic". Being well over fifty feet from the ground they seemed not to be in danger of this, but it was intended, I suppose, not against horses or motor-cars but to deter people from using trolleys for moving antiques, which was our usual practice.

On the night that our Life Room was demolished, fire had also seized the great square room at the head of the main staircase, which belonged to the so-called British and Mediaeval Department of the Museum, which comprised practically everything found in Britain. This had not been empty, because the Trustees, in the interests of morale, had decided not to shut the Museum entirely. The Department had therefore arranged to put on an exhibition of duplicates, consisting mostly of prehistoric flints and pottery. That night the exhibition was com-

British Museum, the Greek and Roman Life Room after its destruction by incendiaries in 1941. This view looks north-west.

pletely burnt out. Among the exhibits had been a curiosity from an old private collection, consisting of a flint split in half, with markings on it which had been supposed to resemble the profile of William Pitt, Earl of Chatham; and the original owner had inscribed on it Chatham's last words. The Keeper of the Department, inspecting the burnt-out gallery the next morning, found this one exhibit lying alone on the ashes, and still bearing Chatham's words "Oh, my country".

On the ground floor of the Museum the new Elgin Gallery, completed just before the war, had had not only a glass roof, but beneath it a complete glass ceiling; a bomb had penetrated, and every panel of glass was shattered – there must have been some thousands. The old Elgin Galleries beside it were not badly damaged, nor was the great Edward VII Gallery – not in my Department – which ran the whole length of the Museum on its northern façade.

Before the war the Elgin and other Marbles had been taken from their pedestals, stacked against the walls of their own galleries and sand-bagged in. But soon a far safer place was found for them. Some years earlier there had been a scheme for extending the Piccadilly Tube from Holborn southwards under the Thames, but it never got further than Aldwych. Like most Tubes it consisted of twin parallel tunnels, and so, while one of the tunnels operated – and still operates – a shuttle-service between Holborn and Aldwych, the other, half a mile or so long, was vacant; and it was here that the most important marbles, the whole of the Parthenon Frieze for instance, were eventually stored. It was an ideal place, because although it was a little damp and naturally very dusty, the constant movement of the train backwards and forwards in the parallel tunnel kept the air circulating, warm, and tolerably dry. The danger would have been if a large bomb between the south end of the tunnel and the Thames had let in the river.

Although we could not yet move the marbles back to the Museum, it was possible to inspect some of them where they were stacked, not so much in the tunnel itself as on the platforms of a ghost-station which existed under the present Aldwych station. Very soon we had visiting archaeologists from abroad. Two of the earliest of these were delightful Frenchmen, Professor Demargne of the Sorbonne, and Professor Metzger of the University of Lyon. Both were engaged on the French excavations at Xanthos in Lycia, and were anxious to see the sculptures found there by British expeditions in the nineteenth century.

Many of these happened to be stacked in the deserted station, so I was able to take them down there several times. It was a dirty and a rather eerie job in the gloom, and it meant squeezing in among the long marble slabs of relief sculptures, mostly a couple of feet thick, three feet high and a dozen feet long, which formed a kind of labyrinth.

Also working independently on the Lycian sculptures was a visiting young American student, Carla Gottlieb; she was extremely diligent, not to say demanding, but I think we did our best for her and she came down to the Tube too. One morning we had been working on the marbles and were making ready to go back to lunch, when we heard a kind of scuttling sound among them and there emerged, crawling from behind one of the slabs, Carla, begrimed from head to foot. We had soap and water down there, and she was none the worse, unless she thought our laughter unkind.

The Edward VII Gallery being the least damaged part of the Museum and with direct access from the north entrance, the Trustees decided to open there as soon as possible an exhibition of the finest objects from our four Departments of the Museum. The Gallery was shabby, but the only visible damage was where a small bomb had gone through from roof to basement without exploding, leaving a trail of superficial damage to the showcases nearby. The hole was repaired, the Gallery touched up, and the Departments started moving in their greatest treasures. The Exhibition, everyone agreed, was an outstanding success. The reasons were fairly obvious. It was partly that people had been starved of such things for years during the war, but it was chiefly that, in a Museum so rich as the British Museum, the Departments were able to select objects that were in absolutely the first class for beauty and interest; everything else was ruthlessly left out in order to give these ample space and a proper setting. The variety of the objects helped matters – terracottas, gold-work, bronzes, vases. And the fact that there were not too many of them; twenty Greek vases of the highest quality are probably quite enough for the ordinary layman.

In selecting and arranging my own exhibits I had the invaluable help of Miss Lodge, my secretary from University College. And it was not altogether easy. My own Department was on the extreme south of the Museum, the Edward VII Gallery on the extreme north; thus I had to make quite a long journey, first out over the roof, which was the floor of the destroyed Greek and Roman Life Room, then through the four vase-rooms, all at that time empty and damaged, then into a long gallery of the Egyptian Department. This too was empty of exhibits, though the showcases were still there, and completely deserted and desolate. I was making this journey one evening just as it was getting dark, and had started to

British Museum, Department of Greek and Roman Antiquities, after patching up, 1944.

walk through the Egyptian Gallery. There were no lights. Now it so happened that I was passing the case in which there used to be kept a mummy with a sinister reputation. I don't think that anyone knew exactly what particular evil it was supposed to bring on you, but its reputation was well known, particularly because, many years ago, there used to be a regular police patrol at night through all the galleries and it was discovered that stalwart London policemen were carefully avoiding this particular part of the Gallery. That however is by the way; the point is that it was a standing joke in the Museum and was naturally on my mind. I have seldom been so frightened as when, at that moment, I clearly heard, in the dusk, a few feet behind me and coming nearer, three distinct footsteps. The explanation was perfectly simple. The Gallery had long been empty; a leak in the roof had loosened some of the cork tiles with which it was floored: I had trodden on them in succession, pressing them down, and after a second's delay they had sprung back into position, one after the other.

We shared the new Exhibition with the British and Mediaeval Department who staged a splendid show, including many early gold treasures. After a while it was thought advisable to safeguard some of the showcases with a special kind of alarm, then the most modern thing of its kind; this alarm, when any showcase was opened, automatically summoned the nearest Police patrol car, guaranteed usually to arrive within three minutes. When the system was first installed, young Assistant Keepers were a little vague as to whether, or when, the showcases were activated; and one of them, wishing to withdraw a couple of gold cups and take them to his office for study, opened a case, took them out, and put them on a tray. The alarm had worked, and before he turned to go away two policemen in plain clothes had him by the arms. Not unnaturally he thought this was a hold-up, and the situation took some time to disentangle.

The second Exhibition planned by the Trustees was one of ancient marbles, and in particular the Elgin Collection. The new Duveen Gallery was wrecked, but the older Elgin Rooms, built a century or so ago, were still almost intact, though very shabby; and here it seemed to me that a fine exhibition, better than that before the war, could be arranged. The Elgin Collection of marbles from the Parthenon consists of three kinds of relief sculpture; one, the pediments, so high that it consists virtually of statues in the round; a second, the metopes, in very high relief; and a third, the frieze, in very low relief. In the old exhibition these had been exhibited together and tended to get in each other's way. They were also rather cramped, and the statues in the round were set too high and too close to the wall to see the backs properly. I planned to take in another adjacent gallery and give the metopes this to themselves, leaving in the old one the frieze, and also the pedimental groups, which were to be mounted on bases lower and better placed than before; and I cleared out all the illustrative matter – pictures, models etcetera – into an anteroom. I redecorated the rooms in a simple colour – a very pale pure Prussian blue.

There remained the problem of getting all the marbles up from the Tube again. The frieze was not stored on the platform of the old Tube station, but actually in the tunnel: the slabs averaged a foot thick and were three feet high, most of them weighing a ton or more. We had to move each slab down the tunnel, which was only eight feet in diameter. We then had to take it across the station platform, round a rather sharp and awkward corner, up a flight of steps, round another sharp corner, along a passage into the ordinary passenger lift (sometimes accompanied by disgruntled passengers), along another passage into the street, into a van, back to the Museum, out of the van and along to the gallery.

Speaking from memory I think it took us about six months working continuously, the team consisting of the Master Mason, the admirable Jack Brennan, and six men; no more could be used because they had to be carefully trained, and the work was extremely delicate. The only way of moving sculpture of this size is to raise it inch by inch with levers (always carefully padded with lead) and wooden wedges, on to a little wooden platform called by courtesy a horse, which had tall detachable wooden sides. When the slab is safely on, the sides are fixed on, padded and bolted together, and the whole thing can then be lifted on to a trolley and moved about. But when getting things up from the Tube, the number of transfers from one trolley vehicle to another would have taken so much time and effort that something had to be done about it. We made one very simple but extremely effective improvement: we fitted four solid steel wheels, four inches in diameter, to each of the horses, and it thus became a mobile unit. So even today it is useful to know something about the siege of Troy. Virgil tells us that the Trojans fitted wheels to the Wooden Horse for a similar reason.

The new arrangement of the marbles from the Parthenon was widely appreciated, largely because of the appropriate scale and excellent lighting of the old Victorian galleries; and the exhibition continued until the new Duveen Gallery, the design for which is shown on page 70, was restored and re-opened in 1961.

This is the only major sculpture gallery built in Britain for a long time, and a word must be said about it. It is, I suppose, not positively bad, but it could have been infinitely better. It is pretentious, in that it uses the ancient Marbles to decorate itself. This is a long outmoded idea, and the exact opposite of what a sculpture gallery should do. And although it incorporates them, it is out of scale, and tends to dwarf them with its bogus Doric features, including those columns, supporting almost nothing, which would have made an ancient Greek architect wince. The source of daylight is too high above the sculptures, a fault that is only concealed by the amount of reflection from the pinkish marble walls. These are too similar in colour to the marbles themselves, and when light is reflected from one wall on to the reliefs on the opposite wall, it tends to flatten them out. These half-dozen elementary errors were pointed out by everyone in the Museum, and by many scholars outside, when the building was projected. Gifts can be a great danger to museums, the larger the more dangerous, especially when they have such strings attached as that the donor must nominate the architect.

The ideal lighting for sculptures is a gently dominant top-light, the source not too near above them, but not too far, so that there is enough diffused light to save the shadows being harsh. But of course one cannot always have daylight, and that

British Museum, Old Elgin Room, 1949. Since the Duveen Gallery had been badly damaged in the war the Parthenon sculptures were placed in a newly restored Old Elgin Room. In 1949 Bernard made the following comments on the colour of the room:

The old Elgin Gallery was painted a deep terracotta red, which, though in some ways satisfactory, diminished its apparent size, and was apt to produce a depressing effect on the visitor. It was decided to experiment with lighter colours, and the walls of the large room were painted with what was, at its first application, a pure cold white, but which after a year's exposure has unfortunately already yellowed. The small Elgin Room was painted with pure white tinted with prussian blue, and the Room of the Metopes was painted with pure white tinted with cobalt blue and black: it was necessary, for practical reasons, to colour all the dadoes a darker colour.

is where the trouble began. The man who set the Victory of Samothrace halfway up a fine staircase in the Louvre, and spotlighted it, showed a touch of genius: the effect is marvellous, especially for that particular statue. The general consequences have been deplorable. In America you can find even important museums from which daylight has been permanently excluded, and a system of powerful spotlights installed. The main point about sculpture is that it is in three dimensions: a powerful spotlight on a statue not only kills the subtler modelling in front, but it casts the back into shadow and makes it either impossible to see, or impossible to look at in detail.

Unfortunately this craze for the sensational and dramatic is spreading to England. The most elaborate devices are employed, with enormous expenditure of electricity, in order to produce effects that are much inferior to simple top-light, and they are often tiring to the eyes because of the amount of brilliant light reflected from the surface of the marble. The sculptor Rodin possessed an ancient Greek torso which he was wont to examine in the dark, moving round it with a single candle in his hand, so that no subtlety should escape him. Every so-called lighting expert should be made to do this before he installs his thousand-candle-power bulbs.

Ideally, one ought to be able to touch sculpture, and feel the subtleties of the modelling. This is obviously impracticable for the general public, but we once made an exception when we had a request from a school for blind children, that some of their pupils should be allowed to come along and handle the sculptures. So we constructed several small platforms in front of various sculptures, so that they could reach them. Nine or ten little girls arrived, aged twelve or thereabouts; some could see a little, and they helped the others both in mounting the platforms and in understanding the sculptures. Even without the help it was amazing to see how quickly the fingers of those who were quite blind moved – almost flickered – over the surface, and conveyed the shapes to their minds. Missing parts didn't seem to worry them: these they seemed able to restore in imagination, just as people with sight can. We offered them reliefs, as well as statues in the round, and here only one thing baffled them. One relief was of a battle-scene, and when they had finished feeling it one of them said "But I thought you told us that Greek shields were round". "Yes," we said, "they were." "But some of these shields are oval" she said. I think it is possible that at such schools they are deliberately not told much about the mechanics of sight, for we quite failed to make clear, and did not like to press, that when an artist shows a circular object in three-quarter view it becomes an oval.

Chapter X

The Department of Greek and Roman Antiquities, British Museum

TOWARDS THE END OF 1947 things were returning, not quite to normal, but nearly enough to make me feel that it was no longer proper to hold two posts; and I had little difficulty in deciding which to relinquish. I clearly had better qualifications for a museum than for a professorship, since I was not a first-class classical scholar and had little confidence in either lecturing or tuition: on the other hand I had a fairly wide knowledge, deep interest in and love for all kinds of classical antiquities, a good eye and memory for sculpture and a quick judgement of value; which is important where purchases are concerned. I also enjoyed the active and practical side of museum life, and the constant contact, through the many visitors to the Department and through correspondence, with the outside world. I should be leaving many friends in University College, but with the consolation that they would still be near, and that I should still be able to help them by giving special facilities to their students in the Museum. It was made easier by the appointment next year of Martin Robertson, my Assistant Keeper in the Department, to succeed me in the Yates Chair: an excellent choice, for he is a sensitive scholar of the highest calibre on both the literary and the artistic side.

After taking up the full-time Keepership of the Greek and Roman Department I tried to make a tour daily of the whole Department: as anyone who has served in the Forces knows, this is the only way of ensuring that everything is as it should be. It also means making the personal acquaintance of the whole staff, and learning exactly how the various sections – Moulders' Shop, Masons' Shop, photographic studio, and laboratory – function; and what their problems are. I found later that Sir Frederic Kenyon, Director of the Museum when I first knew it, had the same custom, but his inspection was a much more formal affair and comprised only the public galleries. I also learnt that the uniformed warders in the galleries then carried rods of office, and that they had developed a bush-telegraph by tapping the butts of these on the floor to signal his approach.

The Departments of Antiquities in the British Museum traditionally performed certain services to the public which were not precisely defined in the statutes. They had to be prepared to pronounce on the genuineness of any antiquity brought in for inspection, to say what they believed it to be, and to date it as nearly as they could. These judgements were given without any claim to authority beyond that of the expert knowledge available in the Department, were not committed to writing, and never dealt with monetary value, for the obvious reason that thus they could not be used to enhance their value in the market. This last safeguard could cause embarrassment, when, as sometimes happened, an object was brought in by a visitor which he was willing to sell and which the Department would like to acquire for the Museum collection. We never tried to buy below a reasonable price, which would have been not only unfair but unwise. The solution here was to give the owner the name of one or two reputable dealers, tell him to see what they would offer him, and then, using that as a basis, return if he wished to us and offer it to the Museum at his own price: we made one or two useful though not major purchases in this way.

A major acquisition that we made in 1945 was of a different kind, for it was already one of the most famous of classical antiquities. This was the Portland Vase, the finest surviving example of a rare glass technique, in which a vessel of deep blue glass was overlaid with a coating of white, and the white glass was then carved with a mythological scene in cameo. The vase, found near Rome, and probably made in the first century AD, had been famous for centuries as the Barberini Vase, had been bought from the Barberini family by Sir William Hamilton (Consul at Naples and Nelson's friend) who sold it to the Portlands in 1785. In 1810 the fourth Duke of Portland deposited it on loan in the British Museum; whilst on exhibition there it had been shattered by a madman into over two hundred pieces, but had been repaired, and had been on exhibition ever since. John Forsdyke, the Director, now [1945] discovered that the Duke was willing to sell, and wrote (I was still in the Air Force) asking me what I thought the vase was worth: I gave a figure which turned out to be what the Duke had suggested, so we bought it at that. Before the war I had had a pleasant visit from Josiah Wedgwood, head of the firm of Wedgwood the potters, and a direct descendant of the original Josiah, founder of the firm. In 1786 they had made a replica in pottery of the vase, and had developed a ware of the same general appearance, called Jasper Ware, which enjoyed immense popularity, and is still being produced. Mr Wedgwood had explained that the prosperity of the firm was largely based on the making of the first replica and the subsequent success of Jasper Ware, but that he had never held the original Portland Vase in his hands: might he do so? Of course I was delighted to take it out of its case and into my office, where he could look at it in comfort.

Most visitors, however, were mainly concerned with discovering what exactly their possessions were, and here we gave them all the help we could, although this might entail a good deal of research. Sometimes they disagreed with our conclusions, and sometimes one could not help sympathising with them. For instance, a visitor one day brought in a model, fragmentary but originally a couple of feet high, of Trajan's Column in Rome, carved in red marble; and a version, abbreviated, but in correct Latin, and also cut on a little tablet of red marble, of the inscription on its pedestal. I pronounced it to be, what it certainly was, a souvenir made in Italy for the tourist trade of the last century; but I did sympathise with the manifest disbelief of the owner when she told me that she had dug it up with her own hands in the garden of her new house on the borders of Sherwood

Forest. Such finds are far commoner than one would expect. They come usually from old private collections, the dregs of which have been left in some cellar or attic: the house is pulled down, or burnt down, or left derelict, and they are thrown out, gradually buried where they lie, or carted away with other rubbish.

A little time after the war, a visitor brought in an archaic Greek bronze statuette of a Spartan warrior, perfectly genuine, and was obviously puzzled, and inclined to be sceptical, when I told him that we already knew of it and where it had come from. His surprise was natural enough, for he explained that he had bought it only a few weeks before, not in a shop but from an Arab in an extremely remote corner of southern Arabia, so remote that it was near the country of natives who apparently live to this day just as they did at the time of Herodotus, nearly two thousand five hundred years ago. He described them as living so far away from the normal trade routes that not only the people themselves, but their animals as well, subsisted entirely on fish.

The explanation was simple enough, and convincing, when I was able to show him a photograph of his own statuette. It had been offered for sale, in the same place, and presumably by the same Arab, to a British officer just before the war. The officer hadn't enough money in his pocket to buy it, but he had set it up on the sand and photographed it with a miniature camera: this was how it came to be published in an archaeological journal. From its greasy condition I should judge that the Arab had been carrying it next to his skin ever since. How a Spartan bronze got to that corner of the world in the sixth century BC or later is another problem.

When I had been visiting Rome in the autumn of 1949, I had met one of my colleagues, a professor from Germany, who told me with some excitement that one of the Italian dealers had for sale what must surely be the head of Aphrodite (a head in profile to the right) from the assembly of Olympian Deities on the east frieze of the Parthenon. This seemed improbable, in fact downright impossible, for although that particular slab was shattered into small fragments, there is already in the Acropolis Museum at Athens one fragment consisting of the right ear and part of the hair of a woman which, from the scale and the subject, certainly belongs to this head of Aphrodite; and no head, whether in profile or not, can have two right ears. We went together to see the head, which turned out to be an expert modern copy of a head of Artemis on the adjacent slab of the Parthenon frieze: it had been slightly altered, and trimmed at the back following the line of the nape of the neck, which gave the fragment a distinctive shape. My German friend and I finally agreed about it, and together we explained the whole thing to the dealer, who apparently accepted the explanation; and the incident quite passed out of my mind. Nearly a year later a visitor arrived in the Greek and Roman Department. He was a dealer from Switzerland, and he carried under his arm a brown paper parcel which contained, he said, a relief sent him by a friend to whom it had been offered for sale. The shape of the parcel was unmistakeable, and I was able to tell him all about the contents before he undid it.

Again, by tradition, the Museum was considered to be the source of information about anything classical, whether a work of art or not. One inquiry on the telephone which seemed to me to come near the limit of what we might be expected to answer was "What was the age of Pontius Pilate at the time of the Crucifixion?" made in an agitated voice just as I sat down to my desk in the morning. This looked like needing a long search but turned out to be quite easy, because I found a vital reference in an ancient author at once, from which it was clear that Pilate had not been a young man at the time, and seemed to have been involved in some sort of trouble with the natives in Palestine before. This appeared to satisfy the inquirer, who then explained that he was a theatrical producer whose leading actor was intent on playing Pilate as almost a youth.

Some inquiries were apt to recur: one was for the measurements of the Venus de Milo – the Aphrodite of Melos. Another, more serious, was "Which was the Greek vase that inspired Keats's poem 'Ode on a Grecian Urn'?" The answer, which, when you read the poem, looks as if it should be easy, is in fact not at all simple, and one of my predecessors had prepared a pamphlet which could be given to inquirers to read. This set out the arguments for believing that Keats was inspired partly by a marble vase of Roman date, with which he was familiar, partly by others of the same kind illustrated in a book of engravings, but above all by the Frieze of the Parthenon, which had recently been brought over by Lord Elgin, and to which Keats had been introduced by his friend Benjamin Haydon, the painter.

As for inquiries by letter, I don't think we ever received a more delightful one than this, which came from a country parish at the time of the Coronation: "Dear

Showing Marshal Tito round the British Museum in 1953.
From left: Tom Kendrick (Director of the museum), Tito, interpreter, Bernard.

Sir, We are having a Coronation Procession, and I am hoping to go as St George, and my brother as the Dragon. I should be very grateful if you could send me a description of a Roman soldier, his dress and his armour." The answer was not too difficult, and mercifully we were not asked to prescribe for the brother.

There is one function of the Department, an important one, which may well be unknown to anyone who has not worked there: it is a meeting place for scholars from all over the world. Those from our own universities and museums also often visited us. Excavators, for instance, travelling from Greece back to the United States would tell us of their latest discoveries and discuss their problems. Scholars from the Continent, who had come to work on our collections, showed us similar material - perhaps recently acquired or unpublished - in theirs. We were sometimes able to put people who were working in the same field in touch with one another and make them collaborators instead of competitors. It is in fact a clearing-house of knowledge, where discussion is free, and without ulterior motive except the advancement of our common studies.

Towards the end of 1948 I had a letter from Sir Frederic Kenyon, who after his retirement from the Museum had been appointed Secretary of the British Academy, and was now about to give up the post. He asked me if I would allow my name to be among those going before the Managing Committee as a possible successor.

This is a more formidable job than it sounds: the Secretary is the senior permanent official and has not only the whole running of the Academy, its Faculties, Finance and publications, but is also involved in negotiations of various kinds with the Treasury and even with foreign representatives about the establishment of British Institutes abroad. It was a post for which I had no hesitation in deciding I was almost totally unsuited. This was well for the Academy, for they eventually appointed Mortimer Wheeler, who had the ideal qualifications - the general character, the organizing ability, the ruthless driving power, and the panache; and who within a few years rejuvenated the Academy and transformed it into something of a far higher standing and greater influence.

By 1954 I was happily settled in the British Museum, with admirable Assistant Keepers, secretary and other staff, when the Lincoln Professorship of Archaeology at Oxford was on the point of falling vacant: John Beazley, who had held it for thirty years, was due to retire in a year's time. By his superb scholarship and unique achievement, particularly in the field of Greek vase-painting, he had made Oxford a major, if not the main, focus for the study of Greek art. The succession would have been obvious had Humfry Payne survived; and the other natural successor, Beazley's Reader, Thomas Dunbabin, a first-rate scholar and archaeologist and a distinguished historian, had also died untimely a year or so before. There now seemed no native scholar old or experienced enough to succeed. The Keeper of Greek and Roman Antiquities at the British Museum was *ex officio* one of the electors, so I was not surprised to have a visit from Walter Oakeshott, the Rector of Lincoln and also an elector, to whose College the Professorship was attached; but I was taken aback by what he had to say, which was that the electors had already met informally and decided that there was no outstanding candidate. "Would I allow my name to be considered for want of a better?" or diplomatic words to that effect.

I explained exactly what I felt: to follow Beazley with anyone but a first-rate classical scholar would be to lower the standing of the Chair more than was anyhow inevitable. I afterwards wrote to Walter amplifying this - that my defective scholarship was only partly due to the First War, that I was now too old, had not lectured for some years, and had failed to keep up with all that had been written even on sculpture, my own speciality, and that this would be evident in discussions with visiting scholars or in giving tuition to advanced students. What assets I had - à love for ancient artefacts, a wide knowledge of sculpture and a fair judgement of genuineness and quality - were only marginally relevant to the exercise of a professorship. I also urged the superior claims of a younger man.

Walter replied with a very kind letter, and also came to see me again; he then invited Dorothy and me to stay with him and his wife Noel, an old friend from the British School at Rome, for the week-end.

I finally agreed to stand, still with some reluctance; looking back now, both Dorothy and I are immensely grateful for his persuasiveness, since our subsequent years in Oxford were full of many different kinds of happiness.

Chapter XI

Return to Oxford, Lincoln Professorship

THERE NOW FOLLOWED the usual problem of finding somewhere to live. We had sold High and Over and had been living in a pleasant flat in Craven Hill, near Paddington, convenient for Kensington Gardens, and, by Tube, for the British Museum. The prospect of a house in North Oxford had no attractions: we looked at several there, mostly impossible, and found one that might have been just tolerable, though clearly not ideal. The College then offered us the Manor House at Iffley, a couple of miles south of Oxford. This was a curious building, with what was evidently an early structure somewhere in the middle; but it had been surrounded by various clumsy additions, resulting in a muddled plan. The price was not outrageous, but it was not low, because at that time the sale of all college properties was regulated by the Ministry of Agriculture, which was charged with ensuring that colleges did not dispose of them at excessively low prices for the benefit of their Fellows. When, however, we had an estimate of thousands of pounds simply for making the building weatherproof, we realized that we could not meet the expense of the thorough renovation and modification that would have been necessary.

Then came a wonderful stroke of good luck, brought about by Philip, who was an undergraduate at Brasenose. He had noticed that another house in Iffley was to be sold by auction in the near future. He looked at it and told Dorothy, who also went to see it. She took one look through the garden gate at its situation, and decided that we must have it if we possibly could: when I saw it I fully agreed with her. It was a mid-Victorian house, not in good repair and of unprepossessing appearance, but set in a splendid position just below Iffley Lock, with a garden terraced down to the river which bounded it on the west. It was called the Mill House, because Iffley Mill, burnt down in 1908, had stood in what was now the north-west corner of its garden. The house was of brick, but the builder, influenced no doubt by Ruskin's Oxford, had inserted, in stone, Gothic relieving arches over two of the windows: otherwise the general feeling, in its simplicity, was of the earlier nineteenth century. The rooms of the original building and of later additions all seemed to have been planned on a module of fourteen feet: fourteen feet square is a decent size for an ordinary bedroom, and 14' × 28' are pleasant proportions for a sitting-room; while almost all the windows were placed to give a view over the river. We found it a delightful house to live in, and we enjoyed it for about eighteen years. The garden especially had great possibilities, as we were to discover, and we remodelled it to a more interesting plan.

The Mill House at Iffley, near Oxford.

There was one strange feature in the house, a spring in the cellar which had been enclosed in a square tank of brick. The surface of the water was normally a foot or two below the level of the floor, and there must have been some hidden overflow which we never found; but with the winter rains the level would rise every year until the whole cellar was flooded to a depth of three or four inches, with the result that the lower part of the supports to the wooden shelves with which it had been fitted had rotted away at that level, and naturally the cellar was unusable then. I found that someone had installed a length of hose which could be made to act as a siphon and carry off this overflow through a window into the garden. This was a poor makeshift, and since the cellar floor was some feet above the level of the main lawn in the garden, it seemed possible to convert the water-supply from the siphon into a fountain; and this we were able to do, and produce a jet up to twelve inches high. (A refinement halfway down in the form of a tank from which the water then fell by gravity made the system self-regulating: it never failed and never froze because the water was at an earth temperature of about 50 degrees.) We then successfully cast in concrete a fountain-basin, using an umbrella as a mould, and created a charming fountain in the middle of the lawn; the overflow formed a stream in the orchard below, then a twelve-foot-long pool fringed with water iris, and finally discharged into the river. In a bank at one end of the garden was another spring, a mere trickle, but enough to supply a narrow curved pool about thirty feet long which we made round one corner of the lawn, matching it with a flower-bed of similar shape at the other corner to balance it.

In the Mill House we had a pleasant little community, with Philip and two of his friends from Brasenose lodging with us: both admirable people of different characters, and rowing men, but highly intelligent. Philip himself had coxed the Brasenose boat in Eights.

Academically I had a somewhat stormy entry to my new post. Before my appointment there had been some dissatisfaction among the four professors of art and archaeology about their access to objects in the Ashmolean. They held that since it was a University museum its first aim should be to provide material for University teaching; whereas it had developed not only into a museum of international reputation, which was all to its credit, but had also become a museum for the city of Oxford, which, finding that a service which it should have provided itself was being given free by someone else, was only too happy to economise.

Professor Edgar Wind, teaching the History of Art, found that he had difficulty in showing – for instance – artists' original drawings to his students, except under glass; whilst Christopher Hawkes, European Archaeology, and Ian Richmond, Archaeology of the Roman Empire, met similar though more easily solu-

The Ashmolean Museum, Oxford

ble difficulties. In my own Department I found that John Beazley, who had immensely enriched the collection of classical antiquities both by gifts, expert advice on purchases, and general scientific rearrangement, had to wait on the convenience of Museum staff, who might not be free to open a show-case when he needed to teach or to examine a particular piece; not being aggressive he had allowed this system to become firmly established.

The solution was not easy, for the Museum staff were scanty, and it was, after all, their responsibility to see that objects were not damaged or lost; if there was a mishap when they were not there they would still be held responsible. Nevertheless, it was clear that there could have been some simpler arrangement by which Beazley could have had a case-key, kept securely with the other keys, to give him ready access to objects he needed for teaching. It was not quite so simple in the Department of Fine Art, where inexperienced students, if not strictly supervised, might have been allowed to finger and perhaps damage irreparably drawings by old masters.

Anyhow, we four professors now came together and drafted a document setting out our difficulties and possible improvements. Although its tone was moderate it became known, one might almost say notorious, as "The Memorandum of the Four Professors", and seems to have caused a good deal of dissension among both the staff and the Visitors, the governing body of the Museum. I don't know that anything positive resulted, but there was more realisation that some changes were needed, and I don't remember having any difficulties myself, perhaps because my teaching was not so thorough as Beazley's.

I had now another and more urgent preoccupation; this was the new gallery for the exhibition of the collection of plaster-casts of ancient sculpture. The site was beside the museum on the north, and had been planned originally to have a frontage on St Giles', but there had been difficulty in acquiring the freehold of the shops which occupied that frontage, and it was decided to cut down the gallery by a third, postponing its completion to a later date when the site could be fully occupied. I knew what such a postponement meant, namely that the gallery would probably never be completed, and anyhow not in my lifetime. This was a great pity, for a gallery of the full size would have allowed a perfect exhibition of the casts the University possessed, but, truncated, would inevitably lead to awkward and unsightly overcrowding. My appointment was just in time, for with the help of Donald Harden, the Keeper of Antiquities who had done the preliminary planning, we were able to modify the building in such a way as to provide a little more space for exhibits. The building was on two floors, but the upper floor – at ground level – was lofty, and I suggested that we should insert a mezzanine over half of it. This proved most successful; the mezzanine not only provided more space, but enhanced the interest of the interior, suggesting as it did a kind of quarter-deck, with a view over the rest of the gallery. We agreed on other improvements: sub-divisions of the space on the lower floor – a semi-basement – to give reserves and a laboratory; a powerful lift, able to take tall and heavy casts, with a large service entrance for the same reason; and in order to

*The Old Cast Gallery,
Ashmolean Museum*

avoid clutter with light-pendants, I suggested that we should combine the powerful electric top-lights with the circular skylights which were one of the main sources of light by day.

A collection of old plaster-casts is one of the most depressing sights possible to imagine, and a powerful deterrent for any newcomer to the study of ancient sculpture. Those in the Ashmolean, a large assemblage which had been steadily augmented by Percy Gardner, were not neglected; they had been faithfully dusted year after year, but they had become increasingly discoloured, and no-one knew how to clean them. Washing tended to dissolve the surface, and painting added another coat over the dirt; both methods, each in its own way, falsified the true modelling. John Boardman (then Assistant Keeper in the Ashmolean) discovered in a German periodical a note that a cast-gallery there had found a method of cleaning by applying a solution of starch; and it was, incidentally, an interesting sidelight on Nazi preparations for war that, two years before it broke out, they had put an embargo on the use of wheat starch for this purpose, and a switch had been made to potato starch. In the Ashmolean the need was urgent in view of the move to the new gallery, although any treatment was bound to continue long after the move had been made. It would in fact be a colossal task taking several years, since every inch of every statue and relief would have to be examined and treated, often more than once. But luck was with us.

Working at University College in London there had been a Jordanian student of archaeology named Mohamed Saleh. He was no ordinary student, but a trained field archaeologist, who had learned his craft under the tuition of Gilbert Harding, the English field-director there. In ruling circles in Jordan it so happened that there were two powerful and rival families, the rivalry between them being sometimes so bitter that one of the two was obliged to go into exile. To the family which had now been driven out Mohamed Saleh belonged, and he was spending his enforced exile in improving his archaeological training, in which one desirable skill is that of making casts in plaster and other materials. In order that he might acquire it the British Museum had agreed with University College to allow him to work in the Moulders' Shop, which was under the control of my Department. His frank and friendly nature soon made him at home there, and he became a welcome and skilful assistant to the two Prescotts, father and son, who were the chief moulders. He was not, however, a British subject, and although he might have been employed on a temporary basis since there was plenty of work to do, he could not have occupied an established post. I remembered this, and thought that he might be willing to come to Oxford and work on our casts; he and I liked each other, and he was grateful for the help that I had been able to give him in various ways in London. He consented to come. The results were more successful than we could possibly have hoped, for he proved to possess just those qualities that were needed – skill in diagnosing the problems and devising and applying remedies, an extremely careful touch, and infinite patience – for the new process, spectacularly successful in straightforward cases, was not miraculous, and it naturally could not be trusted to cope automatically with every variation of surface on old casts which, apart from accretions of dirt, had in the past been treated with paint, oil, shellac, or otherwise doctored in the hope of making them presentable.

The process consisted of making a thick solution – the thickness decided by trial and error – of potato starch, painting or plastering it over every inch of the surface of the statue, leaving it for twelve hours or so to dry, and then peeling it off. If the cast had been in untreated plaster and had simply sucked dirt and dust, as it was apt to do, right into its own pores, however discoloured it appeared to be, the starch had the ability to suck the dirt out and absorb it. The result could be amazing. If, however, the cast had already been treated in some way with paint or other sealer, possibly only in parts, it might resist the treatment and might emerge patchy and unsightly or even completely unaffected, thus demanding some special treatment. Mohamed Saleh persevered for years with this often monotonous task, and when a cast had been treated satisfactorily he gave it a coat of colourless varnish with an eggshell finish which is pleasing in itself and means that the surface is washable.

When the new gallery was completed it was time to transfer the collection there. Casts are not easy things to move because, although most of them are not heavy, they are extremely fragile, especially at the knees, the ankles and the projecting arms and hands. Thus one does want to avoid shifting them about too often, even though Percy Gardner had had the excellent idea of fitting all the bases with castors to make close comparisons possible. My secretary at this time was Mrs Young, efficient, practical, and a skilful artist. She made a scale-model of the two main floors of the cast gallery and we then cut cards, also to scale, for every cast, placing it in a position I judged appropriate in the model. Thus, when the movers began, they knew exactly where each piece should go. The result has been to create a pleasant exhibition, not as comprehensive as one would like it to be, but useful for teaching and of interest to art students generally and to the public at large. Such collections will never be formed in the future, because, apart from the great expense of casting and transport, most museums are now unwilling to have their statues moulded.

The 'New' Cast Gallery, Ashmolean Museum.

CHAPTER XI

I had been holding the Lincoln Chair for just under three years when there happened something that for its sheer unexpectedness passed anything I had ever experienced. The Warburg Institute was a German foundation set up to study the survival of ancient culture in succeeding centuries, and its fine library had been brought to England in 1933 when the Nazis were in power, just in time to escape an embargo on such exports, and had been housed temporarily in Thames House under the auspices of Lord Lee of Fareham and the University of London. Later in the thirties George Hill had presented a memorandum, which I signed with him, to Lord Macmillan, who was then Chancellor of the University, urging the desirability of the University adopting it as one of its central activities; and this was eventually done with great success.

I had naturally been interested in it from the beginning, had continued to serve on the Managing Committee, and had often discussed learned matters with Fritz Saxl its first Director, and Gertrud Bing his Deputy, both first-rate scholars and delightful friends. Saxl died in 1948 and was succeeded by Henri Frankfort, who died only a few years later; and although, since we now lived in Oxford, I did not often attend meetings of the Managing Committee, on this occasion I did because I was interested to know who would be appointed as his successor.

I came into the Committee Room ten minutes before the meeting. There seemed to be some embarrassment, and the Chairman, Professor Edna Purdie, beckoned

Bernard and Dorothy in the garden of the Mill House in 1968.

to me and asked if I would mind going away for a quarter of an hour; I had no idea why. When I came back I was astounded to be told that they were proposing to offer me the Directorship. I at once explained that I was happily settled in Oxford and could not possibly accept it; but they asked me to think it over. This I did, and reached the same conclusion, in spite of receiving kind letters from the Chairman of the Committee, from the Warburg Trustees, and from Gertrud Bing. To her I had explained in detail my unfitness for the task, which was to supervise a body of scholars devoted to the most meticulous research into subjects of which I knew virtually nothing. Her letter was most friendly and persuasive, and if anything could have moved me to accept, it would have been this.

There was a delightful outcome of the whole affair. When I declined, Gertrud Bing herself was appointed and made an outstanding success as Director; I cannot conceive why they can ever have wanted anyone else.

My professorship, otherwise uneventful, did I think serve to soften the loss the university suffered by Beazley's retirement. He and Lady Beazley continued to live and work in Oxford. She died in 1967 and I gave him all the help I could until his death in 1970. My time was also saddened by the death of Llewellyn Brown, my Reader, a loyal colleague and excellent archaeologist. He had just completed his book *The Etruscan Lion* (the lion in Etruscan art) which will be a standard work, and happily his line of study has been continued by his widow Ann, who is an Assistant Keeper in the Ashmolean. John Boardman succeeded Llewellyn as Reader, and has now become the Lincoln Professor. The university has been fortunate in having such able men as Martin Robertson, who succeeded me when I retired at the age-limit in 1961, together with Boardman, to carry on the Beazley tradition, and the possession of the Beazley Archive will always make Oxford the main centre for the study of Athenian vase-painting.

Chapter XII

Retirement from Oxford

Aberdeen

In the same year I was invited by the University of Aberdeen to hold a newly-established Chair of Greek Art and Archaeology. A sum of money had been left some years ago by the Professor of Greek, John Harrower, to found a professorship, but the university had not acted immediately, and by the time they had got round to it the value of money had fallen so much that they were not able to establish a full-time post, but only what was in effect a lectureship, although it bore the higher title; and it was to be held for one term each year by a visiting scholar. This was a most interesting post, for although on the literary side of the classics the tuition and the library had been well kept up, little had been done for archaeology, and it was necessary to expand the library and to build up a reasonably comprehensive collection of slides. I had brought a number of my own slides with me and found a photographer to produce new ones quickly.

I had a warm welcome and every possible help from the academic staff. I lived in a newly-built hostel, Crombie Hall, within a stone's throw of King's College, the older part of the University where my lectures were to be given. They were in fact in the Department of Anatomy, and will always be associated in my memory with the peculiar formalin-laden smell of the dissecting room next door to the theatre. Lanterns were something of a difficulty. I like to have two, in order to make comparisons, but it was not easy to find two with the same focal length, so that they could be operated from a single position; one had to be balanced precariously on a chair behind the other. These, however, are the kinds of anxiety common to all itinerant lecturers, as I was to discover when appointed to the Norton Lectureship in the United States two years later.

My first term as Geddes-Harrower Professor must have been considered a success, since I was asked to come again the following year. This time Dorothy came with me; again we were welcomed, made many friends, and shall always remember Aberdeen with affection. I have since been able to strengthen the archaeological side of the library there by giving them a number of books. The Professorship has flourished, and the list of holders now comprises a highly interesting selection of scholars from all over the world.

United States

Early in 1963 I made my first visit to the United States to deliver one of the

Semple lectures at the invitation of Jack Caskey of the University of Cincinnati, son of our friend L. D. Caskey of the Museum at Boston. In the same autumn I began the Norton Lecture Tour. This is the main travelling lectureship of the American Institute of Archaeology, and is arranged on a tight schedule – about twenty-four lectures in a month – which involves travelling by train or long-distance coach to various towns in New England, and then by air over much of the United States. Only two lectures, however, are needed, and I offered them, as alternatives, to the local archaeological societies.

It was now that I enjoyed time after time the warm and generous hospitality of the Americans, their enthusiasm and their lively and intelligent thirst for knowledge. In the event all the travelling went smoothly, but I had not dared contemplate what would have happened had I missed a day – through illness or one of the mishaps of travel – since it would have disrupted not one lecture only but the whole programme. The hazards were those common to all itinerant lecturers, in whatever country, when they are visiting local societies, since the arrangements are often made by those who have never themselves lectured and are therefore unaware of some of the elementary needs; for instance some means of excluding daylight when necessary; a firm reading-desk with a subdued light; a firmly-based lantern which fits the slides and throws an image which fits the screen, some means of communication, other than verbal, between lecturer and slide-operator, and an operator who has done it before and does not need to have it explained that there are seven wrong ways of inserting a slide; a reasonably light pointer (I was once given an iron bar too heavy to hold out); the screen within reach, and no obstruction between it and the lecturer. I found that it was essential to settle all these points with my host well before the lecture, and made a list of them to give him which proved remarkably effective. I had a few mishaps: once only a lantern bulb exploded; once only did I have a slide essential to the thread of the lecture permanently lost in the dark; and once only did I have an almost invisible wooden Corinthian column in the fairway between my desk and the screen.

One hazard I had not anticipated was competition from other entertainments, but I found that at Dartmouth a meeting at the same time was being held for Malcolm X, a celebrated coloured agitator; and the climax came at San Diego where, walking through the town in the afternoon, I saw a poster advertising contests between Female Pygmy Wrestlers. I had never heard of such beings before, and might have been tempted to go and see them if it had not exactly coincided with my own performance. However, I was able to tell my Chairman, and this was the highlight of his introductory speech.

Some other common disasters I did avoid. I did not see all my carefully arranged slides spilt in disorder on the floor; I did not see them dissolve one by one in the heat of the lantern; I did not have a breakdown of all the electricity; and I met with such universal kindness and consideration that any failure to give satisfaction, for whatever reason, was doubly painful.

Two other major calamities of an unusual kind I also escaped. These were told me by Professor Gjerstad, a Swedish friend, who had a fine stock of such horror-stories. One was of a colleague who had his complete set of slides slip through a porthole into the harbour just as he was setting out on an overseas tour. The other may be well-known – it has even appeared in a book of anecdotes – but it should certainly be preserved for posterity. The lecture was to be given in a brand-new fully-automated lecture hall in California, and when the lecturer went to look at it the morning before his lecture, his sponsor proudly showed him how perfectly it was fitted out. There was a splendid desk, with a row of buttons on each side. "This one," he said, "closes the window-blinds, this one dims the lights, this one extinguishes them, this one changes your slides, and this revolving one works your electric pointer. You needn't worry about the others, they don't really concern you." At the lecture all went well at first; after his opening remarks he blacked out the room successfully, and the first slide, and others, duly appeared when he pressed the button. After a while he became so absorbed in his subject that he leaned forward and rested his elbows on the desk, unfortunately also on both rows of buttons. There was a powerful grinding noise and the whole audience slowly sank out of sight; simultaneously, sections of a dance-floor closed in over their heads, and in exactly a minute he found himself alone in an empty ballroom. "What did he do?" I asked Professor Gjerstad: "What could he do?" he answered, "I think he went home."

HAWAII AND JAPAN

We had arranged the lecture-tour in such a way that it ended in San Francisco, where Dorothy was to fly out from England to meet me; from there we were to join Philip and his family on Hawaii.

Philip had taken a First in Zoology in 1957 and had almost at once been chosen as a member of the Centenary Expedition of the British Ornithologists' Union to Ascension Island, where for eighteen months he made a study of the seabirds there. In 1960 he married, at Iffley, Myrtle Goodacre, also an expert on birds. They lived in a flat above us in the Mill House until early 1963 and their first child, Anna, had been born there in November 1962. Philip's appointment in Hawaii was sponsored by the University of Yale and he was to use it as a base for periodic expeditions to Christmas Island, primarily to investigate the effects on the animal population of the explosion of a nuclear device some years before.

Christmas Island is on the Equator in the Pacific, and thus a counter-part to Ascension Island – also on the Equator but in the Atlantic – where some of the findings of his intensive study of the bird life had been published with Myrtle's collaboration. This was a fine opportunity to extend his research, and Christmas Island being held by detachments of the British Combined Services, the Air Ministry in London allowed him to make occasional use of their shuttle-service from Honolulu.

Dorothy's flight was an exceedingly long one from London to San Francisco, and seemed longer because, flying westwards, the sun refused to set. In San Francisco we were reunited and had several happy days there. Thence to Hawaii, where, thanks to Philip and Myrtle, who met and garlanded us, we spent what was the most marvellous holiday we had ever enjoyed. Our pleasure and interest were immensely increased by having just read that excellent book, James Michener's *Hawaii*, which explains its history and development, how the various racial groups had arrived, and how they lived together in harmony.

Honolulu was just beginning to be fully developed as a modern tourist resort, and there was not yet quite the full range of lofty hotels which now crowd the water-front. Myrtle had cleverly found us a delightful hotel, which, because it occupied expensive land, has now probably disappeared; it consisted of a number of self-contained cottages dotted about a delightful garden. Myrtle had prepared ours with a vase of Strelitzia ("Bird of Paradise") flowers, the first we had ever seen, and a fine selection of local fruits; and the whole area was pervaded by the cooing of innumerable doves. It was magical.

The charms of Honolulu need no elaboration, and we enjoyed them all – the climate with its glorious trade-winds, the scenery, the great rollers and the surfing, the beaches, and the food. Honolulu is on the island of Oahu, among the other delights of which were plantations of pineapple and sugar, rain-forests, and an aquarium where dolphins were being trained. Philip and Myrtle had arranged, after a few days there, a tour to two of the other islands of the Hawaiian group, Maui, and Hawaii itself, known as the Big Island. We flew to Maui and on the first afternoon went to the famous old whaling port of Lahaina. Next morning Philip, who had hired a car at the airport, took us all, with Anna, now just over a year old, up Mount Haleakala, an extinct volcano. We raced against the cloud which often shrouds the summit; it was clear, so that we could look right across the vast crater, seven miles in diameter. Then we flew on to Hawaii, which has an active crater full of molten lava, many other craters active in various ways, such as geysers, fumaroles; a lava tunnel – all on the slopes of a great central mountain, also volcanic but now extinct. On Hawaii is the bay where Captain Cook was killed, and many exquisite beaches, valleys and waterfalls; here we spent two nights, not in a hotel but in rest-houses ten thousand feet up on the mountain-side.

Our plans now were to fly on to Japan and join there a cargo-ship of the Blue Funnel Line, the *Perseus*, on which we had booked a passage back to England. We flew to Tokyo, then by the famous fast train, passing Fujiyama, to Kyoto; but here we had a shock – there was a telegram in the hotel telling us to embark immediately, since the ship was sailing two days early because it was the Japanese New Year when things were at a standstill. We soon came to realise the system on which these cargo steamers worked, and were helped in this by talks with an official of the Company, who, on retirement, had been given a world voyage for himself and his wife; he explained the admirable organization of the Company, which has its own training schools for officers and crew.

The ships, which to an outsider look rather old-fashioned, are extremely sturdy and fitted with powerful engines. It often amused us to see the *Perseus* overtaking with ease elegant liners which to the layman looked far speedier. The point is that if a ship can make three trips to the Far East and back in a year, instead of two, the Company makes more in proportion; but it does depend on perfect planning so that the cargo is ready at a port and can be loaded or unloaded in the minimum time, thus our premature departure from Yokohama saved two days. The ports of call are determined by whether there is cargo to be taken up or unloaded, and the time spent there by how long it took. For instance, we stayed ten days in Hong Kong, one in Penang and two in Colombo; and this uncertainty, provided one is in no hurry to get home, adds to the enjoyment of the voyage. The accommodation for the twenty or thirty passengers is more luxurious than would be possible on an ordinary liner; ours was virtually a state-room, on deck level, with bedroom, sitting-room, bath and lavatory. But cargo clearly came first, and passengers were apt to be an embarrassment – perhaps less profitable – hence the gradual phasing out of this, the most delightful form of travel.

Eventually we arrived in Liverpool, having had a perfect journey except for a battering in the Gulf of Lyons, which was made less severe because the weight of the cargo means that the ship rides with great steadiness.

Bodrum and Greece

In the summer of 1964 I was able to do some constructive archaeology. The Mausoleum of Halicarnassus, the tomb of Mausolos, Ruler of Caria in the second quarter of the fourth century BC, has since given its name to all grandiose tombs. The site, which is on the coast of Asia Minor, north of Rhodes, had been excavated by a predecessor as Keeper of Greek and Roman Antiquities at the British Museum, C. T. Newton, in 1856, and the remains of its sculptures are now in the Department there. One of my Assistant Keepers, Donald Strong, and I had been studying them for publication, and we thought there was a possibility of finding more of them in the walls of the Castle of St Peter at Bodrum (the modern name of the place) which had been built at the entrance of the harbour by the Knights of St John, when threatened by a Turkish invasion. They had used vast quantities of masonry from the Mausoleum which they had discovered nearby, and had even built some of the sculptures into the Castle walls as decoration.

A Danish archaeologist, Kristian Jeppesen, had also been studying the Mausoleum, chiefly for its architecture, and we suggested to him that we should all three go to Bodrum together and see what we could find. We were cordially received there by the Turkish Keeper of the Museum in the Castle, Bey Halouk, and we did actually find – or rather Jeppesen did – a new piece of sculpture embedded. It was several feet of the frieze showing Greeks in battle with the Amazons, of which we already had many slabs in the British Museum. When we had extracted it I saw at once that it was of the same style as three slabs, joining one another, which Newton had discovered lying in a row in his excavation; that same evening we found that it would actually fit the broken end of Newton's right-hand slab, and would complete the composition neatly.

This was a nice discovery, and would by itself have justified our visit, but Kristian and Donald were also able to observe or check a number of other points about the remains of the Mausoleum, both on its own site and in the Castle, and Kristian has since headed a Danish expedition which has completely excavated the site.

Whilst we were in Bodrum we all three wanted to take the opportunity of visiting the site of ancient Cnidus which is about thirty miles further south and – since it was almost at the tip of an exceedingly long peninsula – by road, if roads had existed, the distance would have been no less than a hundred and twenty miles; so the only way was by sea. We spoke to Bey Halouk; he kindly agreed to arrange the hire of a boat, and the next morning we all met on the quay. The boat was ready; it was well kept, but evidently very old, the sails were patched and even the patches were patched. It had a small motor, and the boatman was workmanlike and friendly; so off we set, Bey Halouk coming with us. The wind was northerly, which suited us well. Our plan was to spend the day at Cnidus and wait until after sunset when, theoretically, the wind would drop and we should not have it against us on the return journey.

It was a pleasant trip, marred only by the fact that Donald was feeling very unwell, not seasick, but something more serious, as we were to discover the next day. After landing at Cnidus we had a look at the remains of the ancient city which is finely situated, with its two harbours, just to the south of the tip of the peninsula. It had been celebrated in antiquity and later by having bought the statue of Aphrodite by Praxiteles, which was the first classical Greek statue of a completely naked woman; the original had perished, but copies made in Roman times survive, and so do the scanty remains of the shrine in which it was set up. My own chief interest was not the city itself but a shrine of Demeter in a cleft of the hills half a mile away, where the face of the cliff above had been tooled smooth and a couple of rectangular niches, probably for statues, carved in it. In front of the cliff was a precinct sacred to Demeter, Persephone, and Pluto, God of the Underworld. Here Newton's excavation had revealed a good deal of broken sculpture including a fine seated statue of Demeter, of which he found first the body, and the head, which had been made separately, much later; both are in the British Museum. It was once suggested that the statue, of which I later published a detailed study, had fallen from one of the niches; but both were too shallow. I took some useful photographs of the cliff and the shrine, and we all met again on the main site towards sundown and re-embarked.

Further east, along the south side of the peninsula, is the famous Lion Tomb, a massive pyramidal structure of masonry originally surmounted by a colossal marble lion, which Newton found and transported to the British Museum. We sailed past it but did not land, and turned westward again intending to sail along the south bank of the peninsula, round Cape Krio, a splendid lofty headland at its western end; then head north for Bodrum. Although it was now past sunset the wind had not fallen as we hoped and was almost dead against us. Our tacking was not efficient and we were relying on the motor, but this was of very low power and it was disconcerting to see, by looking at the coast, that we were not

Modern relief (British Museum 673). This is one of several forgeries of the Parthenon Frieze which Bernard recognized.

going forwards but slightly backwards, and Cape Krio was as far off as ever. Mercifully the wind abated a little, and we eventually rounded the headland and made for home. It had turned rather cold, with a roughish cross-sea, and poor Donald was in misery, but we found that the boat was lined inside with a heavy canvas, so we lifted this at one point and tucked him in underneath where it was warmer, reaching Bodrum safely, thanks to some clever seamanship from our captain.

The next morning Donald was no better and Kristian went off to find a doctor. He went to the local club where some friendly Turkish citizens had made us welcome, got in touch with a doctor there and brought him along to our guesthouse, together with his twelve-year-old son to act as interpreter. This was a good idea since neither the doctor nor we were fluent enough in French or German and the little boy spoke good clear English. The doctor soon saw what was wrong; Donald had a stone, and he drew and gave me to keep a pretty diagram of Donald's inside, showing where it was and what he hoped would happen to it. It looked rather as if this was a common affliction there, for not only did the doctor diagnose it at once, but gave us the address of a chemist where a remedy could be had – unexpected in a town so small as Bodrum; this, together with copious draughts of the local soda-water, eased Donald's condition within twenty-four hours. There was a happy sequel; the doctor refused to accept any payment whatever, but Donald, when he got back to England, was able to send him a parcel of books that would be of interest both to him and to the boy.

One other thing I had long wanted to do it was now possible to combine with the visit to Bodrum, namely to publish the sculptures of the temple of Zeus at Olympia, the largest and finest body of early Classical Greek sculpture; to illustrate every piece with a brief commentary in order to make them better known to students and to the general public.

The original publication by the German excavators was a model, both for the speed with which it was produced, its thoroughness and its quality; but it was now a century old, a rare and precious book, indispensible for scholarly research but quite unsuitable for general use. In 1936 Gerhart Rodenwaldt had published an excellent short study, illustrated with spectacular photographs by Walter Hege. But Hege's methods had one grave defect. In order to lighten difficult shadows or soften extreme contrasts he used large sheets of silvered cardboard from which he reflected the sunlight onto the sculpture, moving the sheet about during the exposure. This resulted in smooth and attractive pictures which naturally give little idea of the actual surface of the marble – in fact make it look much like soap. Alison Frantz of Princeton, attached to the American team excavating the Agora at Athens, had shown herself to be the finest living photographer of Greek sculpture, and she and I agreed that we would make a new joint publication; the Phaidon Press in London, still a British firm at that time, were glad to co-operate, so we went ahead.

There was one difficulty: since the time of the German excavation a number of new pieces of sculpture from the temple had been discovered or identified, and it was important to include these in our book. The Greek superintendent of antiquities in the Peloponnese was Dr Nicolas Yalouris, who had made some new discoveries himself, and we thought that the best – indeed the obvious – way of meeting the difficulty was to ask him to join us and write part of the book. He agreed, and Alison Frantz and I went to Olympia together at the beginning of June 1964 to find out exactly what the conditions were, and to take some trial photographs. These were developed and printed whilst I was in Bodrum, and when I came back from there we again went together to Olympia and finished the photographing – over two hundred pictures in all. I cannot imagine a happier collaboration; we both knew what was wanted and how to get it done in the quickest way, and any discussion about the exact view or other problem, such as lighting, could be settled without delay. It was amusing too, for some of the sculptures being nine or ten feet tall and mounted on a base three feet high called for some lofty structures to support the camera – this was before the days of the 'zoom' lens – and we needed many close-ups and details. So our improvised supports of tables and chairs often had an unstudied charm, and indeed appealed to the groups of school-children who are systematically brought to the museum by their teachers, perhaps more than the sculptures did. The processing of the photographs was excellently done at the headquarters of the American excavation in Athens, and the results were as near perfect as one could wish; Phaidon printed them well and produced a most attractive book.

YALE

Towards the end of 1964 I was asked to accept a Visiting Professorship at Yale. Philip and his family were settled there, so that when I agreed, Yale had two Professors Ashmole. Had I known the state of the Department of Archaeology I should have been less willing, for so far as I could infer without access to explicit information, it was riven by feuds and dissensions. The professor, lately dead, had concentrated on Papyrology to the almost complete neglect of any other aspect of classical archaeology, and the departmental library as well as the collection of slides was grossly inadequate. The library arrangements were inherently awkward, as indeed they often are in other universities, because of a conflict of interests between the departmental library and the main library of the university, here about half-a-mile distant, the awkwardness being accentuated by there being no facilities for lecturing or taking classes within the main library. Many archaeological publications are of great size and weight and they had to be conveyed from the main library to the Department in advance. There were no service staff who could do the carrying, so that it was necessary for the professor to be exceptionally able-bodied.

Within the Department, so difficult to reconcile were the various interests, that a professor of classics from Harvard had been appointed to straighten things out; and another personal difficulty – apart from the resentment felt for a professor from the rival university of Harvard and for another outsider imported from England – was the presence in the Department of a number of young graduates for whom there was no prospect of a teaching appointment at Yale itself. This is a drawback of the American system (not unknown now in Britain also, where the number of post-graduate students has vastly increased) because there comes a moment when many of those who have been in direct competition with one another for some years, have to be ejected. As a newcomer I had little idea of the comparative merits of the various graduates, but I was able to secure one from relegation by a protest to the Harvard Professor; and the choice has since been amply justified.

Nevertheless our stay at Yale was enjoyable, and was made more so because we lived in a new college, Morse College (named after the inventor of the Morse code) of which the head and his wife, Dr and Mrs Patterson, were exceptionally congenial; and, as in any institution, the personality of the head affects its whole atmosphere.

On the floor below us too was another visiting Professor from Oxford, Hugh Lloyd-Jones, Professor of Greek, with whom we became very friendly, and it was he who, with Isobel Henderson (Fellow of Somerville and a visiting lecturer) arranged for a most promising student, Donna Kurtz, who had come from Cincinnati to work in my Department, to be accepted in Oxford. She is a first-rate scholar and has since become Keeper of the Beazley Archive there, which she manages with outstanding success.

Being at Yale gave me an opportunity I had long wanted. In the Museum of Fine Arts at Boston there is a marble relief consisting of a front panel nearly five feet wide and two wings projecting backwards from it. Its shape is unique except for that of the so-called Ludovisi Throne in Rome, which is one of the most admired Greek sculptures in the world, dating from the second quarter of the fifth century BC. The Boston relief is not only similar in shape, it is almost the same in measurements; but the style, though similar too in a general way, has some unusual features. It was said to have been unearthed in Rome, near where the Ludovisi Throne had been discovered about ten years before; this was on the site of the Gardens of Sallust, famous in antiquity for their beauty and for containing works of Greek art said to have been plundered from the province of Numidia – much the same as modern Tunisia, west of the Sicilian Channel – of which he had been Governor.

The Boston relief was a puzzle, and from its first appearance had been attacked as a forgery, sometimes by reputable critics, sometimes by others less responsible whose prime weapon was innuendo. I had always believed in its authenticity, and this seemed a good opportunity to defend it. E. P. Warren had bought it from the Ludovisi Collection in 1896, and had exported it with an official permit to Lewes House in Sussex, where he then lived. (He almost obtained a permit to purchase and export the Ludovisi Throne too, which, in view of its subsequent fame, now seems incredible.) Warren had a factotum, Frank Gearing, a skilled and experienced technician, well used to handling antiquities, and in the twenties I had long talks with him about the Boston relief. He explained that when it first arrived in Lewes it was heavily encrusted with an earthy deposit – a photograph showing its condition still exists – and that under Warren's instructions he had for many months worked steadily over the surface of the three reliefs (the front and the two wings) with a razor-blade, carefully removing the deposit, since this proved to be the only way of cleaning it without damaging the surface of the marble.

The kind of deposit generally accepted as the most certainly ancient is the "root-mark", and genuine root-marks have never (so far as I can discover, and I have seen many attempts) been successfully imitated by the forger. They are caused in the following way: roots are slightly acid, they etch the surface of the marble and stain it as they decay; calcium from the marble is re-precipitated and builds up a hard deposit preserving the shape of the original roots; it is difficult to remove, and even when removed by physical means tends to leave a stain.

Having had Gearing's account – and naturally he had not the slightest doubt of its genuineness – I assumed that, somewhere on the surface of the relief, at least some root-marks could still be found; and this indeed proved to be so in one or two places which had been difficult for him to reach. Further, assuming that the lower bed of the relief would not have been cleaned at all, I asked Cornelius Vermeule, our friend who was keeper of antiquities in the Boston Museum, whether he would have the whole block of marble lifted so that its lower bed could be examined; this he kindly did.

It was most fortunate that the laboratory of the Boston Museum was in the charge of a friend of long standing, William Young. He was an Englishman who had been trained at the Ashmolean Museum in Oxford by his father, also William Young; he was therefore known as "young Young", to distinguish him from "old Young" his parent. He had migrated to America to take the appointment at the Boston Museum and had been a great success there; he was the perfect colleague.

When the relief was lifted – a formidable task because of its weight – its lower bed was found to be in virtually the same condition as when it was excavated, and Young's tests proved that it was covered with genuine root-marks. He made tests of deposits elsewhere on the relief, and was able to compare them with samples of deposits on the Ludovisi Throne in Rome which Dr Harold Plenderleith obtained, and which proved to be closely similar. Young also made various scientific tests, petrographic and spectrographic, and together we published our results in the Museum's Bulletin. Our proofs may not be conclusive – although we think them so – but they come as near to certainty as is possible with arguments about ancient sculpture. Others agreed, and A .R. Bellinger, the American numismatist, even exclaimed "They ought to give you the Freedom of the City!"

Chapter XIII

Paul Getty

IN THE LATE SUMMER OF 1970 I had a telephone call at the Mill House. "This is Paul Getty. Do you remember me?" "Yes, indeed I do: you came to look at the Elgin Marbles when we put them on show again." I had remembered the incident particularly well because I had been impressed by his genuine interest in and knowledge of Greek sculpture, and by the complete lack of interest shown by the charming woman who was with him. He went on, "Would you look at some sculptures for me in London?" "Yes, certainly," I said; and we made an appointment to meet at the showroom of a dealer in the West End.

This visit, although I did not realise it until some time afterwards, was the occasion for the most gross failure of judgement of which I have ever been guilty, and looking back I naturally try to explain it. The main reason was the old device employed by the coin-dealer in Athens many years before – here a little more complex but basically the same - namely, that after being confronted with a number of obvious forgeries, the eye over-reacts when presented with a really skilful one and tends to accept it. Here the shop was crowded with forgeries, the dealer was at my elbow most of the time with distracting sales-talk, and Mr Getty was waiting not far off. I normally like to look at an antiquity for hours, to think about it, and if possible to return to it again and again. But these are excuses, and not a valid defence.

I eventually selected a couple of the least pretentious pieces for purchase, a small circular ventilat-

J. Paul Getty, about 1970.

ing panel and an oblong panel with reliefs on both sides. These little marble panels were common enough in Roman times, and were usually carved by minor craftsmen with Dionysiac subjects. The circular one had a naked maenad, and I ought to have been suspicious of the higher polish on her body which made it look more attractive; but it was a slight piece and difficult to fault. Over the oblong panel I was more culpable: one side had a couple of Dionysiac masks - a common subject – but the other had an exceedingly rare one of which I knew only one other example. It was again Dionysiac, with Dionysus shown as young and naked, lying with one leg bent and laid on the thigh of Ariadne, who is sitting, fully clothed, with her hand holding out her veil in the conventional gesture of a bride. This scene was the same as that embossed on a large bronze mixing-bowl found in a tomb in Macedonia. I rashly assumed that since the bowl had been excavated as lately as 1960 it could hardly have been known to a forger: it was sheer carelessness that I did not check the exact dates and follow up this one obvious clue, to see whether a forger could possibly have copied it.

After our session at the dealer's, Mr Getty offered to drive me back to Paddington, and as we went along (driven by an admirable English chauffeur whom I afterwards came to know well, and whose unsolicited, shrewd, but always discreet information about the set-up at Sutton Place, where Mr Getty lived, was afterwards useful) he murmured something about an honorarium. I hadn't ex-

Mr Getty visiting an archaeological site, about 1970.

Sutton Place, Mr Getty's home in England, about 1970.

pected this, because I had regarded the whole thing as being on a friendly basis, so I said "No, don't worry about that; but if you like to send me some claret." The claret soon arrived, and this was the curious beginning of my happy relationship with Mr Getty up to the time of his death.

In the late autumn Mr Getty rang again, asking if I would go to Switzerland to look at some antiquities. I said "I wonder if I could think it over. It will be winter. I must ask my wife." "Oh, take your wife with you!" So I accepted, and Dorothy and I had not only this trip but a series of delightful visits to the Continent at Mr Getty's expense. We agreed that my task should be to report, about any antiquity, first its genuineness; second what exactly it was, whether Greek or Roman, original or copy; and third its condition. I would report its price, but not whether I thought this reasonable or excessive. Mr Getty preferred sculpture to vases, and although I examined a number of these he rarely bought any. Among the sculptures, he disliked anything funerary: this was a prejudice he shared with Randolph Hearst, his neighbour in California at San Simeon, where any mention of death was taboo. In fact I did persuade him to buy one or two particularly interesting grave-reliefs, but these were placed in the old stable when they arrived at Sutton Place. Altogether I bought on his behalf a splendid series of sculptures, of which any museum in the world might be proud; and this had been made easier because so many fine pieces had come onto the market during those five years, partly from the older private collections.

In all my dealings with him I was impressed by his courtesy, kindness and generosity, and especially by his genuine love for ancient art. He never saw his new museum, nor did I (although I knew the little gallery in Malibu that housed his earlier collection); but he took the keenest interest in the building, which was to be a replica of the great Villa dei Papiri at Herculaneum; and when I visited Sutton Place he would always show me on a model how far it had progressed.

Mr Getty would never buy anything which had been exported illegally from its country of origin. Here there are often some delicate distinctions to be made as to the exact meaning of the word "illegal"; and there is also a nice moral problem when an important group of objects, archaeologically connected with one another, is already on the market and will inevitably be dispersed and thus lost to scientific study in private collections. (Mr Getty himself decreed that his own acquisitions should always be accessible to scholars.) An excellent example of what I am sure is the correct procedure was when a museum in Britain decided to buy an entire series of architectural terracottas in order to prevent them being dispersed. A crucial situation of this kind soon occurred. A Swiss dealer offered some wall-paintings, and Mr Getty asked me to inspect them. They were in a secret location near the border with Italy; in itself suspicious. I spent many hours examining the hundreds of fragments into which they had been broken, and decided that they came from the painted plaster walls of no less than five rooms of a Roman house. They were of high though not the highest quality, and would have taken years to piece together again and place on exhibition. I also examined the plaster on which they were painted, and decided that they must have been detached from a building quite a short time ago; I suspected that the plaster contained pozzolana, which is of South-Italian volcanic origin. The inference was obvious, and I explained this to Mr Getty, telling him that on the one hand they would almost certainly be sold piecemeal if he did not buy them; on the other that, apart from the difficulties of restoring and exhibiting them in his museum, they were almost certainly clandestinely exported. This was a dilemma. He consulted his lawyers and decided against the purchase. I am sure he was right in the circumstances.

The solution for this difficult question, which affects every country, but particularly Italy, Greece, and Turkey, should be to recruit a sufficient number of Inspectors of Antiquities for the various ancient sites and the countryside generally - making sure that they are honest - to compensate generously the chance finders of antiquities if they report them, to tighten up the export regulations, issuing export permits, with corresponding taxes, for minor antiquities, and to punish any violations severely. It may be a counsel of perfection, given the difficulty of finding enough honest people, but it would be far more effective than pious resolutions by museums not to purchase illegal exports.

The Peristyle Garden of The J. Paul Getty Museum, Malibu, California

There now came perhaps the most tricky episode of all. A dealer in London offered Mr Getty a life-size head in bronze of the Doryphorus by Polycleitus, the Argive sculptor of the mid fifth century BC. The bronze original, long lost, representing a naked youth carrying a spear, must have been set up at one of the main athletic centres in Greece, probably Olympia. It was very famous in antiquity because it embodied a system of measurements relating the various parts mathematically to one another; and many ancient copies have survived, but almost all are in marble. A good copy in bronze would be of extreme rarity and would be a gem in any collection. This looked good, in fact an excellent copy, and I could not find any fault with its style. But the first question to consider was whether it could possibly be a forgery. Now the forger of a bronze can only produce it convincingly by taking a mould from some ancient piece and then casting the bronze from it. Any damage might well have been reproduced in the modern cast. I worked through every one of the ancient copies which I knew either at first hand or from publication in learned journals, but could not find any one which seemed likely to have served as a model. Another indication of antiquity is patina, that is to say a change in the colour of the bronze as the result of age, weathering or burial. Here there was no patina, but the surface appeared to have been gently worn away somehow, perhaps by weathering, perhaps through having lain in a river or lake, leaving the metal bright.

After a good deal of heart-searching, and assurances from the dealer about the source from which he had acquired it, I recommended it for purchase, and it was bought at a very great, though because of its rarity not excessive, price, in the region of half a million dollars, a huge sum even by Mr Getty's standards. It was selected for the cover picture of the catalogue for an exhibition of new acquisitions in Mr Getty's museum, and the book was already in production; but I had not given up working on the problem, and by the greatest good fortune came across a recent picture of a marble replica of the head of the Doryphorus of which I had not known before. It was not on exhibition, but in the storeroom of the Museum at Naples; and Naples, as I had realised all along, was the most likely place for any forgery to have been made, for the Neapolitans have a long history of excellent bronze-casting, and there is a well-known firm there which has for years been producing copies of objects found at Pompeii or Herculaneum so faithful that they have often deceived experts.

The question now was "Is there anything in the marble replica to suggest that it had been used to produce the newly-purchased bronze?" Fortunately there was. The marble had a slight flaw running vertically up the left cheek from the nostril to the eye, and on the bronze was a crack which might have resulted from it. The point of the chin was flatter than one would expect and this in the marble head turned out to be a restored patch. There was a second clue. The bronze, if genuine, would have been cut or broken from a complete statue. It included the whole of the neck and ended below in what looked like a fractured edge; but the general shape of the whole lower part resembled in an uncanny way the same part of the marble head. It was not an exact match, because the lower edge of the bronze was irregular, whereas that of the marble was smoothly finished; yet it was suggestive and did reinforce the other suspicion.

After thinking the whole problem over for a long time, I decided that the bronze must be false, and at once wrote a long report to Mr Getty giving all the facts in detail, then went to have a talk with him. As always, he was friendly and considerate, and took what must have been a sad disappointment without blaming me in any way, which he might reasonably have done.

In a sense my doubts were no more than doubts, impossible to confirm, and there now came the problem of how to produce proofs to support them powerful enough to convince the dealer that he must take the bronze head back and refund the money. There seemed to me to be two possibilities. One was the recently discovered method of testing the age of pottery by thermoluminescence, and I had noticed that inside the top of the head was a deposit which might be the remains of the clay core of the bronze when it was cast: if this proved to be modern it would imply that the bronze was too. Alas! When tested it was shown to be not fired clay but solidified mud.

The whole thing was made more difficult by the dealer having enlisted the help of Denys Haynes, my successor at the British Museum, and of his wife, both expert on bronzes. They both maintained that the bronze was genuine, and the dealer then produced a long document which he sent to Mr Getty, aimed at showing that it could not be a cast of the marble head in Naples. The arguments in this were mixed, one or two strong though not conclusive, others weak and in effect worthless. I commented on them in detail when asked by Mr Getty, and meanwhile went on with my search for solid evidence. There was one last possibility. The composition of ancient bronzes was rarely identical. Different alloys were used in different places with varying proportions of the basic materials, copper and tin, and traces of other metals; but some, e.g. zinc, were never present. Modern bronzes, on the other hand, are normally, in Italy at least, cast from practically identical alloys calculated to give the best technical results. An analysis of a sample from the head was made, and the alloy was found to be of the regular modern formula, unlike anything known in ancient bronzes. This was enough to convince everyone involved, and the dealer, an innocent party himself (so far as any dealer is ever innocent, for not one can be trusted about how he has acquired an object), admitted the error and refunded the money. It was an enormous relief.

Chapter XIV

Retirement in Scotland

AFTER HIS WORK ON CHRISTMAS ISLAND, Philip had been appointed to a Professorship at Yale. This he held for a little over seven years, and in 1971 it was drawing to an end. A Lectureship in Edinburgh was advertised and we sent the notice to him. He came over to Britain, was called for interview, and appointed to the post, which he took up early in 1972. He and Myrtle, now with a family consisting of two daughters, Anna and Leilani, and a son, Dominic, had decided that the children ought to be sent to one of the State Schools, and hearing that those in Edinburgh itself were of a relatively low standard because of the existence of good private schools there which tended to draw off the most promising pupils, they explored all the country within twenty-five miles of Edinburgh for somewhere to settle, and eventually found an abandoned mill cottage at Kidston, a couple of miles north of Peebles (the planning regulations forbade new building in untouched countryside).

The cottage, roofless but with stone walls still standing, lay within a few yards of Eddleston Water (which flows into the Tweed at Peebles) and of the disused railway line which used to run between Peebles and Edinburgh. Unfortunately, the bridge that carried the line across Eddleston Water had been removed, and since this would have provided the only access to the Peebles Road it was essential to replace it. The cottage had originally faced east, but Philip and Myrtle added a Y-shaped extension on the south. This was built of pinelogs, and gave them a large sitting-room including a kitchen, a workshop at the east end and two little studies at the west end. The old cottage was restored, and provided two bedrooms and a bathroom on the ground floor, and on the first floor several smaller bedrooms reached by a fine staircase of beech-wood which they designed and built with their own hands. They planned and constructed a new garden and outhouses, and planted many trees, both deciduous and conifers, which have since grown so well that they have had to be thinned only ten years later.

Dorothy and I felt that in our old age we should like to be within reach of one of our children and it seemed that Peebles was a possibility. We did not know the town at all, had indeed hardly heard of it. However, we came up to Peebles and stayed for some days in an hotel to see whether we should like to live there, found it delightful, and started looking for possible accommodation. The main feature of Peebles is Tweed Green, through which the river flows, and we decided that we should like to live actually on the Green, and, remembering how we loved the sun, decided that it ought to be on the north side facing south. We consulted Mr Fyfe, the solicitor who had helped Philip and Myrtle acquire Kidston Mill, and explained what we wanted. Naturally enough he thought this was likely to be pretty difficult, but suddenly remembered that there was a little development going on by the same local builder, James Clyde, who had restored the bridge and the cottage at Kidston. He had acquired a derelict building about sixty feet long which had a frontage of about forty feet on the Green. It was a solid stone structure with walls over a foot thick backing on to a house in Peebles High Street, which lies on a ridge of gravel roughly parallel with the Tweed. Within this shell (a wool warehouse that had been converted into a YMCA Hall), he had planned to build three flats, but the local planning committee had cut the number to two – which could thus be set far enough back from the road to allow parking space for two cars. At the back was a walled space for a garden surrounded by walls twenty feet high, the soil consisting of the rocks and gravel originally laid down by the river when in prehistoric times it was vastly greater than at present.

Dorothy and Bernard at Peebles near Edinburgh, 1983.

Of the two flats planned, one above the other, that on the first floor was definitely booked, but the one on the ground floor was not, and we promptly contacted the builder and put an option on it when it should be ready, which would be about a year ahead. The plan seemed excellent, and, with modifications arranged by Myrtle, has since proved so, with a due south aspect on the Green and sitting snugly insulated within the old stone walls.

Before leaving Iffley, and acting on a scheme proposed by our friend Ritchie Russell, we planned to sell the Mill House and its beautifully situated garden as a sheltered housing estate. We persuaded the Guardian Housing Association to whom we sold it below market price to employ one of the leading architectural firms who had already shown their talent for planning elsewhere. They started taking soundings in the garden to discover the position of the local rock which comes near the surface in some places. Owing, however, to determined opposition by one or two local inhabitants the very attractive scheme was finally turned

Dorothy on Tweed Green at Peebles, 1988.

down by the local authorities, with the result, which might have been foreseen, that the village has now been developed with much undistinguished building. Fortunately the Mill House was eventually acquired by Doctor Lawrence and his family, who fully appreciate it, so the site will not be spoiled.

Now for nearly ten years we have enjoyed living in Peebles, among its friendly and generous inhabitants. It is of the ideal size for a small country town. Everything one needs is within five minutes' walk, and its situation could hardly be bettered, since it is surrounded by the fine hills of the Borders, and, besides Tweed Green, with the river running through and often something to watch, there are three parks with many fine old trees, and ample space for every kind of sport. It has many local activities, and its traditional Festival, the Beltane. Here we have been able to watch our grandchildren growing up, both those near us at Kidston and, by mutual visits, those in Sussex and London, and have been happy to see their varied talents.

When I look back on my life I realise, as I have always done, that its main feature has been my extraordinary good fortune: in surviving at all, in my parents, in my friends of every kind - their early loss my great sadness - in my dearest wife and our happiest of marriages; in our healthy and talented children and grandchildren.

The Mill House at Iffley Lock on the River Thames, 1993.

Of gratitude for this I know of no more fitting expression than the prayer used in memorial services in Oxford,

> O Lord our Saviour, who has taught us that thou wilt require much of those to whom much is given, grant that we, whose lot is cast in so goodly an heritage, may strive together the more abundantly, by whatever means thou shalt ordain, to extend to others that which we so richly enjoy; and as we have entered into the labours of other men, so to labour that in their turn other men may enter into ours.

That theme everyone, whether Christian or not, can echo, and surely no scholar can forget.

Appendix I

Adventures of Air-crews of 84 Squadron

THIS IS A RECORD MADE by George Maurice, who was the Observer on MacDonald's aircraft on the flight of 84 Blenheim Squadron from Heliopolis to Sumatra. Miller was the Air-Gunner, Hughes and Collingwood passengers. Passmore was pilot of another aircraft, W/C Jeudwine CO of the Squadron. The account begins with the take-off from Lloknga, north Sumatra, with the intention of flying to Palembang, six hundred miles further south-east, where the Squadron was to be stationed. (ETA = estimated time of arrival).

23 January 1942.
Breakfast at Hotel at 06.00 hrs. Picked up ORs and back to Lhoknga, changing to Staff car on the way. Set off about 08.30 (to avoid Jap. reccos) and followed railway & coast to Medan – a meadow with only one length & that not very long. Parked a/c in the blazing sun and went for gen on edge of the wood. Arr. to fly to Palembang individually but no maps available except the sketch which Holland brought from Sambang and an even worse one held by Sgt Palmer. Our maps went as far as Pakan Baroe & we were told from thence we altered course about 6 degrees and the distance was 619 Kilometres. Our engine was overheating and when we had taxied out we shut off the engine for about 15 minutes. Passmore's port wheel went into a badly filled bomb hole and Fihelly had some engine trouble. However we took off about 13.30 hrs just skimming the trees with 9lbs boost. Climbed on track and on ETA were about 2 miles to the right of Pakan Baroe. We a/c correctly and ETA was about 18.00 hrs. At about 17.30 we passed over a large river with an island visible on our port side. As we had only just about enough daylight we did not investigate but soon after turned to port to rejoin the coast. By ETA there was no island in sight although we should not be more than 10-15 miles from our objective. The light was failing and Mac decided that he must put her down. We passed a river at whose mouth there was a small village visible. With little warning, Mac eased his stick forward, while I scrambled back to sit on Collingwood's toes. We landed smoothly on the mud patch between swamp and the sea and slid along our nose (wheels up of course). Suddenly the gun blister broke and we were blinded by stinking mud, but goggles protected my eyes. At first I thought we had gone under and struggled to reach the top hatch which was opened before landing. The other two, being higher, received

less mud and Mac was able to say: "All right! Keep still! We've got to get out first" or words to that effect. Subconsciously I must have realised that they were above the level of the mud and when Collingwood got out, I sat on his seat and lifted my goggles to find that there was only about 18" or 2ft of mud in the bottom of the nose, although everything had of course been covered with it by the first fountain that poured through. My exit from the plane was greeted with cheers; apparently I caught the dirt worse than anyone and had 'icicles' of it hanging from my helmet and goggles.

THE JOURNEY TO PALEMBANG: 23/1/42 TO 28/1/42.

23rd January.
The first thing was to inflate the dinghies (2) in case the a/c sank. One was punctured but the other was OK & we kept it on the wing still tied to the strut. We then took stock of the position. (although not tabulated at the time) we decided roughly:

1) As long as possible to stay on the a/c, because this seemed fairly stable and stuck in the mud and because the tree-lined shore was probably nothing but swamp.
2) To take vital kit (pyrotechnics, 1st aid kit, rations and some extra clothes) either out of the kite or have them handy inside just in case of a hurried departure.
3) To sleep on the wings, not inside. For this we used some of our bed rolls.
   As it began to get dark we thought we saw a ship on the horizon and sent off one or two of the verey cartridges. Mac went on to the mud to rescue some cartridges & kit and disappeared above his knees but was tugged back. Later the mosquitoes started and we ripped a couple of 'chutes and slept under these. By common consent we only drank a very little water and did not eat but had 2 cigarettes each - my pipe was smashed.

During the night it began to rain & we hurriedly got some groundsheets out. Luckily the a/c was still OK lighting the rear cockpit. A tremendous thunderstorm developed and at one tremendous flash right overhead Bill Miller was only just grabbed by Hughes before the former slid off the main plane. As it died down we all got some sleep but somehow managed to keep one eye on the venturi head to see that it was not sinking. The tide came up during the night and lapped the nose but we hardly sank at all.

24th January.
We woke next morning at the first streaks of daylight and spent an hour watching the light increase, scratching our mossie bites and trying to make out whether this or that bit of flotsam was a native boat. Then we saw something at the mouth of the river (about 2 miles to the north). We gave an organised roar of 'Help' as

on the previous night and waited. The specks got larger so we gave another. Then, as obviously we had been spotted, we kept quiet to avoid frightening the natives. Several times they came nearer and then stopped. Then I alone gave 'Hallo!!' which brought an answer and three boats drew up alongside the main plane. We stripped the kite so far as possible, including the parachutes, accumulators, tool box, personal kit (but forgot the clock and instrument panel) and loaded it into the boats. We dismantled the guns, smashed the bombsight (which was jammed) and destroyed the maps. We were then rowed back to the native village which we had seen the previous evening.

The village was built on mango poles at the side of the river. Laths of bark were laid cross-wise to form the platform and on the rear part of this the various houses were built – also of mango – with a landing stage left clear in front of each. On this front, fish were laid out to dry, the housewife leaves her baked rice and other cookies except at meal-times and the community leave their washing to dry in the hot sun. The houses showed some faint signs of civilisation, a few cheap pieces of carpet, a little earthenwear and bottled mineral waters! The clothes show definite signs of civilisation, mainly in the men's preference for pyjamas.

Here we were made very welcome. Collie and I were in one house, Mac alone in another and Bill Miller & Hughes in a third. First we stripped nearly naked – not quite because of definite local opinion – and were bathed in full view of the community on the main street! Luckily we had enough clean clothes between us to go round (my bedroll had been untouched). The natives then washed everything imaginable and unimaginable & hung them out to dry. They even washed helmets. With bare feet, we then sat down to a feast of rice and chicken & tea following which we paid formal visits to each others' hosts and drank mineral waters.

Of course, none of us could speak the other party's language so we started by saying 'Palembang' and after a lot of pointing, pretending to paddle &c, they arranged to take us upstream which appeared to be the correct way. Of course, we had great fun showing them what the various items of kit were, but did not dare to fire the verey pistol with a cartridge in it.

Apparently we had to wait for the tide and we all watched the ebb anxiously. About 3o/c by my watch (which appeared to be the most accurate) the boats were organised and we loaded up leaving behind the dinghy and its pump and oddments, mainly pyjamas, as presents. Then the boss (Boeme) asked for money in advance and we only had Indian rupees. It took a long time to explain that we would pay at the other end but at last we got away about 4 nm – Bill in one boat, Mac and Hughes, Collie and I. At first only the second of these had a roof: Bill's boatman changed at 'his uncle's' during the night into a roofed boat. Our boatman cut some canes on the way and made a framework. Over this he stretched a groundsheet & bit of blanket, carefully asking our permission first.

We paddled on with the tide through the twilight without more than a short rest occasionally. Then, as the mossies began to operate, a fire of green wood was lit on the prow of each boat and the smoke was extremely effective. Fireflies, literally hundreds of them, lined the banks on each side: these, the usually starlit sky and a gentle paddling of 3 natives per boat might have been a really romantic setting.

Two or three times during the night tea was made on the fire. Although it was swamp water, we felt that it might have been safely boiled and eagerly shared it with the boatmen. Later we all went to sleep and were only temporarily disturbed by the tying up for the night about 3 am.

It was at some time before I went to sleep that I suddenly realised that we had taken a lot for granted upon the seemingly friendly welcome by the villagers. We had no idea where we were nor any real idea where we were going although the boats seemed to be heading ENE. This was about right assuming that the big river we had seen was actually Palembang. We were later told that there were head hunters in Southern Sumatra, but it appears that these are mainly in the mountains on the S-Western coast of the Island.

There was one amusing series of incidents throughout the trip. Soon after we had started, Boeme complained of a headache – probably a 'try-on' to see what we would do. Miller, who had got the first-aid kit, gave him an aspirin and Boeme seemed cured immediately. This was obviously 'fair game' and they all fell sick in turn. Our supply of aspirins was limited & we must keep some for ourselves. After the first few efforts, Hughes had the bright idea and we gave them a few grains of Edward's Dessicated Soup from our rations, which seemed quite efficient as a medicine. Nevertheless, our first aid kit and spare bandages picked up in Libya were invaluable. For instance at Village No. 3 a young chap cut his toe; we promptly applied some iodine and bandaged it. He took it very calmly but seemed grateful. At all halts we held a surgery and had to resist the temptation to be too clever.

The framework made by our boatman (Boeme) was made as follows: we pulled into the side of the river; with a knife he cut down a sugar cane by chipping all round the base; then he stripped the leaves off with the knife; he then made a single series of cuts round the bark and stripped off pieces of bark all round the cane; another series of cuts was made all round and a second flaking made. These long triangular pieces were tied together end to end and provided very strong substitutes for cord, which was to tie the upright poles forming an arched roof.

25th January.
We awoke about 06.00 hrs and all had the inevitable cup of tea. We then set off and about 09.00 hrs arrived at the first native village which we had seen since leaving the mouth of the river. Here we were made very welcome and given breakfast – 'given' being an euphemism, because Boeme pointedly 'chalked it up'. This was a little more civilised including two chairs and showed signs of a river trader. The main house, though still on swamp, had a proper boarded floor. On the right hand side of the door was carved DIATOERIMASOEK and on the left ASSALAMOIAIAIKOEM (?AS SALAAM AI ALAIKUM). What these mean or even what language they are I have been unable to discover. After our meal, the boatmen fed and no doubt finished the huge mountain of rice upon which we had made hardly

any impression. We showed our various treasures leaving a few odd things as presents and were regaled with music from an old gramophone complete with horn. The records were Dutch. The village had even more chickens than village No. 1 but was otherwise unremarkable.

We set off again about 11.30 hrs and Bill showed his skill as a paddler. We stopped about 15.30 hrs and had another meal. The natives would not touch our bully beef and the Resident told us later that probably they feared it was 'pig' which is unclean to them. The natives eat rice with various meats &c and also some 'goolah', which they explained was scooped from the centre of the canes which fringe the river most of the way. Obviously crude sugar. They were at a loss to understand our water bottles and would not drink the water from the 5 and a half gallon tank rescued from the kite.

We started again from our moorings about 16.30 hrs and paddled on until the early hours of the morning. Nothing to report. We passed several villages and were still fringed by swamp 90% of the time. The fireflies appeared, we lit our green wood fires in the prow and later to sleep. By now we were getting really friendly with our boatmen and I had no qualms that night.

26th January.
Woke about 06.00 hrs, had tea and set off. About 07.00 hrs we went up a side stream to our left and came to a single native hut. The two women and one youth here gave our boatmen some fish. Rather like dog-fish, but longer and thinner, which we cooked by the fire on the prow. We had bully and cheese and made some cocoa, which the natives would not touch. About 08.00 hrs we were off again and reached Native Village No. 3 about 10.00 hrs. Here we stayed until about 13.00 hrs.

The village was on dry land and they had ducks and chickens and there were coconut palms growing. The Resident told us later that these trees only flourish near villages and spring up and die out with every settlement. No one knows why. The children spend a lot of their time in the water and at first we had thought that the little huts which one reached via a slippery tree trunk in the river were places where they changed into a dry sarong. It was at this village that we discovered that their purpose was more strictly utilitarian. After that we always took care to bathe up stream of the shacks. There also I remember the surprise of a villager at my understanding Boeme's request for my groundsheet, although we could not speak each other's language. Here again I first displayed my queer collection of money (but took care not to show my Egyptian).

Much refreshed, we set off about 13.00 hrs and paddled steadily, Collie and I also taking turns with the paddles. Later we had doubts as to whether the boatmen knew their way, because they pulled into the side and climbed a tree as a look-out. We knew we were due to arrive at our last stopping place (Sampantiga) that night. After frantic paddling we arrived a few minutes before sunset.

Sampantiga proved to be an excellent rest house. As regards the name – it is not marked on any map that I have seen and I suspect that it means the place where sampans stop (i.e. the highest navigable point of the river for sampans) and is not a proper name (?cf Urdu Tiga). There was the usual collection of floating logs as paths up to the buildings, which were however on dry land. Collie and I made the *faux pas* of entering the house with shoes on & yelled a warning to Mac & Hughes.

We were clearly expected and were soon seated (after the usual bath in the river) at a table drinking glasses of tea which were poured from a large thermos jug. A crowd began to collect including two old chiefs who rather put our boatmen out of countenance by drinking with us. We then had a most sumptious meal (alone) and then sat down to talk to the villagers. Main attractions were the various currencies, the verey pistol and my helmet and goggles. Two native policemen (from Sampantiga and the nearby village) turned up in full white uniform and hats rather like a fez. We exchanged names and promised to tell the Resident that we had met them. Incidentally, this was our first intimation that there was any official at 'Salapan', although we knew there was an 'auto'. About 22.00 hrs, we retired behind a screen stretched across the room - Mac going into the bed - the other four of us slept under a huge mosquito netting on the floor; we had arranged to be called again soon after 05.00 hrs and were due to start again at 06.00 hrs. Our boatmen slept in the boats, but came in to shelter from a terrific thunderstorm, such as we had not had since the day of the forced landing.

27th January.
Called about 06.00 hrs and after going out to see the boats were OK (we were becoming seasoned by now) set down to tea and breakfast (rice with side dishes) when Mac carefully avoided the hot herbs which had burned his tongue the previous evening. As usual, we collected cigarettes before setting off (Dutch make). These (Red Seal &c) were pretty putrid and I personally scrounged a lot off Boeme who rolled coarse shag in young sugar cane leaves about 6" long. This was much better and I regret not having brought any away with me.

The Sampantiga policeman accompanied us as we set off about 06.30 hrs. Immediately afterwards, we took a right hand fork on the river and the stream rapidly narrowed, although there was still land each side most of the time. The policeman was at first very prim and proper but later unbent when he found that the white man took his turn at the paddles.

We had one stop for tea and then about 10.00 hrs thought we heard the sound of aircraft. Mac was leading, Bill Miller second while Collingwood and I were in the third. The river was winding the whole time; I heard the engines grow faint and then a hail in English 'Good Morning, Gentlemen!' from an unseen source. Our boat turned another bend of the river to disclose a European standing up in a motor boat dressed in immaculate white drill. There flashed through my mind that other meeting epitomised by 'Dr Livingstone, I presume'.

This person, who turned out to be the Dutch Assistant Resident, explained that the police at Sampantiga had sent a native ahead the previous evening in a light skiff. This lad had paddled hard and arrived at Toeloang Selapan (the place where the auto was) about 02.00 hrs. The local chief had then telephoned the Asst. Resident, who lived about 60 Kilometres away, and he had come down to see the messenger immediately. All he could gather was that there was that night at Sampantiga five 'big men with big feet and square money' (reference to India 2 As pieces). He had packed the motor launch with drink, food and cigarettes, armed all four boatmen & himself and set out to explore. He also knew that there was a 'caporal' (i.e. flying thing) mixed up in it somewhere.

He was very shaky at first, but seemed rather surprised on hearing what we had been doing that we were so obviously well and chirpy. In fact we were all a little bit sorry that the adventure was drawing to a close.

We ourselves transferred to the motor boat and went on ahead, leaving the lightened native boats to come along at their own pace. There was much to talk about on the way up the river but I personally felt as if a weight had been lifted and slept most of the way up. We duly arrived at Toeloengselapan and up to the local asst residency, where we had some food – still native but served European fashion with the Asst Resident and the local chief.

From conversation we gathered that we had been extremely lucky to land at the mouth of that particular river. A glance at the map showed a large number of streams, none of which came up near a road; this would have meant two or three days in litters. We could not know this then, but February 13th might have seen us still struggling back to Palembang minus much of our kit.

The other boats turned up just before 15.00 hrs, were unloaded on to the wharf, to the amazement of the locals, during pouring rain and carried to the two waiting motor cars. Even the Resident seemed rather surprised at the amount of salvage. Boeme & co had planned to come to the Big City (Palembang) but the Resident vetoed owing to lack of room in the cars. Their bill came to about 30 guilden (roughly £4). We wished to make them a present in addition and suggested making it up to 200 guilden. The Resident advised however that this was too much: the native would look upon it as out of all reason & therefore not appreciate it as much as a smaller amount. Eventually we paid them, so far as I can remember, 60 G. (roughly £8) which was under £2 for saving each man's life and bringing him 3 days journey up the river with food and smokes thrown in!

About half-an-hour after we arrived, the air raid siren (rather like in England) went and I went out alone with our host to look at the local ARP post. In addition to the telephone, they have arranged an ingenious system of cross-country warning by rattle (Palembang to Kajeogoeng, a distance of 60 kilos, takes about 4 minutes). I also inspected the air raid shelter under the garage.

Our hostess could speak little English but a few words of German helped considerably owing to their similarity to Dutch – a fact which I first noticed with the police at Sampantiga. The others cleared off to bed soon after the News from Singapore (21.00 hrs) but I stayed talking for about an hour.

Incidentally, we got through that evening by telephone to Palembang and eventually reported to W/Cdr Jeudwin that the kite was probably a complete write off, but that all 5 of us were safe.

So ends the real adventures, but for sake of completeness, a short account of our return to the RAF and report to Group HQ must be added.

28th January.
I woke about 06.00 and crossed from my bedroom annexe to the house to find the Resident and his wife having an early cup of tea. The dog, who had been extremely shy the night before, became a little more friendly and chased round the garden. After breakfast we set off by two cars about 09.00 hrs and crossed the ferry into Palembang, a distance of about 60 km. We went to the Resident's office and had our identity confirmed by the RAF. We then went to AHQ and reported to the ops room also arranging for the service to pay our expenses. From there we drove by service lorry to Maria School (where the Squadron was billeted). The squadron were all at the drome so Mac & I went out to lunch at the Smit Hotel with some of the 34 Squadron officers.

The next day I went along to ops room and discovered that the distance from Pakan Baru was 519 Km not 619 Km and told the ops room just what I thought of them.

That evening, W/Cdr Jeudwine returned from P2 and I gave him a brief account of what had happened. He told us that Brian Fihelly had come through the day after us from Medan giving the first news that we had left. A Sgt Pilot reported that we had not landed at Pakan Baru. He then went to AHQ and requested a search be made for us by air. HQ, however, replied that after 24 hours in the jungle or swamp we had almost certainly 'had it' and in any event they could not spare the aircraft. This attitude made us realise once again how lucky we had been.

Appendix II

The Log of the *Scorpion*

Foreword

84 Squadron, Royal Air Force, was withdrawn from the Western Desert on 3.1.42, re-equipped on an increased establishment, and sent to the Far East as a reinforcement. The Squadron operated from Singapore, Sumatra and Java, where it lost all its aircraft by land attack (1.3.42). The ground personnel were left at Bandoeng with the Equipment, Cypher and Engineering officers, while air crews were sent to Tjilatijap, a port on the South coast, for evacuation.

No ship arrived and the Squadron was given the choice of returning inland or making an escape as best it could. An effort was made to escape in two ship's lifeboats, all that could be rescued from the fires raging in the port, but this was found to be impracticable owing to the crowded state of the boats and personnel were put ashore in a cove, one boat being wrecked in the process.

It was decided that the remaining lifeboat with a crew of twelve should try to reach Australia and get help for the people left behind. The CO and F/O Streatfield were the only two people who knew anything about sailing, P/O Turner was chosen as Navigator as he could handle a sextant, and S/Ldr Passmore was taken as Second-in-Command and to look after the rationing. The remainder of the party were chosen from the Australian air crews as it was felt that they should be given the chance of reaching their home country. The crew consisted of:

W/CDR.	J. R. JEUDWINE	Captain
S/LDR.	A. K. PASSMORE	2nd i/c and Purser
F/O	C. P. L. STREATFIELD	1st Lieut. and 2nd Helmsman
P/O	S. G. TURNER	Navigator
P/O	M. S. MACDONALD	
SGT.	W. N. COSGROVE	
SGT.	G. W. SAYER	
SGT.	A. C. LONGMORE	Crew
SGT.	J. LOVEGROVE	
SGT.	A. C. E. SNOOK	
SGT.	P. M. CORNEY	
SGT.	P. HAYNES	

Personnel remaining behind consisted of 3 Officers and 50 sergeants and aircraftsmen. In addition four other officers who had come to Tjilatjap (S/LDR

Tayler, F/LTS Wylie and Holland and F/O Owen) were in the vicinity but had become separated from the main party.

Before leaving Tjilatjap a considerable quantity of rations and other foodstuffs had been collected and divided between the two boats. Also a quantity of American canned beer had been obtained from a Dutch canteen. This latter undoubtedly largely contributed to the well-being of the crew of the *Scorpion* as the water had to be very strictly rationed and the beer was a food in itself.

It was calculated that the nearest port on the Australian coast was Roebourne, nine hundred miles and fifty nautical miles away, with Port Headland and Onslow a little further away and to the West and East of the aiming point. It was hoped to cover the distance in sixteen days as an illustration in Bartholomew's Atlas showed favourable winds and currents at this time of year, but double this time was allowed for. Some rations were therefore unloaded from the serviceable boat until it was estimated that there was ample food and water for twelve men for thirty days. Water was contained in three breakers, one full and the others two thirds full, and seven tubs each holding about twelve gallons.

Aids to navigation consisted of a marine sextant, a 1/15,000,000 Mercator's projection of the World, a portion of the Nautical Almanac giving declination tables and time apparent noon, a large scale chart of Java and Bali, and a general navigation chart of the World. This was not found until after land had been reached. There was no chronometer, so the CO's watch was used, which was estimated to lose four minutes a day.

In view of these preparations, or lack of preparations, the following pages show the enormous luck which attended the *Scorpion* and her crew on their forty seven days' voyage.

Log of HMRAFS *Scorpion*

Tjilatjap to Frazer Islet. March 7 to April 20, 1942

Sat. March 7.
1700. Crew embarked. A very haphazard procedure. Found 13 people on board so after a count had to send Sgt Jeanes ashore.
1730. Under way. Boat had to be pulled out of "Scorpion Cove" as wind was against us.
2300. Heavy thunderstorm and a little wind. Made a few miles SSE. Resorted to oars as soon as wind fall. Navigator much to his own surprise was sea-sick.

Sun. March 8.
0800. Rudder came adrift. Damage had been caused by tow-rope fouling on night of 6/7. Repairs effected by lashing hinge pin with rope. Ration fixed at 10 ozs. "M & V" or "Camp Pie", half pint water, and four ration biscuits per man per day. If Bully Beef was used, rations fell to 9 ozs per day. Cigarettes limited to 3 per man per day, 2 good ones and 1 "good-bad" i.e. one which had been soaked and dried out. Crew suffering from cramped positions in boat and from sunburn. One or two people got bad burns on their feet.

Considerable mental effort required to move about. The hot sun seemed to sap our strength and although an awning was found and rigged, the heat under it was stifling. Any moving about had to be done on all fours and this in itself was quite an effort.

1615. Breeze from SSW. Made slight Easterly progress.

Mon. March 9.

0300. Heavy rain squall which enabled us to collect some extra water. Becalmed again at 0530.

1200. Position approximately 20 miles SE of Tjilatjap.

1545. Moderate breeze from SW. No sooner had we got under way when a Japanese submarine bearing the markings "56" surfaced about a mile astern and steered towards us. She closed to within 100 yards and we were scrutinized through a pair of binoculars by an officer on the conning tower. One rating was standing by the 6 pdr gun forward and another was manning a machine gun on the conning tower. We expected to be shot at or captured, but after describing a half circle around us the submarine made off towards the East and eventually submerged. This was regarded as a lucky omen. Passed round a can of beer each on sighting submarine in case we were captured and killed or the submarine turned out to be an American and therefore dry. Typical 84 Squadron.

1800. Very heavy thunderstorm broke and all water casks fully replenished. Most of the water casks had leaked considerably, but they were now soaked enough to hold water. Rain was so heavy that a 12 gallon cask was refilled in half an hour. All members of crew drank a lot of water which revived them considerably after two days of calm under a blazing sun. Wind very variable and gusty so hove to. Tot of whisky issued to combat the soaking rain which turned from a blessing to a nuisance. Whisky enabled everyone to sleep in the most extraordinary postures.

Tue. March 10.

1530. Set sail to fresh breeze, course SSE.

1200. Wind dropped to flat calm. Position approximately 40 miles SE of Tjilatjap. Rudder giving trouble but temporary repair effected. Rough check of provisions shows we have enough for 45 days. We hope it will not take us as long as that.

1500. Sighted two large whales.

1700. Crew bathed, shark watch being kept. Exercises very welcome after cramped positions in boat. This bathing was adopted as a daily practise when possible. Crew encouraged to swim once round the boat for exercise and also to scrape marine growth off the boat's bottom.

Wed. March 11.

0130. Ran into heavy thunderstorm. A fireball rested on the stern for a few seconds, only a couple of feet from two of the crew. It took the form of a bright light and was presumably caused by a static change. Lightning was flashing all round the boat incessantly and the noise was terrific. No damage no casualties. Began to run before NW wind but rudder came adrift so hove to and spent another miserable night.

0830. Serious repairs begun on rudder. The handle was cut off an 8" screwdriver and the metal portion driven into the keel by Sgt Cosgrove and self. This was to serve as the bottom pintle. A ¼" iron ringbolt was filed down to a spike and driven into the rudder for the centre attachment. Utilizing the remains of the original fittings the rudder was then replaced, the operation being made very difficult and very painful by the heavy swell. Tools used: 3-cornered file, small screwdriver, cold chisel, small axe, Javanese knife and twins. Sgts. Corney and Lovegrove put up most magnificent effort in fixing rudder in face of great difficulties.

Thu. March 12.

1230. Ran into thunderstorm which gave us a sailing breeze. Course SE. Rudder came adrift again so carried on steering by oar but boat very difficult to hold so limited spells to 15 minutes.

0600. Rudder repaired. A comparatively simple job this time.

1900. On our way to a slight breeze. Although the general course has been SE we have been close hauled most of the time. Can Mr Bartholomew be wrong?

Fri. March 13.

0300. Got a good wind then lost rudder again. Only to be expected on a day like this. When we tried to repair the rudder we found that the metal pintle had dropped out so we made a wooden one.

1200. Estimated noon position 200 miles on track to Roebourne but longitude very doubtful. Becalmed since 1130 so lay sweating under the awning. A shark paid us a visit during the forenoon. Fired about 20 rounds .303 at it but he was too deep.

1630. More trouble with the rudder.

Sat. March 14.

0715. Extra ration of water from barrel into which a case of Lifebuoy soap had fallen a few days previously. This was intended as a laxative as we had no "No. 9's" on board and most of the crew were suffering from constipation. Results not all we hoped for.

1730. Seven days at sea and Saturday Night. Extra rations and a tot of whisky issued. Drank the King's health and followed up with "Sweethearts and Wives". Youngest member, Sgt Snook, called upon to reply to toast but for once words failed him.

The crew had become more acclimatised to living in an open boat, but it is obvious from various conversations how few realise the hazards of this voyage. Some people seem to think that they are being taken for a nice pleasure trip and that there is no need for them to exert themselves. Luckily these are very few and morale is generally high.

Rudder gave way again during night.

Sun. March 15.
1630. Rudder repaired.
1200. As the navigator gets more proficient so the results become less optimistic. Estimated noon position 111 deg. East, 10 deg. South.

Mon. March 16.
Fair sailing all day in choppy sea with big swell running. Sky gives indication of coming storm.

Tue. March 17.
Storm has not materialized but that has not prevented the rudder from parting company with the stern post. The two chippies got it fixed again.

Wed. March 18.
Have been befriended by a sea bird, who sits on the rudder head performing amazing balancing feats. He is, however, inclined to peck away string round the tiller.

Received a visit from a shark. This time the First Lieut. put a .38 bullet in him.

Most of the crew suffering from pimples on the posterior. These very painful when at the tiller as we have no Rumbold upholstery on the quarter deck. Cures for pimples were Mercurcrome of which there was a small bottle on board, and sun bathing. Former cure produced some astonishing sights, while the latter was apt to be painful if applied for too long a time.

Thu. March 19.
Very light sailing conditions with sea still choppy. Crew's sleeping quarters re-arranged to take some weight out of the bows. Positions were then two in the bows, where they always got wet if there was any sea running, two on the thwart abaft the mast, two on the next thwart aft, two on side benches amidships, and four on the stern.

A small snack (two biscuits and two sardines or a little potted meat and a mouthful of water) being issued at noon each day. This gives us something to look forward to and helps pass the time.

Fri. March 20.
0100. Becalmed, with very heavy rain storms all round. These eventually met overhead and a good water catchment was made.

Under way soon after dawn. One of the Queen's garters (type Barbara) hoisted on the signal halyard. Wind from SSE as usual in this bloody ocean.
1630. Wind increasing and heavy clouds forming.
1800. Wind dropped and rain storms visible.

Another foul night, pouring rain and no wind. Whisky passed round to keep out the wet and cold, and to enable us to sleep in spite of the discomfort.

Sat. March 21.
0630. Under way. Breeze freshening.
1830. Had to heave to as we were shipping water over the bows faster than we could bale. The boat started to become waterlogged and the lee gunwale

remained awash. As soon as we hove to the rudder came adrift. Our position is pretty serious.

The "Saturday Night at Sea" customs were observed with the evening meal.

Sun. March 22.
1030. Rudder fixed. This was a very difficult job owing to the mountainous seas and the very sharp movement of the boat. More praise to the chippies. Under way again making about 5–7 knots. A very wet process.
1130. Hove to again as sea and wind too great. There is no reefing device on these sails and we cannot afford to run before the wind which is from the SW. Found that even with the sea anchor streamed the *Scorpion* still insists on lying beam to the sea and wind, so hoisted sail and put jib aback. This made her ride easier and she was actually making headway without a rudder which of course had come adrift again. Our actual track was E by S, speed approximately one and a half knots.

According to our sailing plot we are about half way to Roebourne. Another foul night but everyone taking it very well. Still think that in most cases it is a question of "where ignorance is bliss".

Am later proved right.

Mon. March 23.
0630. Wind dropped sufficiently to start sailing again as soon as rudder was fixed. Found we had to jettison three water barrels as the sea water had got into them.
1200. Rudder came adrift again. Position 113 deg. East 14 deg. 15 min. South. Very strong repairs made to rudder. This held until we reached land.
1445. Under way. Sun coming out which enables us to dry one or two garments. First Lieut. and I sharing all watches at the helm.

Sea still running very high.

Everyone given two quinine tablets as a precaution against the recent wettings.

Tue. March 24.
A gentle day's sailing with a favourable wind. Sea going down but still coming on board every now and then.

Wed. March 25.
1200. Becalmed. Most uncomfortable in the swell which is still very heavy. Will we never break in the way of a constant wind? Mr Bartholomew is a complete liar about the winds in this part of the world. I bet he has never been here. Think there are grounds for an action against him as he is misleading school children.

Thu. March 26.
Under way most of the day, but only just. Luckily there is quite a lot of cloud about so it is not too hot.

Had a really thorough check of the foodstuffs and found that we are very well placed, there being enough to enable us to increase rations and still have plenty in hand. This is a great relief. Also a number of delicacies such as canned plums and tomatoes were found.

Fri. March 27.
Still becalmed. Sea like glass. We have been adopted by another sea bird.

Noon position showed that we had drifted North but some doubts expressed as to the accuracy of the sight.

Crew playing "Crosswords" to pass the time.

Sat. March 28.
Same old calm. Noon position shows a further drift to the North but everyone refuses to believe the Navigator who keeps his temper remarkably well. General impression is that sextant suffered damage during the gale.

Sun. March 29.
Becalmed. Rations reduced to former scale as things do not look too good. A few more of these calms and we would be up the creek. Northerly drift still apparent, but everyone except Navigator expressing silent disbelief. Navigator's attitude is "Take it or leave it".

First Lieut nice and gloomy about our chances of reaching Australia. As the diarist said "Mr Streatfield's morals very low". Had to give him (Stretty) a pep-talk. Not the first but rather excelled myself this time.

Mon. March 30.
'As idle as a painted ship...' Am not at all surprised that the Ancient Mariner went nuts.

Noon position now confirms the Northerly drift. This is very upsetting, as if this current has been present all the time our sailing plot which has been used a check on our estimated position is quite false. The Navigator, with great forbearance, has not yet remarked "I told you so". Northerly drift since March 28th reckoned at 82 miles.

Tue. March 31.
Still becalmed. Further check of rations shows that the tinned fruit and some of the rations are going bad through heat, rust, and being shaken about. In view of our drift, the uncertainty or our position, and our lack of progress generally things are starting to look most unpleasant.

A blissful air of unconcern reigns forward. During this calm we have rigged the awning after breakfast and organised games competitions between the quarter deck and fo'c'sle. These have kept us occupied and helped pass the time but we found that the mental exercise made us very hungry and the talking and arguing brought on thirst. These are easier to bear than the monotony.

Wed. April 1.
Still becalmed, and not many April Fool jokes. The penalty for April Fools about ships or land was loss of beer ration for the rest of the voyage.

Slight breeze sprang up during the morning. No notice taken in spite of

MacDonald's continuous comments as we were busy with the finals of the 'letters' competition. Eventually MacDonald became so insistent that we had to set sail. Score in competition - eight all and one to play.

Wind increased from NW during afternoon. Is this our break?

Thu. April 2.
Still sailing at dawn. Noon position puts us about 390 miles from Roebourne. Wind has backed and we are close hauled again. Obviously Mr Bartholomew is a liar of the first water and has no idea of what he is talking about.

We still have our bird companions.

Fri. April 3.
Wind fresh but variable. Course SSW Sgt Haynes, i/c roundhouse declared closing time at sunset as he has rigged his bed there.

Sat. April 4.
Sailing comfortably but course still W of S. The *Scorpion* will not sail at all close to the wind so we are making our Southing while we can.

We have been joined by another bird. If this goes on we shall become an aviary. They are the most peculiar creatures. Apparently they do not keep regular mealtimes and they are very tame. Also they keep their balance remarkably well for web-footed birds, even when asleep, but if a particularly sharp roll almost upsets one of them it always puts the blame on its companion. Perhaps everything goes nuts in the Indian Ocean.

Had an issue of soi disant *Crème de Menthe* for the Saturday Night at Sea celebration. A most peculiar concoction, later identified as a patent cough cure.

Sun. April 5.
Nothing of interest. Wind refreshing.

Mon. April 6.
Wind veered enough for us to make due East. We do not want to go Westwards more than we can help.

Wind dropped in the afternoon.

Tue. April 7.
1345. Put about to S.W as wind backed. Had to pinch to make that course, but better than making NE.
2300. Becalmed.

Wed. April 8.
1200. Becalmed all morning, but noon position shows us 140 miles from Barrow Island and 180 miles from Onslow.

Smoked last cigarette this evening. Had made a contract with four members of the crew to save their butts. These were carefully saved and kept in a tin. It meant that I could have an occasional pipe. Will never again despise old men picking up fag ends from the gutter - I know just how they feel.

Thu. April 9.
1045. Becalmed. Young whale, 50–60 feet long, or about twice the size of the

Scorpion, surfaced about 200 yards away and decided to give us a close inspection. Eventually came to rest lying in a curve with its tail no more than 3 feet from the rudder. We could see the eyes and mouth under water. "What does 'A' do next?". We hoped that it would not become playful or try to make its toilet on the bottom of the boat, and luckily, after looking at us for about half a minute which seemed like half an age it submerged and went to join another whale which looks about four times as big. I hope that the other one was its mother and the she tore him off a strip for going and staring at strangers. When we had regained the power of movement we passed around a bottle of Australian '3 Star' brandy which we had been keeping for an emergency, after which we did not care if we saw elephants, pink or otherwise, flying over us in tight formation.

Wind sprang up in afternoon, probably as result of this morning's vertical breeze, but possibly as result of hoisting red garter in place of Barbara.

Fri. April 10.
Wind strong and increasing in force. Sea also getting up. Unfortunately wind is from SE so we have to tack and pinch to make E and W of S. As the *Scorpion* will not go about in a seaway we have to wear ship every time and it is tantalizing to see the speed she gets up with the wind abaft the beam.

First Lieut. and self sharing watches at the tiller. We demanded extra issue of food to keep us awake and were allowed to open a tin of ship's biscuits. Found these very palatable and also a magnificent laxative - presumably due to increased bulk.

Rest of crew dodging waves, or trying to.

Sat. April 11.
Wind, which reached gale force during night, now moderating but considerable sea running. Lack of swell and shortness of sea make me think that we are E of North West Cape.

1200. Noon position shows plenty of Easting but only 13 miles of Southing. This not compatible with sailing plot. Reviled Navigator who both kept his temper and refused to be shaken from his calculations. He was right of course.

Got inspected by another whale during afternoon, but from a safe distance, thank God. These visitations occur when I am trying to write up the Squadron History so am giving this up for the time being.

Sun. April 12.
0600. Wind dropped until we barely made steerage way. Most of crew very depressed, wondering whether we are going to have another long calm after the last gale.
1800. Becalmed.

Mon. April 13.
During the daylight catspaws kept us moving. It is better to pretend to sail than to lie about doing nothing. Boat making water fast. The last gale opened up a seam. Becalmed after sunset.

Tue. April 14.
1200. Noon position 115 deg. 45 min. E. 20 deg. 9 min. S. We are now on the same latitude as Port Headland.

Wind sprang up during afternoon. Squadron Colour garters hoisted in place of red one.

Wed. April 15.
Noon position shows that we have made 45 miles Easting. Regard this as extremely doubtful but am now wary of arguing with the Navigator. Made some Easting during the day but breeze slight.

Thu. April 16.
Sgt Corney swore he smelt Spinnefez on the dawn breeze. Soon he had everyone smelling something but personally put it down to the Purser who suffers from flatulence. However, everyone very cheerful. Plans made for first meal widely discussed.
1200. Noon position 118 deg. 50 min. E. 20 deg. 11 mins. S. or 30 miles from Port Headland. Great excitement all round.

Fri. April 17.
Dropped a bombshell this morning. Had spent a sleepless night working out times of sunrise and sunset during the past few days and had come to the conclusion that the recent large amount of Easting shown by the moon sight was due to my watch - the only one to have survived - losing more than four minutes a day and that it may have lost as much as 40 minutes. This would put us 600 miles W of Port Headland and about 250 miles W of the westernmost point of Australia. Rations, water, and beer drastically cut down, and an accurate check shows that we can last for another six weeks on this new scale. We shall all be in pretty poor condition by the end of that time. Thank God the water will last that time, as that is one of the most important items, ranking equally with the beer.

A breeze sprang up during the morning and lasted until evening. We were becalmed by sunset and tried to row, but we were already so weak from 6 weeks on the boat, that it was not very effective.

Sat. April 18.
0200. Breeze sprang up. Much seaweed noticed but nobody dare say whether it indicates the proximity of land or whether it is commonly found right out to sea. We assume the latter to avoid disappointment. A Swallow-tail butterfly seen during the afternoon. That must mean that we are somewhere near land.

Sun. April 19.
0300. Wind sprang up. If we do 10 miles a day in the right direction our rations will last out even if we are right out to sea. During day several butterflies seen and some new type jellyfish. Even I think that we must be nearer land than I had feared, but still dare not increase rations.
2230. Most members of boat thought they heard a motor working, possibly a small motor-boat. Lit a distress signal flare but had no reply.

Mon. April 20.

0200. First Lieut. electrified everyone by shouting 'Land ho'. Sure enough there was a beach about 50 yards away. It appeared to be a small island, and as the only island marked on our map was Barrow Island, which was quite a big piece of land, we reckoned that this was a spit of the mainland and decided to carry on until we could make certain. We soon discovered that we were surrounded by small islands and reefs which we had crossed at high water and which were now appearing as the tide went down, so we decided to wait for the dawn.

Daylight showed us a sea dotted with small islands, but no mainland, so we put ashore at the point where we had first struck land, almost too literally, which we found to be Frazer Inlet from a plate on a beacon which had been erected there. This did not convey much to anyone, but the mere fact that it was land was very heartening.

0730. Put foot on dry land for the first time since March 7th - our 45th day at sea. All members of crew very weak but looking forward to a hot breakfast. Food issued ad lib. and cocoa made, but people found that they could not eat as much as they thought, with the exception of the First Lieut who proved a fine trencherman. Purser feeling sick, probably reaction but may be the sight of so much food being issued at one meal.

1000. Navigator reported finding a chart (general navigational) of the World in the boat. We would after 45 days. Chart showed we had reached Dampier Archipelago between Onslow and Roebourne so decided to make for mainland not far distant.

1030. Set sail course SSE.

1300. Sighted mainland, or perhaps Barrow Island. Hard to tell but think that it is mainland. Later proved correct.

1500. Altered course NE along coast. Winds appear favourable for us to reach Roebourne. Sighted unidentified aircraft high and about 10 miles to the West. Probably a Catalina. Flashed mirror and waved clothing but failed to attract attention. Some people rather disappointed but general feeling that we have reached Australia by the grace of God and little else matters. Also, if Catalinas are about the Japs are not in occupation of the coast.

1600. Anchored in the lee of a small island as not considered safe to carry on through the night. Spent the night ashore after a hot meal. What a joy to lie on a stationary bed, and a soft one too. (Sgt Corney made up Spinnefex mattresses. His sense of smell was proved to be in good working order and accusations against Purser withdrawn.)

Tue. April 21.
Boat grounded on ebb tide so crew spent morning ashore fishing from beach. Several Butterfish caught and cooked for an early lunch. Called island "Butterfish Island" as a result. Fish damned good to eat after tinned food. Found boat leaking all along one of starboard strakes.

1145. Under way, course NE.
1230. Sighted several kangaroos ashore. This proves that we are off the mainland and also indicates the presence of fresh water in the neighbourhood. A suspected water pump and tank turned out to be a tree.
1430. Flying boat (Catalina of Patrol Squadron 101, US Navy) appeared dead ahead at about 1500 feet. Pyjama jacket hoisted to peak in best 'Razzle' style and all members of crew waved clothing etc. Afterwards learnt that Catalina crew thought we were having a free fight. After much signalling persuaded Catalina to alight, but its crew very suspicious and displayed artillery. After exchange of semaphore signals (of a sort) I swam over to flying boat, beating all existing records for ocean swimming in my anxiety to dodge any sharks that might be around. Was given a rope to hang on to but in spite of the fact that I was mother naked except for my beard I was menaced by a man with a Colt .45 who would not let me on board until he was quite satisfied that I was harmless. Captain of Aircraft offered to take six of us off to their base but only three of our crew accepted the offer - Sgts. Cosgrove, Longmore and Haynes. Remainder of crew determined to sail the *Scorpion* into port.
1700. Anchored for the night in a creek. Intended having a bit of a party since we had so much liquor left, but after an enormous hot meal everyone felt drowsy and went to sleep.

Wed. April 22.
0830. Set off again. Decided to call our stopping place 'Catalina Creek', but some members of crew gave it a less euphonious name owing to increased bowel activity caused by large meals. Continued to coast on NE course and expected to turn East fairly soon, but as each headland was passed another one was raised. However, no alarm felt as food and drink were plentiful and we were off the mainland.
1200. Noon position gave our latitude just North of the Fortescue, much further from Roebourne than we thought. If latitude five miles out we should be much nearer Roebourne, in fact where we estimate we should be, so for once we take the optimistic view.
1230. Catalina appeared from SW and made towards us. This time we displayed little interest, thinking that the Catalina was merely being curious.
  The Catalina however, alighted and signalled that she had orders to take off all remainder of crew. Great disappointment as having got so far it seemed a pity not to complete the trip.
  Lowered sail, unstopped mast, and gathered all belongings, such as they were.
1300. Crew all transferred to flying boat and *Scorpion* cast adrift. Unfortunately in the hurry the Squadron shield was left in the forward locker. Had intended hoisting it to mast-head as we sailed into port. Discovered that information given on previous day re our position was inaccurate, and we were nearly 100 miles from Roebourne. So after 47 days, having sailed approxi-

mately 1500 statute miles, leaking like a sieve but still serviceable, with a jury rudder fitting in use since the second day out, HMRAFS *Scorpion* was cast adrift off the NW coast of Australia without the honour of being sailed into port. She was a cow into wind and would not go about without assistance, but she was a very strong and magnificent sea boat. No member of the crew wishes to make another trip like that, but if fate should ever decree that any of us are again at sea in an open boat, we all pray that it will be as good as the *Scorpion*.

Epilogue

The crew of the *Scorpion* spent the night of April 22/23 on board USS *Childs*, captain Lieut Commander Frank O'Bierne, USN, who was the pilot of the Catalina which picked up the main party on April 22. Great hospitality was shown and everyone made very comfortable.

On April 23 the whole party was flown to Perth in another Catalina. OC, 84 Squadron got in touch with US Naval authorities through the ACC Western Area, Air Commodore de la Rue, RAAF, and arrangements were made for a US submarine, the *Sturgeon*, to call at "Scorpion Cove" on her way back from Corregidor and attempt to pick up the 84 Squadron Air crews who had been left there with orders to wait for two months if possible.

The *Sturgeon* went into the cove on the night of Thursday April 30 and sent her boat to within 50 yards of the beach. The officer in charge of the boat, who had been notified of the signal arrangements flashed the recognition signal and later hailed, but got no reply. A hand searchlight was then shone ashore, but all that was seen was a deserted lean-to. There was no sign of a cross of stones on the beach, denoting a voluntary departure, so the fate of the stranded air crews of the Squadron is problematical.

Thus apart from personal satisfaction and the escape of twelve members of the Squadron the voyage of the *Scorpion* was a failure, for although help was sent within the time limit the rescue of the remainder was not effected.

Notes

The Queen's Garter
S/Ldr Passmore, F/L Streatfield and P/O Turner called their aircraft "Queen of Shaibeh". Stretty carried a selection of feminine garters around with him which were put on the pitot head fairing when going on an operational flight or on a special occasion. During the voyage the garters were used as pennants and as one set failed to produce a favourable wind so another set would be hoisted. The garters had nothing to do with "Mr Streatfield's morals".

Our Feathered Friends
These were a type of sea gull. Owing to lack of human contact they were very tame, and even if knocked off their perch for becoming too free with their beaks

or insanitary habits they would come back for more. Their first efforts at decklandings were pretty poor but they improved with practice until they were able to make landing with negative ground speed.

Other birds seen were Stormy Petrels, Man-o-War birds, Albatross, some curious gulls with a long tail feather, and some small sea birds which looked very like sand martins.

Flying Fish

From a close and prolonged study it appears that these fish always leave the water into wind. The 'wings' are used to keep the body of the fish airborne, but as the tail touches the water it gives a few flicks, thus regaining flying speed and lifting the whole fish to shimmer and gives the appearance of flying.

On one or two occasions the 'flying fish' turned out to be young squid. These would leap out of the water to a height of about 6–8 feet, and on one occasion one came on board striking the First Lieut. a shrewd blow on the left ear.

Other denizens of the deep seen during the voyage were sharks with their pilot fish, whales (and how), porpoises, dugongs (sea-cows), tunny, sting rays, skipjack, blue mackerel, garfish, schnapper, sea-snakes, butter-fish, turtles, and a variety of jelly-fish including 'Blue-bottles'.

Deportment

In order to get the most out of every meal it became a habit to lick one's plate clean. This became a bit awkward when our beards grew, but the habit persisted and we had to watch ourselves very closely when we got back to civilisation. Also there was a great competition to get any tins after their contents had been dished out in the hopes of finding a few scraps in the less accessible corners. Sgt Cosgrove earned himself the nickname of "The Alley Cat" from his habit of begging twice scoured tins and opening them out flat with a tin opener so as to get any bits which could not be extracted with a knife. He was lucky not to get lead poisoning.

Part II

The Published Writings of Bernard Ashmole

1921
The so-called Sardanapalus. *BSA* (1919–21) 78.

1922
Locri Epizephyrii and the Ludovisi Throne. *JHS* 42 (1922) 248–53.

Notes on the Sculptures of the Palazzo dei Conservatori. *JHS* 42 (1922) 238–47.

1924
Review of F. Poulsen, *Greek and Roman Portraits in English Country Houses*. *JHS* 44 (1924) 134–5.

Review of O. Walter, *Beschreibung der Reliefs im kleinen Akropolis Museum in Athen*. *JHS* 44 (1924) 135.

1925
Review of C. Blümel, *Zwei Strömungen in der Attischen Kunst des V. Jahrhunderts*. *JHS* 45 (1925) 138–9.

Review of G. H. Chase, *Greek and Roman Sculpture in American Collections*. *JHS* 45 (1925) 139.

1927
Hygieia on Acropolis and Palatine. *Papers of the British School at Rome* 10 (1927) 1–11.

1928
An Attic Relief of the Late Fifth Century. *Antike Plastik, Festschrift W. Amelung* (Berlin, 1928) 13–15.

Details of Roman Sculpture. *JHS* 18 (1928) 179–180.

La tecnica della scultura sotto l'Impero. *Atti del I Congresso Nazionale di Studi Romani, Aprile 1928*.

Photographs for the participation in E. Strong, *Catalogue of the Greek and Roman Antiquities in the Possession of the Rt. Hon. Lord Melchett* (Oxford, 1928).

1929
Suggestions for the New Exhibition of the Sculptures of the Parthenon, with J. D. Beazley and D. S. Robertson (1929).

A Catalogue of the Ancient Marbles at Ince Blundell Hall (Oxford, 1929).

Photographs for R. Carpenter, *The Sculpture of the Nike Temple Parapet* (Cambridge (MA), 1929).

1930
An Alleged Archaic Group. *JHS* 50 (1930) 99–104.

Sardanapalus Again. *JHS* 50 (1930) 142.

1932
Hellenistic Art. *Cambridge Ancient History* VIII, Chapter 21. Reprinted in *Greek Sculpture and Painting*, with J.D. Beazley (Cambridge, 1932, 1966).

Female Torso in Burlington House. *Brunn-Bruckmann Denkmäler* nos. 747-8 (Munich 1932).

Review of C. Blümel, *Staatliche Museen zu Berlin: Katalog der Sammlung antiker Skulpturen. Band IV, Römische Kopien Griechischer Skulpturen des fünften Jahrhunderts v. Chr.* *JHS* 52 (1932) 135–6.

Review of O. Waldhauer *Die antiken Skulpturen der Ermitage* I-II. *JHS* 52 (1932) 137–8.

Art in Ancient Life – I. Reconstructing a Greek City. *The Listener*, 19 October 1932, 545–547.

Art in Ancient Life – II. History and Art in Greece. *The Listener*, 26 October 1932, 587–589.

The Achievement of the Greek Potter – I. The Maker of the Pot. *The Listener*, 2 November 1932, 627–629.

The Achievement of the Greek Potter – II. The Decorating of the Pot. *The Listener*, 9 November 1932, 644–666.

Art in Ancient Life – V. From Drawing to Sculpture. *The Listener*, 16 November 1932, 699–700.

Art in Ancient Life – VI. Discussion with R. H. Wilenski: Is there any Greek Sculpture? *The Listener*, 23 November 1932, 754–757.

Art in Ancient Life – VII. What do we look for in Sculpture? *The Listener*, 30 November 1932, 790–792.

Art in Ancient Life – VIII. Architecture as an Art. *The Listener*, 7 December, 1932, 821–3.

Art in Ancient Life – IX. Coinage. *The Listener*, 14 December 1932, 865–867.

1933

Review of *Brunn-Bruckmann's Denkmäler Griechischer und Römischer Skulptur: Text und Register zu den Tafeln 501-750*. JHS 53 (1933) 127–8.

1934

Review of C. Blinkenberg, *Knidia*. JHS 54 (1934) 85–6.

Late Archaic and Early Classical Greek Sculpture in Sicily and South Italy. *Proceedings of the British Academy* 20 (1934) 91–123.

1936

Review of A.J.B. Wace, *An Approach to Greek Sculpture: An Inaugural Lecture Delivered before the University of Cambridge on 17th May 1935*. JHS 56 (1936) 245–6.

Review of H. Payne and G.M. Young, *Archaic Marble Sculpture from the Acropolis: A Photographic Catalogue*. JHS 56 (1936) 247–9.

Review of R. Boehringer, *Platon, Bildnisse und Nachweise*. JHS 56 (1936) 250–51.

Review of T. Fyfe, *Hellenistic Architecture*. CR 50 (1936) 189–190.

Review of R. J. H. Jenkins, *Dedalica*. CR 50 (1936) 233–5.

The Relation between Coins and Sculpture. *Transactions of the International Numismatic Congress* XVII (London, 1936) 17–22.

Manners and Methods in Archaeology. JHS 58 (1938) 240–6.

1937

Griechisches Relief mit Reiterkampf. Oxford, Ashmolean Museum. *Brunn-Bruckmann Denkmäler* no. 768 (Munich, 1937).

Review of O. Waldhauer, *Die antiken Skulpturen der Ermitage* III. JHS 57 (1937) 91.

1938

Review of F. Dornseiff, *Der sogennante Apollon von Olympia*. CR 52 (1938) 87.

Review of W. Otto, *Handbuch der Archäologie im Rahmen des Handbuchs der Altertumswissenschaft*. CR 52 (1938) 33.

Correspondence by F. Dornseiff, *Peirithoos or Apollo*. CR 52 (1938) 205.

Review of G. P. Stevens, *The Periclean Entrance Court of the Acropolis of Athens*. CR 52 (1938). 40.

1939

Review of J. Jantzen, *Bronzewerkstätten in Grossgriechenland und Sizilien*. Gnomon 15 (1939) 424–7.

The Same Methods. JHS 59 (1939) 286.

Review of F. Dornseiff, *Der sogenannte Apollon von Olympia* (ed. 2). CR 53 (1939) 152.

Review of *Études d'Archéologie grecque sogenannte*. CR 53 (1939) 142–3.

1946

Greek Art at Burlington House. *The Listener*, 21 February 1946, 235–6.

Kalligeneia and Hieros Arotos. JHS 66 (1946) 8–10.

1949

Preface to Arthur Smith's, *A Short Guide to Sculptures of the Parthenon in the British Museum (Elgin Collection)* (London, 1949).

The Elgin Marbles at the British Museum/Les Marbres D'Elgin au British Museum.
How the Elgin Marbles came to England. *The Listener*, 25 August 1949, 308–10.

1950
An Archaic Fragment from Halicarnassus. *Festschrift Andreas Rumpf* (Krefeld, 1950) 5–9.
Guide to Ince Blundell Hall (Liverpool, 1950).

1951
Demeter of Cnidus. *JHS* 71 (1951) 13–28.
The Poise of the Blacas Head. *BSA* 46 (1951) 2–6.

1952
A Relief in Silver. *British Museum Quarterly* 15 (1952) 62–4.

1953
The Bicentenary of the British Museum III. *The Listener*, 2 July 1953, 17–18.

1954
Five Forgeries in the Manner of the Parthenon, *Neue Beiträge zur klassischen Altertumswissenschaft, Festschrift B. Schweitzer* (Stuttgart, 1954) 177–80.
A Greek Relief Re-discovered. *Nederlands Kunsthistorisch Jaarboek* 5 (1954) 91–100.

1956
Cyriac of Ancona and the Temple of Hadrian at Cyzicus. *Journal of the Warburg and Courtauld Institutes* 19 (1956) 179–191.

1957
A Lost Statue Once in Thasos. *Fritz Saxl Memorial Essays* (London, 1957) 195–8.

1959
Not by Agoracritus. *Nederlands Kunsthistorisch Jaarboek* 10 (1959) 1–3.

1960
Cyriac of Ancona (Italian Lecture, British Academy 1957). *Proceedings of the British Academy* 45 (1960) 25–41.
Graphic Art in Ancient Greece: Review of M. Robertson, *Greek Painting*. *The Listener*, 28 January 1960, 183.

1961
Forgeries of Ancient Sculpture: Creation and Detection. *First J. J. Myres Memorial Lecture* (Oxford, 1961).
A Selection from the Ince Blundell Hall Marbles (Liverpool, 1961).

1962
Arcaico and Skopas in *Enciclopedia Universale dell'Arte I* (Venice, 1962) 554–98.
Torch-racing at Rhamnus. *AJA* 66 (1962) 233–4.

1963
Some Nameless Sculptors of the Fifth Century BC. *Proceedings of the British Academy* 48 (1963) 213–33.

1964
The Classical Ideal in Greek Sculpture. *Lectures in Memory of Louise Taft Semple* (Cincinnati, 1964).
Iphigeneia in Tauris. *Essays in Memory of Karl Lehmann* (New York, 1964) 25–6.

1965
The Three-sided Relief in Boston. *Boston Museum Bulletin* 63 (1965) 59–61.
Introduction to *Captain E. G. Spencer Churchill. Exhibition of Antiquities & Coins. Ashmolean Museum* (1965).

1967
Art of the Ancient World I, with H.A. Groenewegen-Frankfort (New York 1967, Englewood Cliffs 1972).
A New Interpretation of the Portland Vase. *JHS* 87 (1967) 1–17.
Sir John Beazley: a Biographical Note in *Select Exhibition of Sir John Beazley and Lady Beazley's Gifts to the Ashmolean Museum 1912-1966 Oxford.* (Oxford, 1967).

1968
The Boston Relief and the Ludovisi Throne, with William J. Young. *Boston Museum Bulletin* 66 (1968) 124–66.

1969
A New Join in the Amazon Frieze of the Mausoleum. *JHS* 89 (1969) 22–3.

1970

Aegean Marble: Science and Common Sense. *BSA* 65 (1970) 1–2.

Greek Art. *Encyclopaedia Britannica*, 14th ed. (1970) Volume 10, 833–849.

1971

The Ludovisi Throne and its Boston Counterpart Reconsidered. *Antike Kunst* 14 (1971) 159–60.

1972

Architect and Sculptor in Classical Greece. Wrightsman Lectures VI (London, 1972).

Sir John Beazley: 1885–1970. Obituary: *Proceedings of the British Academy* 56 (1972) 443–61.

1973

Menander: an Inscribed Bust. *AJA* 77 (1973) 61.

1974

Ancient Greek "Painting, the History of Western Art" *Encyclopaedia Britannica* 15th ed. (1974–85) Volume 25, 325.

Ancient Greek "Sculpture, the History of Western Art" *Encyclopaedia Britannica* 15th ed. (1974–85) Volume 27, 62–63.

1975

Review of J. J. Pollitt, *The Ancient View of Greek Art. AJA* 79 (1975) 299–300.

1977

Solvitur Disputando. *Festscrift für F. Brommer* (Mainz, 1977) 13–20.

Aim and Method in the study of Ancient Art, the Value of Casts

THE IMPORTANCE OF CASTS in the study of ancient art was emphasized by Professor Bernard Ashmole in the lecture at University College, London, on "Aim and Method in the Study of Ancient Art," with which he opened his course on Greek Sculpture. His insistence on the need of casts was based not only on their value to the student who cannot travel to examine all the originals, but also on the more complete examination which they permit, and this aspect, concerned with the lighting of statues and heads from various angles and their examination in various positions, he illustrated with lantern slides.

He spoke of the advances in the knowledge of works of art which had been made possible lately by the intensive study of originals, casts and photographs. For the study of sculpture, though drawing by the student himself might be useful, photography was supreme. One of its many dangers, however, was that of trusting photographs too fully, of imagining that they could thoroughly comprehend a three-dimensional object by means of a two-dimensional medium. Side by side with photography as a factor of progress they must set plaster casts. This is not a new invention nor an invention which had been improved in any way. The making of a collection of casts had long been recognised as one of the first pieces of apparatus necessary for the scientific study of ancient sculpture. In 1885 the collection in Berlin contained over 2,000 casts and it had been growing steadily since. There were great collections, numbering their casts in thousands, in other German towns, in Paris, and elsewhere on the Continent. London to-day had in the basement of the British Museum something under 300. The potential loss of efficiency could easily be gauged.

Among the slides shown was a photograph of casts of the so-called Westmacott athlete in the British Museum and the statue of a boy at Dresden placed side by side to illustrate resemblances and differences. Remarking on the difficulties of obtaining this and hundreds of similar comparisons needed without a cast gallery, Professor Ashmole said it would be almost impossible to secure that two photographers in different places should take photographs on the same scale and with the same lighting and quality. He also showed slides taken lately in the cast gallery at Oxford. These illustrated a cast of the archer from the east pediment of the Temple of Athena Aphaia at Aegina. Dealing with one of these, which showed clearly how the line of muscle strain from the arm is continued down under the cuirass, he said that if a cast was valuable because it could be turned about and lighted in a way which was impossible with an original, the photograph of a cast was valuable in that it constituted an enduring record of features suddenly made clear by a particular aspect or a particular kind of lighting. He looked forward to the time when the cinema would be adapted to taking all-round views of sculpture, which would be printed for study. The value of the photography of details was that, like the child's telescope of a plain cardboard tube, it helped them to see things more clearly because it cut out the objects around.

A particularly good example was a set of photographs of a cast of the head from the island of Chios, probably the work of Praxiteles, which was exhibited at the Burlington Club at the beginning of this century, and is now in Boston. It had been the subject of a most able monograph by the late John Marshall, by whom these photographs had been prepared. One view showed how this particular sculptor solved the ever-recurring problem of adjusting the segment of a cylinder represented by the forehead to the ovoid of the lower part of the face. Another, secured by means of a gelatine cast which avoids the 'joints' of the piece-mould, showed the full beauty of the lips. Professor Ashmole showed by means of this example that the modelling of the lower lip, which without careful examination appears to be a continuous curved surface, is in reality made up of four planes which dissolve into each other with extreme subtlety. He explained, too, that the cast showed what the photograph could not - the great beauty of the recession of the upper lip. Speaking of casts in general he said they discounted any discoloration there might be in the marble. They also lost the translucency of marble, and, with it, one of the later Greek sculptors' chief media. On the other hand they enabled the student to see not the effect, which would only be seen in the marble, but the means by which the effect was obtained and so added to his knowledge of the sculptor's methods. But they must never forget that the aim of study is to know everything that there is in the original.

Discussing later the possibility of a cast museum being set up in London, Professor Ashmole mentioned some of the difficulties that would have to be met. A large space, he said, would be needed, in a central position, and there would have to be not only provision for filtering the air of the gallery and for cleaning the casts regularly but, in addition to the director, there would have to be an assistant travelling round the museums to secure that the right casts were ordered and carefully made, and that cast-makers should not foist upon the museum casts from moulds which had already been used an excessive number of times. He added, on the subject of cleaning, that the experiment at Oxford of spraying an exceedingly thin coat of oil paint on to the casts appeared to have been successful and allowed the casts to be washed satisfactorily at intervals.

The Times
24 October 1929

Part III

An Appreciation

by Martin Robertson

A COPY OF *One Man in his Time* was first shown me when I was writing an extended obituary of Bernard Ashmole for the British Academy. We had got to know each other shortly before the war, and we were friends for the remaining fifty years of his long life. Before that we had met occasionally, and of course I knew much about his work; but he was seventeen years my senior and I had only vague notions about his earlier time. An appeal to his charming family brought the warmest and most helpful response, including a loan of the autobiography. This of course eased my task immensely; but I was also very much impressed by the work itself, and I am delighted by the decision to publish it. At the same time I share a feeling expressed to me by some of the family that, while the book gives a fascinating picture of the changing world through which Bernard lived and of the not inconsiderable part he played in some of the events of those times, his natural modesty mutes the strength as well as the charm of his own personality. There was a quality in Bernard which nobody who met and talked with him could fail to feel; and the family have asked me to contribute a sketch which might indicate something of that quality to a reader who comes to this book cold. It is a task which I am far from sure that I can carry out effectively; but at least that strong and delightful personality is very clear to me and I am happy to do what I can to conjure it up for others.

Reading the book crystallized in my mind a feeling, already present but hardly formulated, which I think is important for a realization of Bernard's personality and of the character of his work. He was of course a scholar, in the field of classical archaeology and art. That was the career he chose and in which he made his name, and it is for his work in that career that he is remembered. Indeed he was a remarkable scholar, with a gift not too many have for expressing what he had to say in words which are a pleasure to read. He held important professorships as well as museum posts, was a Fellow of the British Academy for fifty years, showered with the highest academic honours – but somehow the word 'academic' does not apply to him. I am not decrying Academe. I was born into it, have never left it and shall die in it. I have a great respect for the academic world and for many academics, and Bernard was unquestionably a very good academic. Yet somehow when I compare him to most of my other teachers and colleagues the word does not seem right. I do not intend the facile contrast between Academe and the 'real world' outside, between academics and men of action. Bernard's record in two world wars is remarkable, but something of the sort could be said of not a few academics. What I feel about Bernard is that he was an outstandingly *practical* man, challenged by practical problems and a solver of them. It is above all, I think, this practicality which gives his art-historical writing its own special character; and this character makes his scholarship in an unusual degree a part of the way he lived life in general.

I have begun with this aspect of Bernard's make-up because I think it is a key one, and I shall return to it, but it was not the first thing that struck one about him. That, surely was his charm: true charm, which really is what it seems. When one met him it was natural to like him; soon inevitable to love and trust him; and that proved right. He was as reliable as he was delightful.

I first got to know Bernard in circumstances which might have been difficult. I was then Assistant Keeper in the Department of Greek and Roman Antiquities in the British Museum, my first job. Before that I had been a student at the British School at Athens. There I had fallen in love with Greece and Greek art, and my work had been guided by the young Director, Humfry Payne, a deeply exciting and inspiring teacher who had fired me with a determination to make my career in this field of study. Payne died suddenly in 1936, and later the same year I took up the post at the British Museum; but after the excitement of the years in Greece and the tragedy of Payne's death I found it hard to settle into the museum work, and then, within about two years, the Department was disrupted by events which ended in the departure of the two senior officers. In this crisis Bernard, then Professor at University College London, was asked to act as Keeper of the Department. He accepted (not the first awkward situation in which he was asked and agreed, not very happily but from a feeling that it was what he ought to do, to step in and pick up the pieces); and for some years he held the posts of Professor and Keeper together. Thus I now found myself working closely under him with another young Assistant Keeper, my contemporary and friend Denys Haynes; and the museum work seemed suddenly to take on a different character.

I say Denys and I worked 'under' Bernard, and so of course we did; there was no question who was in charge. Yet somehow it felt much more like working 'with' him. He treated one as a person, sharing his knowledge and ideas with open generosity and asking for and respecting any ideas one might have oneself. He made us feel that he saw us as fellow-enquirers, learning together, instead of (what we much rather were) learners to be instructed; and yet he did instruct and guide, gently but genuinely. For the detail of the particular fields I was already specializing in (painted pottery of various kinds, never one of Bernard's main interests), I learned much more from others; in particular first from Humfry Payne and then over a long period from J. D. (Sir John) Beazley. The special thing which, looking back, I feel I got from working with Bernard Ashmole is a sense of proportion: of the relation of any particular specialism one might be engaged in to the whole field; and beyond that perhaps of scholarship and study to the rest of life as one was living it.

Here perhaps is the place to say more of what I mean by Bernard's practicality in relation to his scholarship. In relation to his life outside it is evident enough. Look, for instance, at his account of his experiences in the second war or of the way he coped with the problems of the British School at Rome or those of the Department in the British Museum; or, in a different mode, at his involvement in the design and building of the great modern house, High and Over, which he put up in the early thirties on a hill above Amersham, or the charming fountain-basin he cast in concrete with the help of an umbrella for his garden at Iffley twenty years later. Striking examples of the recognition of this character by others are the facts (new to me when I read *One Man in his Time*) that he was offered in 1948 the Secretaryship of the British Academy, and even more unexpectedly some ten years later the Directorship of the Warburg Institute: a most prestigious institution specializing in a field well outside his own. In his scholarship this practical bent showed itself in an every-growing curiosity, rigorously pursued, about questions of how and under what circumstances works of art were actually produced. He had very fine aesthetic appreciation and could express it beautifully, but he became more and more concerned with the practical problems of how the work of art came into being.

Bernard's first and enduring love in ancient art was sculpture, but through architectural sculpture he became deeply interested in architecture too; and what I mean by his practical scholarship is most perfectly illustrated in two books produced, like much of his most exciting work, after his retirement: *Olympia: the Sculptures of the Temple of Zeus*, and *Architect and Sculptor in Classical Greece*, which deals with the Temple of Zeus again, the Parthenon at Athens and the Mausoleum of Halicarnassus. All these monuments he loved for their art and he writes of it with fine appreciation. At the same time, however, he is deeply concerned to consider in detail how they were actually brought into being: how many men would it take to produce the architectural members and the sculptures in the time allowed; how much work was done in the quarry; how were the carvings put in place; and so on; and this concern gives his writing here a *gravamen* and an edge which set it apart among art-historical studies.

Architect and Sculptor in Classical Greece started as lectures, as did other of Bernard's books. In more than one passage of the autobiography he speaks dismissively of his lecturing, but this is strange to anyone who heard him. He was in fact in demand as a lecturer, and with reason. Indeed I would place him on his day as perhaps the best lecturer I have ever heard, combining as few can impeccable scholarship, originality of thought, exquisite presentation, and wit. I think I have not used this word before, but it was another important feature of his make-up. I have spoken of his charm, but he could be also extremely sharp. His wit, however, was only on occasion of that kind; generally it was just part of the natural flow of his thought and conversation, part of the pleasure of his company. And here another word comes to mind which it would be a shocking mistake to omit from an attempt to evoke Bernard. He was *fun*.

Bernard Ashmole and the British Museum

by Ian Jenkins

BERNARD ASHMOLE WAS Keeper of Greek and Roman Antiquities at the British Museum from 12 January 1939 until August 1956. His appointment, following close on the incident of the cleaning of the Elgin Marbles, was intended to restore confidence and stability to the Department. The relative calm of his early Keepership, however, was shortlived, and he had little time to realise his own priorities for the collections before the whole Museum was precipitated into emergency preparations for war.

At first Ashmole held his Museum post jointly with the Yates Professorship in Classical Archaeology at University College, London. There he was one of a distinguished line of scholars of Greek art to hold the Chair. In holding both posts simultaneously, Ashmole repeated the experience of his predecessor Charles Newton who, as the first incumbent of the Yates professorship in 1880, had also occupied it while retaining his post of Keeper. Ashmole devoted two and a half days during university terms to the Museum, and five days a week for the remainder of the year. It is an indication of the extent to which both the university and museum professions have changed since his day, that such an arrangement is now unthinkable.

Ashmole took over a department where the Academic staff had been depleted by the early retirement of F. N. Pryce as Keeper, and the resignation of R. P. Hinks as Assistant. He could, however, draw upon the assistance of Martin Robertson, who had joined the Museum in September 1936 with responsibility for the Greek vase collection, and the strength of Assistant Keepers was brought up to two in February 1939, when Denys Haynes, a specialist in ancient bronzes, was transferred from the Victoria and Albert Museum.

One of Ashmole's first acts as Keeper was to have a number of antiquities stripped of their old restoration. The restored heads of the Muses on the Apotheosis of Homer relief, signed by Archelaos of Priene were removed; plaster additions to the head of the so-called Mausolos from the Mausoleum at Halikarnassos were taken off; and a number of vases had their overpainting erased. In such matters Ashmole was a purist, and this same tendency can be seen in his approach to the major task confronting him both as Keeper and as the Department's sculpture expert, namely to preside over the completion of the rearrangement of the Parthenon sculptures.

Already in 1928 at the request of the Royal Commission on National Museums

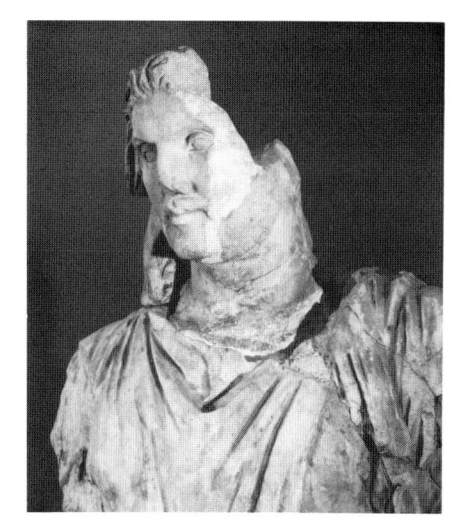

'Mausolos' from the Mausoleum at Halikarnassos (British Museum 1000).

A. Before nineteenth-century restorations were removed by Bernard

B. After restorations were removed.

and Art Galleries, with Donald Robertson and John Beazley as co-signatories, he had put his name to a document making detailed and impassioned proposals for a new exhibition of the Elgin Marbles (see p.69). At that time they were still in the room designed for them by Robert Smirke, completed in 1832. For nearly a century the Elgin Room of the British Museum had served as a laboratory of Parthenon studies, where the original body of material salvaged by Lord Elgin from the wreck of the Parthenon was under constant review. Every new discovery by way of joins among the Elgin Marbles themselves, or of material uncovered on the Acropolis following the Greek war of Independence, or of stray finds in European private collections, was added to the sculpture, whether in the original or in the form of a cast. Such was the extent of the casts that by the end of the century the frieze as displayed in the Museum (including casts of the west frieze of the Parthenon made for Elgin in 1802) consisted of sixty percent marble and forty percent plaster. In the metopes and pediment sculptures, too, there were extensive plaster additions representing the labours of generations of scholars and masons who had endeavoured to render the sculptures of the Parthenon as complete as possible. More than once the sculptures had to be rearranged in order to accommodate the accumulation of knowledge. Ashmole and his colleagues disapproved of this combination of marble and plaster, and took a different line in their report to the Commission arguing for a simpler exhibition, restricted to original fragments only. One of the aims in the Elgin Room had been to show as fully as possible how the design of the Parthenon sculptures was dictated by their intended function as architectural ornament. Ashmole took the other view, namely that although the sculpture was in origin architectural, it now had a status of art, and this should be acknowledged in the exhibition. All supplementary information by way of models and photographs was to be removed, along with the casts, and displayed in a separate exhibition, leaving the beauty of the unimpeded sculpture to speak for itself.

The opportunity to make these recommendations a reality came about when Lord Duveen offered to build a new gallery for the reception of the Marbles on open ground to the west of the Elgin Room. At first, the scheme drawn up by Duveen's chosen architect J. Russell Pope was not to the liking either of the Museum's Trustees, or of Ashmole and the other experts. It was criticised especially for having reduced the Parthenon sculptures to the status of an ornament to Pope's design (see p.70). A compromise was reached, and some ten years after voicing his opinion, Ashmole now found himself charged with the physical task of putting the sculptures into the newly completed Duveen Gallery. First, the position of the sculptures was tried out using casts and then piece by piece, the sculptures were removed to their new setting. The project was not completed, however, when the long-expected outbreak of hostilities with Germany necessitated a hasty dismantling of all the Museum's galleries.

Martin Robertson, who had been attending the Sixth International Congress of Classical Archaeology in Berlin, cut his visit short. On the evening of 24 August he hurried home to escape the risk of internment and to join in the effort to safeguard the collections. Ashmole's report to the Trustees of 9 October 1939 describes the progress that had been made in the interim. The removal of the collections of smaller objects, vases, terracottas and bronzes, displayed on the upper floor of the Museum proceeded with haste and already a good number had been packed and despatched, either to Boughton in Northamptonshire or to the Aldwych Tube (see p.72). Safeguarding the sculptures on the lower floor was, however, of necessity a slower business. Three small pieces went first to the Tube: the horse's head of Selene, the Charioteer relief from the Mausoleum frieze and the head (only) of the Demeter of Knidos (see p.71). The remainder of the sculptures were sandbagged at strong points in the galleries or in the basement. The Parthenon sculptures with a number of others were collected together at the north and south ends of the Duveen Gallery, under a large "pent-house" erected behind the pediment base of reinforced concrete. This makeshift shelter was built of massive timbers roofed with corrugated iron and covered with a double layer of sandbags.

Although Ashmole technically remained Keeper of Greek and Roman Antiquities throughout the war, he ceased to serve the Museum actively after November 1939 when he was transferred to the War Office, before joining the Royal Air Force on 21 July 1940. Haynes went to the War Office in October 1939 and subsequently enlisted in the Army. Martin Robertson, therefore, was temporarily left behind to oversee the collections until August 1940 when he too transferred to the War Office before enlisting in the Army.

By October 1940 the Museum was beginning to suffer damage from enemy bombing. In January 1941 the first substantial move of the Parthenon frieze was made to the Aldwych Tube and this transfer was complete by April 1941. Meanwhile the pediment sculpture was taken down to the Sepulchral Basement, so-called from its having served as a repository for funerary sculpture when first built in the mid nineteenth century. These precautions were well-advised, since on the night of 15 November 1940 the Duveen Gallery had "suffered when a bomb exploded in it, piercing the floor, blowing out the glass in the roof, doing much damage to the heating and the lighting arrangements and to the walls at the north end". The sculptures that remained at either end were unharmed. How much happier was the effect of this bomb than that which wrecked the Parthenon two and a half centuries earlier!

After the war Ashmole was the first of the academic staff of the Department to be demobilised and already in October 1945 he was contemplating the renewal of the emptied and bomb-damaged exhibition galleries. Haynes did not return to his Museum duties until September 1946 and Robertson two months later. The latter was destined to succeed as Yates Professor, when in 1948 Ashmole gave up his University appointment to concentrate full-time upon the considerable task of reconstructing the Museum. In May 1947 the Department was further strengthened by the arrival of Reynold Higgins and, after Robertson's departure, Peter Corbett joined the Museum service in October 1949.

In the short term little could be achieved since not one of the galleries upstairs was weather proof and, of those on the ground floor, only the Old Elgin Room was serviceable. Meanwhile the basement was overcrowded and chaotic with the mass of sculpture that had been taken down there and sandbagged. The immediate priority was the retrieval and re-exhibition of the sculptures of the Parthenon. The first sculptures came out of the Tube on 25 November 1948 and, in what seems a remarkably short time, the new exhibition was complete by early September of the following year. The re-emergence of the sculptures from their makeshift sanctuary was seen by the press as a symbol of Britain's post-war revival. A generation of young people, it was remarked, had grown up without seeing them, and now at last they were returned. There is an ancient apocryphal saying, "Pheidias belongs to Peace", and it was at the end of a protracted war with France that in 1817 the Elgin Marbles first went on display at the British Museum. The post-Napoleonic *Pax Britannica* did not prove as long-lived as might then have been hoped, but only in this century, first in the Great War and then in the Second World War, have the sculptures been forced to leave the inner sanctum of the British Museum. One may wish that they should never do so again.

Ashmole, who twenty years before had voiced strong opinions upon how the Marbles should be displayed, clearly relished the opportunity to resume the work rudely interrupted by the outbreak of war. Never having reconciled himself to the Duveen Gallery as a setting, he was now free to experiment with the Old Elgin Room. Here he placed the frieze around the walls and the sculptures of the east pediment on freestanding bases. In a smaller room to the north, the remainder of the south frieze was arranged on one side and on the other stood the sculpture of the west pediment (see p.127). Then in a further gallery to the north of the last were displayed the metopes and Erechtheum Caryatid. In his own account Ashmole describes the colour of the walls as a pure Prussian blue. Only the metope room was so coloured, however, while the rest was painted blue below the line of the frieze and white above.

A *Short Guide* to the Parthenon sculpture was edited by Ashmole and in the Preface he reflects upon the difference between this and the earlier arrangement. He may well have felt he owed something to A. H. Smith, a former Keeper, who had remained bitterly opposed to the scheme for dismantling the old exhibition. He more than any other scholar knew the virtue of the casts as a resource for understanding the sculptures and his monumental publication of 1910 had gone further than anybody before or since to gather all the fragments together in one volume and render them intelligible. Ashmole praises the work of Smith and his other predecessors, and acknowledges the importance of the casts: "this unique collection still exists", he says, "much of it is in frequent use by students, and the whole will, it is hoped, eventually be made accessible again". This was more than mere platitude. Ashmole was firmly committed to the value of casts of ancient sculpture as a resource for students and scholars, as his own account of the collections at University College and Oxford bears out. The ambition, however, to reconstruct the entire Parthenon sculptures in plaster in the basement under the Duveen Gallery was never realised and still today London lacks what the Old Elgin Room had once provided.

Ashmole was not entirely satisfied with his own work. The separation of some of the south frieze from the main body of material was an acknowledged fault. Nor did he care for the utilitarian lighting which, through lack of funds, was forced upon the rooms. He was convinced, however, that his arrangement was an improvement upon the Duveen Gallery and when, eventually, plans were laid for repairing the damage there, he proposed that it should be put to some other use, namely for the display of the Lycian sculptures from Xanthos brought back from south-west Turkey by Charles Fellows in the early 1840s, and for the collection of mostly Roman sculpture, once belonging to Charles Townley. While a reconstruction of the Nereid Monument from Xanthos was a possible option, in keeping with the scale of the Gallery, it must be said that the suggestion to include the Townley marbles was not really practical. Many of these are less than life-size and would certainly have been overwhelmed by the grandeur of the room.

Nothing was resolved before Ashmole left the Museum for Oxford and was succeeded in 1956 by his senior Assistant Keeper, Denys Haynes. The latter adopted his predecessor's line of resisting the return of the Parthenon sculptures to the Duveen Gallery and even went so far - in the event of Duveen's heirs refusing its use for another purpose - as to suggest measures for toning down the architecture. These included stripping out the gris d'Alésie panels, many of which were damaged or loosened by the war and making good the walls with plain plaster and paint. Further, he proposed taking out the ornamental columns flanking the entrance to the transepts at either end of the main gallery, in order to insert crosswalls pierced by simple door-ways. Finally, he conceived of lowering the ceilings so as to bring the source of natural light closer to the sculptures. None of these measures was carried out, however, and in 1962 the Duveen Gallery, newly repaired to its original design and with the Parthenon sculptures returned, was reopened to the public. Nearly seventy tons of the pink-cream stone used to repair the walls was quarried near Ales in southern France and black marble was imported from Trieste to renew the floor.

Ashmole's criticisms of the Duveen Gallery are justified: the colour of the walls is too close to that of the sculptures, the natural light source is too far removed and the architecture is somewhat overbearing. Nevertheless the space is dignified and dramatic. At night when the sculptures are illuminated by artificial lighting and the upper parts of the interior recede into shadow, the room is very splendid indeed. It is difficult to judge from photographs only, but Ashmole's arrangement in the Old Elgin Room seems somewhat stark. Having seen the Duveen Gallery grow, as it were, from seed, he was all too aware of its shortcomings and perhaps, did not fully appreciate its virtues. When it was reopened to an entirely new audience it was greeted by an expression of delight, which is commonly the response of every new visitor today.

By the time Ashmole handed over the Keepership to his successor, the collections of classical antiquities had been largely returned to public view. Ashmole's rare combination of practical as well as scholarly ability was ideally suited to the exceptional and difficult problems to be faced by a war-time Keeper. His practical side went hand-in-hand with a profound respect for craftsmanship, which came out in his writing about sculpture with its emphasis on the technique of carving stone. Such a study was his analysis of the position at which the British Museum's colossal head of Asklepios from Melos, the so-called Blacas head, should be viewed.

A. Old poise.   *B. New poise.*

Blacas Head (British Museum 550). Bernard applied his knowledge of the techniques of Greek sculpture to determine the correct poise of the head.

Demeter from Knidos (British Museum 1300).
In a magisterial publication Bernard attributed the style of the statue to the sculptor Leochares.

This was published in the *Annual of the British School at Athens* for 1951. The versatility of his talents was demonstrated by another article which appeared that same year in the *Journal of Hellenic Studies*. This was his magisterial publication of the Demeter of Knidos, combining a full discussion of all technical aspects of the sculpture with a virtuoso commentary upon its style. Scholars interested in the methods of ancient craftsmen sometimes show a tendency to lose sight of the artistic ends to which those methods were put. This, fortunately, was not the case with Ashmole, who published works exhibit that blend of practicality and aesthetic feeling, which characterises the best of English art history.

The Ashmole Archive at King's College London

by Geoffrey Waywell

BERNARD ASHMOLE's personal archive of photographs of ancient Greek and Roman sculpture, which he had built up during his long lifetime of distinguished research, came to the Classics Department at King's College in the University of London in May 1982 at his personal insistence. The venue must have seemed strange to uninformed outside observers, for Ashmole had no academic contact hitherto with London University's second oldest College on the Strand, although as a result of his generous gesture he was elected a Fellow of King's College London.

Ashmole was justifiably proud of his collection of sculpture photographs. It was substantial, consisting of more than 10,000 black and white photographs, stored in sixty box files, nearly as many glass negatives and slides, and large quantities of notes, letters and off-prints. He assessed it in the following characteristically understated terms:

> It is not by any means comprehensive, but it has all the heads of the Parthenon frieze (published in *Jahrbuch* many years ago and copied by Becatti in *Problemi Fidiaci*), many unpublished details of the Amazon frieze of the Mausoleum, and details of all the heads of the Phigaleian frieze, together with various oddments I photographed in Greece and Italy, as well as Alinari's and Anderson's from there and elsewhere.
>
> Letter (5 March 1981), Ashmole Archive

It reflected therefore the special interests of Ashmole's academic career, with a strong pioneering input of personal photographs of sculptures in the collection of the British Museum. At the same time it was extensive enough to form the basis of a really fine research archive on ancient Greek and Roman sculpture.

King's College was not the London home originally intended. When Ashmole left the Mill House at Iffley to retire to Scotland in 1973, it was to University College London that he decided to hand over, or 'bequeath' as he put it (letter 10 January 1973, Ashmole Archive), his collection of photographs, more specifically to the person of Peter Corbett who was then the incumbent of the Yates Chair in the Department of Classical Archaeology formerly held by Ashmole. This of course was an entirely appropriate thing to do. Ashmole had spent most of his academic life in London, either at University College or the British Museum, and it seemed natural to leave his photographic collection there for the benefit of future generations. He did not offer it to Oxford because, as he put it quite simply, that "will eventually have Beazley's". He was, however, determined that it remain in Great Britain which lacked an ancient sculpture archive of such international quality, and to this end decided not to give it to the British School at Athens (another important institution to him), and had "refused a very handsome offer to buy it from abroad" (letter 5 March 1981, Ashmole Archive). The intention was that the photographs be removed from their somewhat battered box-files, be sorted, mounted on card (as many were curling), identified and annotated, and then made "freely accessible" to students and scholars.

A start was made on this not particularly ambitious project, but soon, for a variety of reasons, progress slowed and eventually halted, and it was in some exasperation that Ashmole asked in 1981 if anything could be done to restart the momentum. Given the well-known (mostly friendly) rivalry that has existed between University College and King's College in London since their foundations, the situation was potentially delicate, and no precipitate action was taken. Fortunately a convenient catalyst existed in the person of John Barron, who had for long been a colleague of Peter Corbett's at University College, and was then Professor of Greek and Head of the Classics Department at King's College London. Thanks to his negotiating skills and the active promotion of Ashmole, a perfectly amicable agreement was drawn up between all parties that the collection of photographs should be transferred to King's College, so that the programme of sorting, mounting and identification could be actively pursued and brought to completion. So it was that the Ashmole Archive came to be established at King's College London in 1982.

The College was extremely grateful. Personally I regarded the transfer with pride as a generous accolade to my own work on Greek sculpture. Despite the great difference in our ages and status, we had been sculptural colleagues since the 1960s, and it was largely through Ashmole's support that I embarked on the study of the free-standing sculpture of the Mausoleum at Halicarnassus, working as part of a team alongside himself, Donald Strong and Kristian Jeppesen, who was re-excavating the site.

Funding for archives such as that which was to be established in Ashmole's name is always problematical. In this case, although King's College provided the space, funded the overheads and supplied some minor equipment, it was not in a position to pay the salary of a specialist archivist or research assistant of the kind desperately needed. The transfer and maintenance of the photographic collection was made on the understanding that it be self-financing. Funds needed to be raised if any real progress were to be made. The College agreed that I should be appointed Honorary Curator, with overall responsibility for the Archive and its development, but my other academic duties allowed me very little time to devote to its organisation on a regular basis. Fortunately applications to grant-awarding bodies and trusts, including the British Academy, the Derby Fund of Oxford University, and the Esmée Fairbairn Charitable Trust, enabled sufficient funds to be raised to allow the appointment for two years of Dr Carlos A. Picón as Research Assistant.

Picón was an extremely able student of ancient sculpture. A graduate of Haverford and Bryn Mawr, and a postgraduate of Oxford University, he had recently come to the end of his term as Junior Research Fellow of Christ Church, Oxford. Later, in 1990, he was to be appointed Curator-in-Charge of Greek and Roman Art, at the Metropolitan Museum of Art in New York. It was largely thanks to Picón's energy, knowledge and vitality that the initial sorting, mounting and identification of the photographs took place. He was also the driving force behind the organisation of a Loan Exhibition at Sotheby's in January 1986, the purpose of which was to raise further funds in aid of the Archive, in the hope of putting its finances once and for all on a sound footing. It did not quite do this. The final sum raised from donations and catalogue sales was, however, enough to keep the wolf from the door for a few more years, and it did bring the Ashmole Archive to the attention of the international academic and artistic establishment.

A fine group of sixty-seven antiquities, sculptures, vases, bronzes and paintings, was borrowed from a wide range of mostly private collections, and displayed in an imaginative arrangement for two weeks between 15th and 31st January 1986. The costs were generously met by Sotheby's, and much of the support work was carried out by Felicity Nicholson, Head of the Antiquities Department. An excellent catalogue of the objects exhibited was put together by Picón, entitled *Classical Antiquities from Private Collections in Great Britain*. This contained not only full photographic and bibliographic documentation, but also an appreciative thumb-nail biography of Bernard Ashmole by Martin Robertson, and a list of his published writings by Donna Kurtz. Ashmole was then ninety-two and was too frail to make the long journey to be present at the opening ceremony, but he was represented by his daughter Dr Stella Ring at the well-attended gathering, and the exhibition was formally launched by the Earl of Jellicoe, who had the fortunate credentials of being both a Director of Sotheby's and Chairman of the Council of King's College London. In a short address the present Honorary Curator of the Archive spoke as follows:

> Bernard Ashmole is one of the most distinguished scholars of ancient sculpture this country has produced. His career and his publications listed in the official catalogue to the exhibition make that abundantly plain. The Ashmole Archive is his personal collection of working photographs and related material. It is very extensive, very individual, full of insights and information to be found nowhere else. It is infinitely worthy of preservation, organisation and utilisation. That is what this appeal is about. We want to draw attention to the existence of this Archive and its potential as a research centre in London, and we would like to raise the necessary money to be able to make fullest and best use of it. What we are looking for is longer-term sponsorship or endowment from private sources. Sotheby's have launched us on our way by sponsoring this exhibition and reception, and many of you have already helped by lending

objects or making donations. I take this opportunity of publicly offering you my warmest thanks, and of hoping that the good start we have made will lead to still richer fruition.

Proceedings were well recorded in the national and international press, most of whose art-correspondents were present, even a representative from the *News of the World*, attracted, as he blithely confided to me, by a combination of free drinks and naked torsos. Gervase Jackson-Stops, who wrote a long and well-illustrated account in *Country Life* (January 30, 1986, pages 238-9), described the exhibition as "a truly Lucullan feast of Greek and Roman art, chosen from private collections all over Britain", the aim of which was "both to raise funds for this worthwhile enterprise and to honour the achievements of a great scholar." And Souren Melikian reported in the *International Herald Tribune* (January 25-26, 1986) how "Sotheby's has put together an enchanting display of Greek and Roman works of art. For once these are not for sale. They tell more about the cultural contribution of Britain than volumes of social history."

When all the excitement died down, and the exhibits were returned to their rightful owners, the Archive subsided into its quiet, academic routine. Picón left about a year later to take up a curatorial post at the Denman Collection in San Antonio, Texas, and was replaced as Research Assistant by Claire Davison, who continued the still considerable task of recording and cataloguing with equal skill, panache and persistence, and eventually brought the work to completion. A considerable portion of the money raised from the exhibition was spent on acquiring a specialist sculpture library in support of the photographs, and fresh grants were obtained for the transfer of the old silver nitrate negatives to safer modern cellophane, and for the acquisition of new photographs to fill gaps in the sequences. This expansion was further supported by the donation of significant collections of photographs to the Archive. These included prints and negatives of Lycian sculpture taken by the late Professor F. Tritsch (Universities of Vienna and Birmingham), and copious illustrations of Roman sculpture and architectural ornament from the estate of the late Professor D. E. Strong, courtesy of his widow, Shirley Strong.

Since 1991 the research profile of the Ashmole Archive has been enormously enhanced by the award of a major grant from the Leverhulme Trust in support of a programme of computerisation. Two new research assistants have been appointed, Dr Hafed Walda and Dr Birte Lundgreen, who are working with Claire Davison and the Professor of Classical Archaeology on the creation of a Greek sculpture image database named *Daedalus* after the first legendary Greek sculptor. The aim of the project is to draw upon and utilise the extensive photographic documentation of the Ashmole Archive in order to create a computerized database combining written word and visual image of all the textual, epigraphical and sculptural evidence relating to the life, work, and style of all known Greek sculptors from the Archaic through the Hellenistic periods (c. 650–30 BC).

A pilot scheme devoted to Pheidias, the best-known and biggest-name of them all, has proved to be encouragingly successful, and gives great hopes for the continuation of the research at the forefront of developing computer technology. Problems associated with rights to image reproduction have been eased by the transfer to the Archive on long-term loan of the photographic records of both the Hellenic and Roman Societies from the vaults of the Institute of Classical Studies at Gordon Square.

More than ten years on, therefore, it can be stated that the establishment of the Ashmole Archive at King's College in the University of London has been a success. Thanks to the efforts of a number of scholars of differing ages, outlooks and career stages, and thanks to the generosity and wise support of many individuals and institutions from all over the world, a fine, diverse photographic archive of international quality has been set up with all the best resources, both traditional and modern, to carry out effective large scale sculpture research at post-doctoral level. It is an Archive, and a project, fit to carry the distinguished name of Bernard Ashmole and to commemorate all that he stood for in academic excellence related to the sculptural image.

COUNTRY HOMES • GARDENS OLD & NEW

HIGH AND OVER, AMERSHAM, BUCKS.
The Residence of PROFESSOR BERNARD ASHMOLE

Designed on an original plan by Mr. Amyas Connell to provide the amenities of modern life with the greatest economy of materials and means.

THIS house is the conception of young men, and of young men educated in the classic tradition. Professor Ashmole is the youthful Yates Professor of Classical Archæology at London University. Mr. Connell was the winner of the Rome Scholarship some years ago, and met his future client at the British School in Rome. It is useful to know these personal details because they had considerable bearing upon this challenging exposition of modern architecture. The affinities of "High and Over" are with the flat white houses of the Mediterranean, and ultimately with the lucid and practical ideals of classic civilisation. It is natural that, at first sight, the building should startle. But the more closely one studies the whole arrangement the more reasonable and pleasing does it reveal itself to be. It may sound paradoxical to say that it is a pure expression of the classic mentality. We are apt to confuse the essentially rational basis of classic art with the humanist gloss which, derived from the Roman misapprehension of it, has sentimentalised the clear outlook of the Greeks. This is not to suggest that the building is in any respect an attempt to revive an antique style. It is rather to say that client and architect approached the problem of designing a home with the whole-hearted respect for the elementary amenities of life that characterised Greek civilisation. This house has been built round a clear conception of reasonable contemporary life. Its sanction is that it works, on the whole, more easily and more enjoyably than houses of conventional type.

Architecture, however, cannot be viewed, as it may be conceived, in the abstract. It inevitably forms part of a landscape, and this house, perched on a bare hillside above the old brick town of Amersham, has, of course, come in for a good deal of hostile comment. For the most part this is really directed against the novelty of the building, for people hate novelty. But it must be frankly admitted that the white house, with its adjuncts, particularly the water tower on the skyline above it, does not fit in with the traditional view of English landscape. It will be wedded with the hillside to a much greater extent than it is at present when the garden planned for it is completed. But houses of this type, which are certain to become commoner in the immediate future, can never fit into the English landscape in the same way as buildings constructed of local materials and in traditional styles.

RELATION TO THE LANDSCAPE

Much is rightly made of the need for preserving the character of the countryside by the use of suitable materials in new buildings, and under the Town and Country Planning Bill it should be possible to compel their use in regions of especial rural or picturesque character. But it is essential that residential zones, such as the Amersham district has become, and in which every sincere experiment in architecture is to be encouraged, should not be hampered by restrictions fundamentally narrow minded. The old nuclei, such as Amersham village, should be jealously preserved, and this house is far enough off not to jar on the traditional scene. Considerable difficulty

Architect and Building News.
1.—FROM THE SOUTH-WEST
The slope below the terrace is to be planted as a wild garden
Copyright.

Sept. 19th, 1931. COUNTRY LIFE. 303

2.—LOOKING DOWNHILL FROM THE SOUTH-EAST
In the foreground the terraced rose garden

3.—THE HEXAGONAL HALL
From left to right: living room, entrance door and dining room

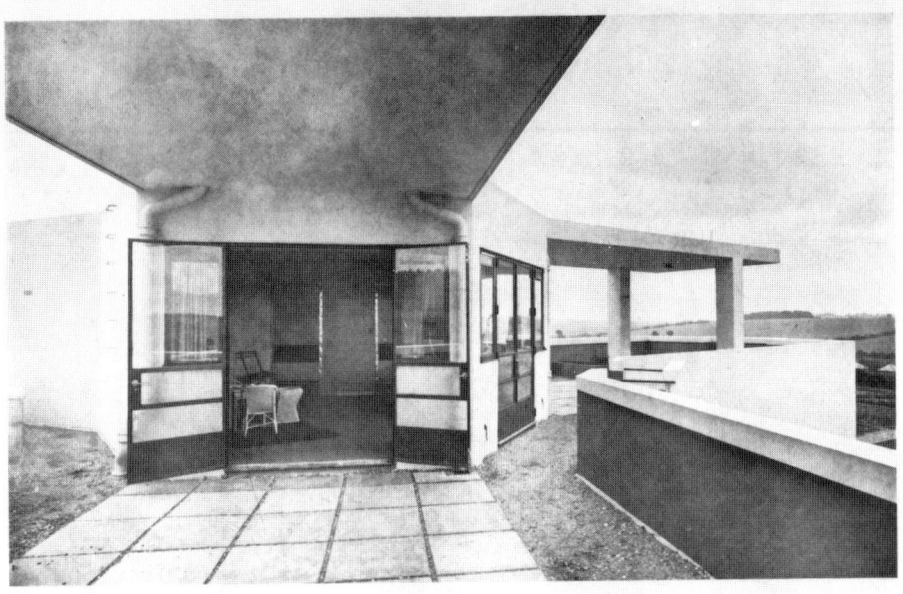

4.—THE ROOF AND DAY NURSERY

was met by the architect in getting his plans passed by the local authority, who only did so at length "with extreme reluctance." Yet every facility is afforded by the same authority for the erection of the most bogus types of "engagement ring" domiciles, which are true neither to standards of good architecture nor to the spirit of the age. "High and Over," on the other hand, is sound and stimulating architecture, a brilliant synthesis of contemporary thought with contemporary materials. And there is nothing in its clean level lines nor in its whiteness that does not harmonise with the rolling chalk uplands. It does, in fact, conform carefully to the contours of the site. But it makes no pretence to having grown out of the soil, a fiction singularly inappropriate to the homes of city workers, but says frankly, "I am the home of a twentieth century family that loves air and sunlight and open country."

THREE MAIN OBJECTIVES

In the owner's own words, it "was built with three main objectives: to take utmost advantage of the scanty English sunshine; to enjoy to the full the magnificent view across and up the valley of the Misbourne; and to conform to the immediate contours." The plan is in the shape of a Y—that is, a sun-trap to the west and south and a screen to north and east. The windows are continuous towards the favoured quarters, and, consisting of plate glass in steel frames that allow of varying adjustments for ventilation, admit the maximum of light and

5.—THE STAIRCASE BAY

6.—THE STAIRCASE, LOOKING ACROSS THE UPPER PART OF THE HALL

7.—THE LIVING ROOM. JADE GREEN CELLULOSE AND CHROMIUM STEEL

8.—THE STUDY. SELF-COLOURED WOODWORK AND CONCEALED LIGHTING

9.—A SMALL BEDROOM

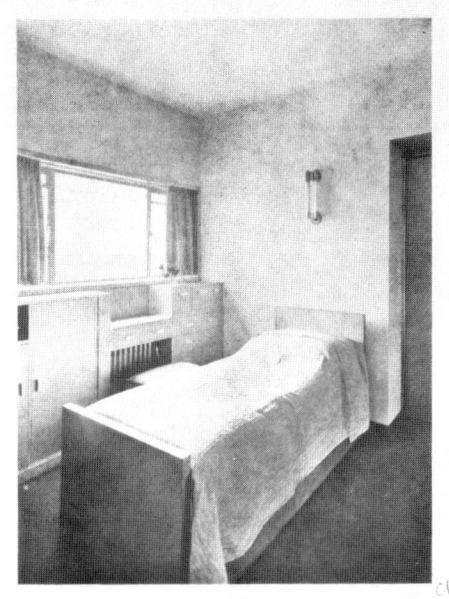

10.—THE DINING ROOM. WALLS OF A ROSY ORANGE

view. It happened that my visit was on a grey and rainy day of the kind that one might expect to make a house of this kind depressing. On the contrary, the rooms being so much lighter than the ordinary, one had the impression indoors that it was a bright day.

The construction is a reinforced concrete frame with brick filling externally, rendered with cement whitewashed; a cavity wall; and internal filling of concrete blocks. The roof, a great feature of the house, is paved with waterproofed concrete covered with fine shingle and concrete setts. Above it are flat hoods of concrete to give shade and shelter and to support the children's hammocks. From a distance these hoods remind some people of the wings of an aeroplane, but, while the association of ideas connects the building with contemporary engineering, it is unintentional.

The entry is from a level forecourt to the north, to the left of which is the tradesmen's entrance to the service wing, and to the right a ramp down to the garage and coke store,

11.—BEDROOM IN THE NORTH-WEST WING

where is also the boiler, in the basement allowed by the slope beneath the living-room. The front door, in common with doors throughout the house, is flush-surfaced, in this case faced with chromium-plated steel and flanked by a band of windows lighting the lobbies. It gives into the hexagonal hall that occupies the centre of the plan, with the three living-rooms opening off it, a glazed garden loggia in the south-west face, and the staircase on the south-east. The compact dining-room adjoins the kitchen, with which it communicates by a hatch. All the room doors can be folded right back on a festive occasion, throwing the whole ground floor into a single space. In the centre of the hall floor is a fountain in a sunk glass basin that lights up at night, its jet capable of being thrown through the circular space above it in the first floor landing. In hot weather this is said to be very cooling for the atmosphere, and at all times the prattling of the minuscule jet is agreeable. The floor is paved in black marble, with insets of cast glass. The steel doors are cellulosed silver and glazed, partly to insulate sound and partly as providing means for a subtle method of decoration, the inside surfaces of the glass being cellulose-sprayed in semi-translucent patterns.

LUXURIOUS EFFICIENCY

The fitting up of the rooms has been designed to incorporate the needs of comfort and storage in the fitments. Its success is well seen in Fig. 8, Professor Ashmole's study. This has electric heating and recessed lights in ceiling and bookcase lintels. Bookcases, drawers and desk (a dream of a desk for the literary) are constructed of self-coloured woods and built in. The living-room (Fig. 7), similarly treated, but in cellulose and chromium steel, has a built-in radio set. It also has the only open hearth in the house, constructed to burn either coal or peat. A novel and ingenious arrangement is a hopper at the back of the hearth into which all ashes can be swept and dropped to the boiler house below, to be collected with the boiler waste. The main heating of the house is by radiators, but heating panels are built in behind the plasterwork in the library and drawing-room. The armchairs in the living-room are designed by the architect.

Opposite the living-room, across the hall, is the staircase, contained in a three-sided bow walled entirely with glass (Fig. 5). Beneath the stairs is a recessed external fountain. The stairs themselves ascend in a continuous angular spiral (Fig. 6) with a solid inner balustrade. The glass walls allow the morning sun to flood the whole hall, and through them is gained a prospect of the garden up the hill (Fig. 2). This is yet very incomplete. But a flight of rose terraces is already finished. To the south, in prolongation of the study, a clean rectangular pergola has been begun, and below the house is projected a little natural lake and wild garden.

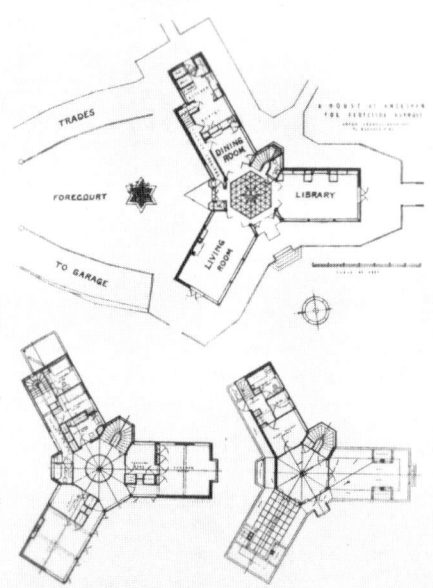

Architect and Building News.   *Copyright.*
13.—THE EAST SIDE OF THE HOUSE, SHOWING THE WATER TOWER AND FIVES COURT BEYOND

Above, along the crest of the ridge, runs a long, broad grass walk, at the top end of which is a water-tower and fives court (Fig. 13). The tower consists of a tubular staircase giving on to a circular view platform on the top of the tank. It is the least successful item in the experiment, from the scenic point of view, for, viewed from below, the tower and tank look like a gigantic cross on the skyline. A tower was absolutely necessary for the water supply of the top floors, but the "mushroom on stalk" effect is not happy. Better for the tower to have been a solid tower, related to the simple mass of the fives court at its base.

The bedrooms, grouped round the circular hall gallery, are designed to give the maximum of light and privacy. The master and mistress's rooms are in the south wing, the former provided with a shower bath in a recess, and all with ample built-in cup boards. The bathroom is across the landing and an ingenious arrangement gives it a hatch to a section of the linen cupboard, where a warm, dry towel can be had. A maids' bathroom is fitted in above the front door and in communication with their bedrooms in the north-east wing.

At the top of the house is the jolliest room of all, the day nursery, a hexagonal room opening on to the two roofs (Fig. 4). On the roofs are a sandpit and large soil boxes for the children's garden. Adjoining it is the night nursery and nurse's bedroom, and a lift from the kitchen brings up meals.

"THINGS ARE WHERE THEY ARE WANTED"

What, to sum up, are the chief impressions left by this courageous experiment in home-making? First, the success with which the elementary, but often-compromised, requirements for comfort have been met. Each room serves its purpose extraordinarily completely, gives its users a maximum of privacy if they want it, and yet is centrally situated. Each room has abundant light, view and warmth, and is so furnished as to provide a maximum of ease with a minimum of trouble. Things are where they are wanted and have been eliminated where they are not. Sanitary and domestic offices are placed so as to reduce footwork to the utmost. The façades, being based on so balanced a plan and conceived in terms of mass and plane, can ignore symmetry of fenestration. The irregular placing of the voids is, indeed, a relief to the severity of the masses, forming a pattern at first sight wilful, but, on examination, subtle and logical. As with all things new, the daring originality of the whole may at first sight be resented, but quickly compels interest greater than that elicited by any traditional building, and ultimately pleases by the sheer beauty and simplicity of the synthesis of purpose with construction. Here is architecture pure and unalloyed by sentiment, reminiscence or clap-trap. One goes away exhilarated as by a fresh and fertile mind or by the consummate simplicity of a Greek vase.   CHRISTOPHER HUSSEY.

12.—GROUND, FIRST AND SECOND FLOOR PLANS

Part IV

List of Illustrations

The Ashmole Family in 1896	2
William Ashmole (father), about 1900	3
Caroline Ashmole (mother), about 1940	3
Gordon Ashmole (brother), about 1935	4
Constance Ashmole (sister), about 1917	5
Gladys Ashmole (sister), about 1917	6
Bernard Ashmole, about 1938	7
Bernard in the uniform of the Eleventh Royal Fusiliers, 1914	11
Bernard in the rifle-butts at Colchester, 1915	12
Oxford, High Street, 1920. Photograph: *Courtesy of the Oxfordshire County Council Central Library*	18
Hertford College, Oxford. Senior and Junior commonrooms dining together, 1919	19
In the garden of Grove Cottage, Wanstead (Bernard's mother's house, near Ilford, Essex), about 1920	20
Dorothy on her wedding day, Newent, 1920	21
The British School at Athens, 1937. *Photograph: Courtesy of Lady Helen Waterhouse*	22
Bernard, about 1920	23
'Confrontation with the housekeeper' (British School at Athens), 1920. Drawing by Winifred Lamb, reproduced from Helen Waterhouse's *The British School at Athens* (London, 1986)	24
Group at British School at Athens, 1921	25
Ince Blundell Hall and the Pantheon façades. *Photograph: Courtesy of the Liverpool Museums*	33
Ince Blundell Hall, the Pantheon (interior), 1959. *Photograph: Courtesy of the Liverpool Museums*	34
The British School at Rome, main front, about 1925	37
The British School at Rome, Entrance Hall, 1925	38
The British School at Rome, the Cortile, 1925	39

Credits are given only for those prints which are not from the Ashmole family collection

'Guy' made by the sculptors D. Evans (Rome Scholar in Sculpture 1923), J.A. Woodford (Rome Scholar in Sculpture 1927) and H. Wilson Parker for Guy Fawkes celebrations at British School at Rome, 1925	40
Virgil celebration at Mantua, 1927	41
Dorothy and Bernard beside the fountain designed by J. R. Skeaping, Rome Scholar in Sculpture, 1926	43
John Marshall, about 1925	44
Dorothy and Bernard in fancy dress dance at British School at Rome, 1925	46
Terracotta bust of Bernard by H. Wilson Parker, Rome Scholar in Sculpture, 1927-29. *Photograph: R. Wilkins*	47
Fancy dress dance at the German Academy in Rome, 1926	45
Ian Richmond (left) and Rex Whistler at the Farewell Dinner for Bernard and Dorothy in 1928	48
Rex Whistler's menu for the Farewell Dinner	49
George Hill, about 1928	50
The site at Amersham before building started on 'High and Over' in 1929	52
'High and Over' from the south west, 1935	53
'High and Over', summer 1993. *Photograph: John Boardman*	54
Bernard and Stella (eldest daughter) in the Hollow at 'High and Over', about 1934	56
Bernard in the uniform of a Pilot Officer RAFVR at 'High and Over' with Philip (only son), 1939	59
Vestal Virgins in Michael Korda's film 'I Claudius' shot at Denham near London, about 1931	67
The British Museum, Elgin Room, about 1920. *Photograph: Courtesy of the British Museum (Neg. IS217855)*	69
The British Museum, Duveen Gallery. J. Russel Pope's design, 1932. *Photograph: Courtesy of the British Museum (Neg. PS265778)*	70
Crates of sculpture from the British Museum stored in the Aldwych underground station with sand bags, 1939. *Photograph: Courtesy of the British Museum (Neg. PS 064175)*	71
Sculpture from the British Museum in the Aldwych underground station, 1939. Photograph: *Courtesy of the British Museum (Neg. PS 064176)*	72
A Blenheim in flight to the Far East about 1940	78
Bernard in Karachi, 1941	102
Air Marshal Robb presenting decorations to Czech Officers at Stanmore in 1944	112
The Greek and Roman Life Room in the British Museum, after bombing in 1941. *Photograph: Courtesy of the British Museum (Neg. A 3178)*	121
British Museum, Department of Greek and Roman Antiquities, after bombing in 1941	122
British Museum, Department of Greek and Roman Antiquities, after patching up, 1944	124

British Museum, Old Elgin Room, 1949. *Photograph: Courtesy of the British Museum (Neg. 132687)*	127
Showing Marshal Tito round the British Museum in 1953	132
The Mill House at Iffley, near Oxford	136
The Ashmolean Museum, Oxford. *Photograph: Ashmolean Museum*	137
The Old Cast Gallery, Ashmolean Museum. *Photograph: Ashmolean Museum*	139
The New Cast Gallery, Ashmolean Museum. *Photograph: Ashmolean Museum*	141
Bernard and Dorothy in the garden of the Mill House in 1968	142
Modern Relief, British Museum 573. *Photograph: Courtesy of the British Museum (Neg. PS096347)*	150
J. Paul Getty, about 1970. *Photograph: The J. Paul Getty Museum*	155
Mr Getty visiting an archaeological site, about 1970. *Photograph: The J. Paul Getty Museum*	156
Sutton Place, Mr Getty's home in England, about 1970. *Photograph: The J. Paul Getty Museum*	157
The Peristyle Garden of The J. Paul Getty Museum. *Photograph: The J. Paul Getty Museum*	159
Dorothy and Bernard at Peebles near Edinburgh, 1983. *Photograph: Donna Kurtz*	163
Dorothy on Tweed Green at Peebles, 1988	164
The Mill House at Iffley Lock on the River Thames, 1993. *Photograph: Donna Kurtz*	165
'Mausolos', British Museum 1000. *Photograph: Courtesy of the British Museum (B: Neg. PS145917)*	203
Blacas Head, British Museum 550. *Photograph: after BSA 46 (1951) pl. 3*	207
Demeter from Knidos, British Museum 1300. *Photograph: Courtesy of the British Museum*	208

General Index

AA Guns 114–8
Aberdeen, University 144
(SS) Abosso 76
Aldwych Tube Station, London 71–2, 123–6, 204–5
Alföldi, András 50
Ali, Rashid 86–7, 104, 107
Ambler, Air Commodore 116
Amelung, Walther 36, 46
American Institute of Archaeology 145
American School, Athens 21, 48
Aphrodite – see Praxiteles 149
Arab Legion 88
Architecture, modern 51–61, 217
  ancient 148
Art Market 43–44, 129–131, 155–61
Ashby, Thomas 28, 36–42
Asklepios (head from Melos) 207
Ashmole Archive, London 209–13
Ashmole, Bernard viii, 1–9
  Family history 6–9
  Oxford 18–20
  WWI 10–17
  British School, Rome 36–50
  University College, London 62–3, 120
  WWII 74–119
  British Museum 120–134
  Lincoln Professorship 135–143
  Geddes-Harrower Professorship 144
Ashmole, Dorothy, née de Peyer 20–24, 39, 43–46, 142, 163–164
Ashmole, Constance 20
Ashmole, Elias v, 1, 6
Ashmole, Elswitha 20
Ashmole, Gladys 20
Ashmole, James xv
Ashmole, Myrtle (née Goodacre) 146–7, 162–3

Ashmole, Philip ix, 58–9, 110, 137, 146–7, 151, 162–3
Ashmole, Silvia (Ebert) 10, 45–6, 57, 110
Ashmole, Stella (Ring) xv, 30, 45–6, 56–7, 110, 211
Ashmolean Museum, Oxford vi, 1, 31–2, 47, 137, 139, 141, 143, 153
Attlee, Clement 120
Australian Air Crews 102

Balliol College, Oxford 50
Barnard, F. Pierrepont 31–32
Barron, John 210
Bartholomew's Atlas 175, 177, 179, 181
Baynes, Norman 62
Beazley Archive, Oxford x, 143, 152, 210
Beazley, John Davidson, vii, 20, 30–31, 42–44, 104, 133, 138, 143, 200, 203
Beazley, Marie 143
Bell, Charles 46
Bellinger, A. R. 154
Bing, Gertrud 142–3
Blenheim Aircraft 78
Blenheim, 84 Squadron 78–103, 166–73, 174–87
'Blacas Head' 207
Blacker, L. H. D. 19
Boardman, John v, xv, 139, 143
Bocconi, Settimo 28
Bodleian Library, Oxford 31
Böhringer, Erich 80
Boethius, Axel 23, 36
'Bomb Alley' 115
'Boston Relief' 152–154
Boyd, Henry 6
Brasenose College, Oxford 135, 137
Brideshead Revisited vi
Brennan, Jack 126

INDEX

British Academy, London   133
British Museum, London   vi-vii, xv, 31, 63, 68–73, 120–35, 140, 148–50, 200, 202–8
British Ornithologists' Union, Centenary Expedition   146
British School, Athens   viii, x, 20–7, 48, 79, 210
British School, Rome   vii, ix, 27–31, 36–51
Brittain, Vera   18
Brewis, G.   19
Bronzes   159–61
Brown, Ann   143
Brown, David   xv
Brown, Llewellyn   143
Buckley, C.   80–1
Buren van, A. W.   36
Burroughs, E. A.   8, 19

Campbell, J. E.   7
Campbell, John McLeod   7
Campbell, Pat   7, 110
Campbell, Percy   7, 18
Carpenter, Rhys   48–9
Caskey, Jack   145
Caskey, L. D.   145
Cassano Medal   65
Casson, Stanley   21, 25
Casts   63
   London, Inaugural Lecture   120, 195
   Galleries (general)   120
   University College, London   138–41
   Oxford   139–40, 195–6
   Cleaning   141
Moving   203–4, 206
Catalina (Flying boat)   184–6
Chamberlain, Neville   72
Chambers, R. W.   62
Chandler, Miriam   23
(I) Claudius   ix, 66–8
Collingwood, Sergeant   166–73
Collotype   33
Concrete, reinforced   55
Connell, Amyas   viii, xiv, 51–61,
Conway, R. S.   41
Corbett, Peter   205, 209–10
(Le) Corbusier   viii, 51
Corney, P. M. Sergeant   174
Cosgrove, W. N. Sergeant   174

Cottage Hospital, Chesham   60
Country Life   viii, 57, 212, 217–222
Cow-gun   75
Chandler, Miriam   24–5
Creswell, H. B.   55
Cruttwell, C. R.   19
Cumont, Franz   42
Daedalus   212
Cyriac of Ancona   vii, x

Daniel, Augustus   57
Davis, Dick   103–107, 109
Davison, Claire   212
Demargne, Pierre   123
Demeter of Knidos   149, 204–8
Denman Collection, San Antonio   212
Denniston, J. D.   8, 19
Derby, Bishop of   32
Distinguished Flying Cross   xiv
Doodle-bug (V1)   113
Doryphoros   159–60
Dossena, Alceo   44
Dream, of river   92
Dunbabin, Thomas   133
Duveen Gallery   viii, 68, 70, 125–26, 204–8
Duveen, Lord   69, 204

Elgin Marbles   vii, 68–71, 73, 123, 125, 155, 202–8
Elwes, Simon   106
Evans, Arthur   22, 47
Evans, David   viii, 40, 47

Farrow, Wing-Commander   103–4, 108
Fellows, Charles   206
Fihelly, B.   166, 173
Flatt, Leslie, Mr and Mrs   104
Florence Bursary (RIBA)   68
Flying Bomb (V1)   113–9
Forest School   5
Forgeries   153–61
Forsdyke, John   36, 69, 85, 130
Fountains   ix
   Rome   43
   Amersham   52
   Iffley   136–7
Frankfort, Henri   142
Frantz, Alison   vii, 151

INDEX

Gardens (Amersham) 59–60
Gardner, Ernest 46-7
Gardner, Percy 8, 20, 31, 32, 46, 139, 141
Geddes-Harrower Professorship, Aberdeen University 144
General Strike 44-5
German Institute, Rome 36, 45-6
Getty, J. Paul v, x, 31, 155-61
Getty Museum, Malibu x, 159
Gibbings, Robert x
Gill, Arthur (Flight Lieutenant) 97–101
'Girl with Doves', Brocklesby 43
Gjerstad, Einar 145-6
Glasgow, Edwin 6
Gottlieb, Carla 123
Goodbye To All That vi
Graves, Robert vi
Great Western Railway 4, 75
Gurkhas 89
'Guy' (Fawkes) 40
Guy, R . C. 5

Hadcock, Neville 18-19
Halikarnassos vii
Halouk, Bey 148-9
Hamilton, M. A. 32
Hamilton, William 130
Harden, Donald 138
Harding, Gilbert 140
Hardy, Brigadier 109
Hawkes, Christopher 137
Hawtrey, Group Captain 104-5, 108
Haynes, Denys 161, 200, 202, 204-6
Haynes, P. Sergeant 174
Hearst, Randolph 157
Hege, Walter 151
Heithaus, Claude 64, 72
Henderson, Isobel 152
Hepworth, Barbara viii, 39
Herford, Mary 24
Hertford College, Oxford 6-9, 19
Higgins, Reynold 205
'High and Over', Amersham viii, ix, 51–61, 74, 104, 107, 109–10, 217–000
Hill, George 20, 34, 48, 50, 57, 69, 74, 110, 111, 142
Hill, Geoffrey 74, 110
Hill, Roderic, Air Marshal 74, 111-9
Hilton, Gwen 56

Hilton, Reginald 56, 110
Hinks, R. P. 202
Hirsch, Jacob 44
Hitler 72
Hogarth, D. G. 46
Holland, Flight-Lieutenant 166, 175
Hollerith machine 107
Home Guard 74
Honeywood File 55
Hoyt, A. 19
Hughes, Sergeant 166-173
Hunter, Air-Commodore 98
Hussey, Christopher 57

Ince Blundell Hall, Liverpool 32-4
Influenza 17

Jackson, Flight-Lieutenant 100
Jackson-Stops, Gervase 212
Jacobs, W. W. 3
James, Squadron Leader 96-7
Janacek, Air Marshall 112
Jasper Ware 130
Jeffery, G. B. 62
Jellicoe, Earl of 211
Jenkins, Ian xiii, xv, 202
Jeppesen, Kristian 148-50, 210
Jeudwine, J. R. Wing-Commander 97, 166, 173-87
Johnson, John 32-3, 46
Jury, Philip 56

Karouzos, Dr and Mrs 80
Keats, John 132
Kendrick, Tom 65, 132
Kenyon, Frederic 129, 133
Kerr, Philip 76-7
Kings College, London vii, 209-13
Knowles, David 19
Korda, Michael ix, 66-7
Korda, Vincent 66-8
Kurtz, Donna 152, 211

Lamb, Winifred 23-5
Lane, Allen 120
Laughton, Charles 66-8
Layard, Henry 89
Lawrence, Arnie 36
Lecturing 41-2, 145, 201

INDEX

Lee, Group-Captain 83–4
Lee, Lord 142
Leeds, E. T. 31, 46
Leverhulme Trust 212
Lewes House, Lewes 42, 153
Lion Tomb 149
Lloyd-Jones, Hugh 152
Lodge, Alice 121,124
London Gazette xiv, 111
Longmore, A. C. Sergeant 174
Lovegrove, J. Sergeant 174
Lucas, F. L. 23, 25
Ludovisi Throne 152–4
Lundgreen, Birte 212
Lutyens, Edwin 27

Macdonald, M. S., Pilot-Officer 98–100, 166–73
MacMillan, Lord 142
Magdalen College, Oxford 30
Malraux, Musée Imaginaire 106
Marble, identification of types 29
Marshall, Howard 57
Marshall, John 42–4, 196
Masaryk, President 112
Maurice, George, Pilot-Officer 98, 166–73
Mausoleum vii, 148, 202, 210
Mausolos 148, 202–03
Mawer, Allan 63
Maxse, Leo General 10
Melchett Collection 35
Melikian, Souren 212
Menander (Bust) 31
Metropolitan Museum, New York 43–4
Metzger, Heuri 123
Michaelis, Adolf 32
Michener, James 147
Military Cross xiii
Mill House, Iffley ix, 135–6, 142, 163
Miller, Bill Sergeant 166–73
Milne, J. G. 31
Minenwerfer 11
Mobile launching pads 115
Montague (Weld-Blundell) 33
Morse College, Yale University 152
Moulders 68, 70, 129, 140
Mountbatten, Admiral Lord Louis 107
Museum of Fine Arts, Boston 152

Museums (displays) 29, 126–8
Navy (Royal Navy) 84–5
Neate, Nelson 13, 18
Newton, C. T. 148–9, 202
Nicholson, Felicity 211
Norton Lectures 145
Noshy, Ibrahim 78

Oakeshott, Noel 134
Oakeshott, Walter 133–4
Oberon, Merle 66
O'Bierne, Frank, Lieutenant-Commander, US Navy 186
O'Neill, Robert J. xiv
Orient Express 48
Owen, Flying-Officer 175

Palmer, Sergeant 166
Parker, H. Wilson viii, 40, 47
Parthenon (see Elgin Marbles and British Museum)
Passmore, A. K. Squadron-Leader 166, 174–87
Patterson, Dr and Mrs 152
Payne, Humfry 104, 133, 200
Peel, R. T. 19
Plenderleith, Harold 154
Penrose, F. C. 21
Pereschitch, General 85
Pevsner, Nicholas viii
de Peyer, Dorothy (see Ashmole)
Pfuhl, Ernst v
Pheidias 212
Photography 32–5, 64, 151, 195–6, 209–13
Picón, Carlos 211–2
Pile, General 116–7
Pitts, Squadron Leader (WAAF) 113
Plaster and plaster-casting (see 'Casts' and 'Moulders')
Portland Vase 130
Polycleitus 159
Pope, J. Russell 70, 204
Praxiteles, Aphrodite 149
Prescotts (Moulders) 140
Prince Paul of Yugoslavia 85
Prior, Sir Henry 105
Protesilaos 43
'Proximity fuses' 116

INDEX

Pryce, F. N.   202
Purdie, Edna   142

Radar   115-6
RAF pocket-book   94
Rats   14-15
Richmond, Ian   48, 137
Ring, Peter   110
Ring, Stella (see Ashmole)
Rizzo, G. E.   65
Robb, Air Marshall   112
Robertson, Donald   203
Robertson, Martin   v, xiii, xiv, xv, 119, 129, 202, 204-5, 211
Robinson, Stanley   20, 64
Robson, Flora   66
Rodd, Rennell   8
Rodin   128
Rodenwaldt, Gerhart   150
Root-marks   153
Royal Fusiliers   10-11
Royal Geographical Society, London   74
Royal Institute of British Architects, London   ix, 68
Russell, Ritchie   163

Saleh, Mohamed   140
Salisbury, Edward   62
Sanders, Air Vice-Marshall   117
Sandys, Duncan   117-18
Sayer, G. W. Sergeant   174
Saxl, Fritz   vii, 142
Scorpion, Log of the   103 and Appendix II (174-187)
Sculpture (lighting of)   29, 64, 126-28, 195-6
(The) Secret War   118
Semple Lectures (Cincinnati)   145
Simovitch, General   85
Skeaping, John   viii, ix, 39, 43, 47
Smith, Arthur   30, 206
Snook, A. C. E. Sergeant   174
Sotheby's, London   211
Spitfire   114
Spooner, Dr.   6
Sternberg, Josef von   66-7
Stevens, Warrant-Officer   83
Streatfield, C. P. L. Flying-Officer   174-87
Strong, Mrs Arthur   28, 32, 35, 36-7, 42

Strong, Donald   148-50, 210, 212
Studniczka, Franz   44
Submarine, Japanese   176
   US   186
Sutton Place   x, 156-7
Sweet Thames Runs Softly   x
Syme, Ronald   86

Tanks   13
Tayler, Squadron-Leader   98, 100-1, 175
Tempest (Fighter aircraft)   114
Thermoluminescence   160
Thomas, M. D.   19
Tigris River   ix
Tito, Marshall   132
Tokens   31-2
Townley, Charles   206
Tritsch, F.   212
Trojan Horse   126
Trout Inn, Godstow   ix, 30
Tube (See Aldwych)
Turner, S. G. Pilot-Officer   174-87

"Ulster Prince"   81-2
University College, London   vi-vii, 46, 51, 62-5, 120, 129, 195-6, 200, 202, 205, 209
University Press, Oxford   32

V1 (flying bomb)   113-19
V2 (rocket)   119
Victoria and Albert Museum, London   63
Vestal Virgins   66-8
Venus de Milo   132
Vermeule, Cornelius   153
Victory of Samothrace   127
Vickers Vimy (aircraft)   80
Virgil's Birthday   41

Wace, Alan   21-2, 85
Wade, A. de V.   6
Walda, Hafed   212
Walker, Pilot-Officer   95, 101
Warburg Institute, London   vi, 142-3
Warren, E. P.   42, 43, 153
Watson, D. M. S.   62
Watson-Watt, Sir Robert   116
Waugh, Evelyn   vi
Wavell, Lord   106
Waywell, Geoffrey   xiii, xv, 209-13

Wedgwood, Josiah 130
Welch, F. B. 23–5
Weld-Blundell, Ince-Blundell Hall, Liverpool 32–3
Whatley, Norman 7
Wheeler, Mortimer 133
Whistler, Rex viii, 47–49
Whiteleys, London 63–4
Williams, Emlyn 66
Williams, Elswitha 107
Wilson-Parker, H 40, 47
Wind, Edgar 137
Wooden Horse vii
Woodford, J. A. 40
Woolley, Leonard 23, 25
World War I
    Declared 9
    Trenches 11–7
    Tanks 13–4
    Rats 14–5
    Demobilization 17
World War II
    Greece 74–8
    Japanese 96
    Dutch 97
    Poles and Czechs 111
    Demobilization 120
Wylie, Flight-Lieutenant 175

Xanthos (excavations) 123

Yale University 62, 146, 151–2
Yalouris, Nicolas 151
Yarborough, Lord (Brocklesby relief) 43
Yates Chair (University College, London) 46, 205
(SS) Yoma 95, 101
Young, Gerard 79, 104
Young, William 153

Zanotti-Bianco 37
Zeus, Temple (Olympia) vii, ix, 150

Geographical Index

Aboukir 85
Aberdeen 144
Allahabad 96
Amersham 51-61, 74, 104, 107, 109-10, 217-222
Aquir 85
Argos 82-3
Ascension Island 146
Ashford 114
Athens, 21, 48
  20-7, 48, 79, 210
Australia 97, 102-3, 174, 180, 183, 186

Baghdad 86
Bahrain 96
Bali 175
Bandoeng 100, 174
Barrow Island 181, 184
Bassae 26-7
Batavia 101
Batoeradja 101
Beachy Head 114, 117
Belgian Congo 76-7
Bodrum 148-50
Bombay 102
Boston 152-4
Brocklesby, Lincolnshire 43

Cairo 77-8, 109
Calcutta 96, 107
Chaeronea 26
Chesham 60
Chittagong 105
Christmas Island 146
Cincinnati 145
Colchester 10, 12, 17
Colombo 102
Corinth Canal 80

'Cox's Bazaar' 105
Crete 81, 86
Cross Kirk (Peebles) 25

Delhi 103-09
Delphi 24-5, 103-9
Dampier Archipelago 184
Denham 66-68
Dover 114, 117
Dum-dum (Calcutta) 96

Forest School 5
Fortescue 185
Franvillers 15
Frazer Inlet 184
Fricourt 10

Gambut 94-5
Gibraltar 109
Godstow 30
Gold Coast 76
Greece 20-7, 78-84
Gythion 81

Habbaniya 86-8, 96, 104
Hawaii 146-7
Haywards Heath 114
Heliopolis 95, 166
Honolulu 147
Hosios Loukas 25-6

Iffley 135-7, 142, 163-5
Ilford 1
India 102-9
Iraq 86-93, 104, 107
Ithome 27

Japan 146-8

234

INDEX

Java   100–102, 174–5
Jerusalem   92–3

Kajeogoeng   172
Kalamata   27, 81–4
Karachi   96, 102
Khartoum   77
Kidston Mill   162–4
Kotabeomi   101
Kotaradja   97
Krakatoa   97
Kythera   83

Lagos   77
Lewes   42, 153
Lhoknga   96–7, 166
Liverpool   32–4, 76, 148
London, Aldwych Tube Station   71–2, 123–6, 204–5
   Ashmole Archive   209–13
   British Academy   133
   British Museum   31, 63, 68–73, 120–35, 140, 148–50, 200, 202–8
   Cast Galleries   120, 195
   Inaugural Lecture   63
   Kings College   209–13
   Royal Geographical Society   74
   Royal Institute of British Architects   68
   Sotheby's   211
   University College   46, 51, 62–5, 120, 129, 195–6, 200, 205, 209
   Victoria and Albert Museum   63
   Warburg Institute   142–3
Lydda   85, 87
Lyneham   109

Malibu   158–60
Mantua   41
Maria School (Sumatra)   98–9, 173
Medan   96, 173
Menidi   78–81
Methana   23
Moes River (Sumatra)   97
Mosul   89, 93
Mouquet Farm   15

Naples   160
Natar   101
Nauplia   80–82

New Haven (Connecticut)   114
New York   43–4
Nineveh   3, 89
Normandy   118–9
North Downs   114–116
Northolt   112

Olympia   150–51, 159
Onslow   175, 181, 184
Oosthaven   101
Oxford   6–9, 18–20, 135–143
   Ashmolean Museum   1, 31–2, 47, 137, 139, 141, 143, 153
   Balliol College   50
   Beazley Archive   143, 152, 210
   Bodleian Library   31
   Brasenose College   135, 137
   Casts   138–41
   Hertford College   6–9, 19
   High Street, No. 64   30
   Lincoln Professorship   133–43
   Magdalen College   30
   Mill House, Iffley   135–6, 142, 163
   New College   6
   University Press   32

Pakan Baroe (Pekanbaru, Paken Baru, Pakan Baru)   97, 166, 173
Palembang   96–99, 103, 166–9, 172–3
Palestine   85–6
Partapoera   101
Peebles   162–4
Perth   186
Port Headland   175, 183
Port Tewfik   95, 101
Rangoon   96–7
Roebourne   175, 177, 179, 181, 184–5
Rome   27–31, 36–50
   British School   27–31, 36–51
   Conservatori   28–9
   Fountains   43
   Gardens of Sallust   152
   German Institute   36, 45–6
   Hotel Hassler   29
Romney Marsh   119

Sambang   166
San Antonio (Texas)   212
Schaffhausen   8

Scorpion Cove (Java) 175, 186
Sharjah 96
Shetland 75-6, 109
Sinai Desert 85
Singapore 95, 102-3, 174
Somme xiii, 10-13
Stanmore 111
Srinagar 107
Sumatra 95-103, 105, 166-174
Sumburgh 75
Sutton Place 156-58
Syrian Desert 87

Takoradi 76
Thiepval 13
Tigris ix, 89-92
Tjilatjap (Cilacap) 102, 174-6
Toeloengselapan 172
Toungoo 96
Tripolitza 81

United States of America 144-7

West Cape 182
Western Desert 93-5, 105, 174

Xanthos 123